ENVIRONMENTAL JUSTICE

D1601492

ENVIRONMENTAL JUSTICE

Discourses in International Political Economy

Energy and Environmental Policy
Volume 8

Edited by
John Byrne, Leigh Glover,
and **Cecilia Martinez**

Transaction Publishers
New Brunswick (U.S.A.) and London (U.K.)

Copyright © 2002 by Transaction Publishers, New Brunswick, New Jersey 08903.

This book is printed on acid-free paper that meets the American National Standard for Permanence of Paper for Printed Library Materials.

Library of Congress Catalog Number: 2001055689
ISBN: 0-7658-0751-3
ISSN: 0882-3537
Printed in the United States of America

Library of Congress Cataloging-in-Publication Data

Environmental justice : discourses in international political economy / edited by John Byrne, Cecilia Martinez & Leigh Glover.
    p. cm.—(Energy and environmental policy series ; v. 8)
    Includes bibliographical references and index.
    ISBN 0-7658-0751-3 (pbk. : alk. paper)
    1. Environmental justice. I. Byrne, John, 1949- II. Martinez, Cecilia. III. Glover, Leigh. IV. Series.

GE220 .E58 2001
363.7—dc21
                                               2001055689

Contents

Part I

Defining the Discourse

1

A Brief on Environmental Justice

John Byrne, Cecilia Martinez, and Leigh Glover

Introduction

Contemporary usage of the term 'environmental justice' arose from resistance movements organized to expose the socially unequal environmental risks and effects of industrialization. While 'at-risk' communities had experienced the problem for much of the 20th century, documentation of environmental injustice as a legacy of industrialization has only occurred in the last 25 years through the pioneering studies of Bullard (1983, 1990, 1993, and 1994a), Gibbs (1982), Goldman (1991, 1993), Lee (1987, 1993), and others. As a result, Bullard could draw on empirical evidence when stating (1993: 15):

> Communities are not all created equal. In the United States, for example, some communities are routinely poisoned while the government looks the other way. Environmental regulations have not uniformly benefited all segments of society. People of color (African Americans, Latinos, Asians, Pacific Islanders, and Native Americans) are disproportionately harmed by industrial toxins on their jobs and in their neighborhoods.

Inquiries into the causes and distribution of environmental injustice in the U.S. ranged from historical critiques of capitalism (Foster, 1994) to analyses of inequality founded in race, culture, and gender. A hallmark of this research is that explanations moved beyond an exclusive focus on the class structure of industrial capitalism (Bullard, 1993: 22-24). The exchange of ideas on sources of environmental injustice prompted new questions that opened fresh avenues of inquiry into political economy.

By the late 1980s, structures of environmental injustice had been identified across the world. A globalized phenomenon of unequal risks and effects was revealed by writers such as Agarwal and Narain

(1991), Bryant (1995), Esteva (1992), Hofrichter (1993), and Khor (1993). Their critiques pointed to a pattern of 'environmental colonialism' as an explanation for a worldwide condition of environmental injustice. Additional analyses by Crosby (1988), Alvares (1991 and 1995), Shiva (1991, 1994a, 1994b, and 1994c), Escobar (1995), and others suggested that unequal patterns extended biologically as well as socially, with the advance of modernization. Their critiques of 'ecological imperialism' suggested that threats to human livelihoods were coincident with threats to ecosystems. An important insight of this work is that it raised the prospect of altered biologies supporting a less diverse specie structure *and* a less diverse social structure.

Learning from the environmental justice debate, the discourse of political economy is presently searching for an appropriate understanding of national and global structures of ecological injustice. Below we review the evolution of the discourse on environmental justice in international political economy for the purpose of offering a context for the contributions to this volume.

Birth and Growth of a Social Movement

Conceptually, environmental justice has its roots in theories of social and political power and social movements. The priority placed on race, gender, and culture as explanations of environmental damage distinguish this movement from the more traditional political economy critiques of capitalism. The latter predicted patterns of environmental risk as outcomes of the logic of capital and explained demands for environmental justice as phenomena of class struggle. By contrast, the new theories of environmental injustice emphasize social and political power, in addition to class, as explanations of unequal environmental risk.

This turn in theoretical strategy recognizes that the toll of industrial life has continued to mount disproportionally, not only for workers and the poor, but also for women, indigenous cultures, and communities of color. Long-standing dominance of the American environmental movement by affluent, white, and middle-class communities with an agenda shaped largely by self-interest and symbolic ecological issues, would now be challenged. Increased local protest in the 1960s and 1970s by communities of color, highlighted the awareness in these communities of the unequal hazards of industrialization. Through the studies of Bryant and Mohai (1993), Bullard (1983, 1990, 1993, 1994a, and 1995), Goldman (1991, 1993, Goldman and Fitton, 1994), Lee (1987, 1993),

Pulido (1996), Wright (Wright, 1995; Wright and Bullard, 1990; and Bullard and Wright, 1987), and others, the racial geography of environmental hazards in the U.S. was exposed.

A breakthrough study by the United Church of Christ Commission for Racial Justice, entitled *Toxic Wastes and Race in the United States* (Lee, 1987), connected what had previously been largely isolated stories of risk into a racially identifiable pattern of injustice. While this pattern was of no surprise to communities of color, it was a revelation to policy-makers and mainstream researchers. Of the many factors that might influence a community's risk of exposure to toxic wastes, the study found race to be the most significant predictor. Those communities with the highest composition of residents of color were revealed to have the highest concentration of hazardous facilities. Every three of five African and Hispanic American communities had uncontrolled toxic waste sites in their midst, meaning that over 15 million African Americans and over 8 million Hispanic Americans live in the vicinity of such sites (Lee, 1987). A 1994 study by Goldman and Fitton (1994) updated these results and revealed that the percentage of people of color living in areas with commercial hazardous waste facilities had increased between 1980 and 1993, so that by 1993 people of color were 47% more likely to live near such a facility than in 1980.

As Gottlieb (1993), Faber (1998), Szasz (1994), and others noted, protests of this condition by grassroots groups composed of workers, minorities, and women differed from those of mainstream environmentalism. Their interests were in correcting industrial causes that fouled the air and water, and which created extreme health risks through the spread of lead and radioactivity, pesticides, waste, and hazardous material. Unlike mainstream environmentalism, this movement located nature in the workplace, in the places we live, in the air we breathe, and the water we drink. For too long, many environmental groups had ignored this nature in favor of the protection of untouched wilderness and endangered species.

Women were prominent in the rise of the new environmentalism as leaders and spokespersons (Hamilton, 1993; Krause, 1993, 1994). As Krause describes: "For women of color, it is the link between race and environment, rather than between class and environment, that characterizes [. . .] environmental justice." (1994: 270). Community and family health were directly affected by environmental injustice and some in the women's movement sought to address the threat as part of a general effort to counter women's historic exclusion from decision-making. Working class women had gone outside the traditional mechanisms in the past and used protests and other means to prompt action on behalf of community needs, thereby drawing attention to the inadequacies of traditional political processes. Women-led environmental activism would similarly go beyond convention to challenge linkages of color, gender, culture, and risk.

Another important dimension to this social movement has concerned worker's risks. Research highlighted the dangers of working in industrial societies, especially in its factories and mills. Through the efforts of César Chávez and others seeking to organize agricultural labor, the effects of pesticides on farm workers became a central concern (e.g., Moses, 1993). Workers and their organizations could not rely on government and corporate action, instead having to gather knowledge of the risks of the industrial process directly, and using their own political power, in seeking corporate compliance with existing health and safety regulations, and in lobbying for workforce protection. For workers, therefore, "[e]nvironmental justice is not merely a battle against pollution, but a kind of politics that demands popular control of corporate decision making for workers and communities" (Mann, 1993: 177).

A key insight of this work has been to show that the patterns of inequality that marked economic and social relations in industrialized nations carried forward an expression in environmental conditions as well. Studies of race, class, and gender characteristics of at-risk communities have revealed undeniably unequal environmental threats of those most marginalized by the American political economy. Although limited in scope, studies by U.S. government agencies (notably EPA, 1992; GAO, 1983) have confirmed the general association of communities of color with contaminated areas. Failure to enforce existing anti-discriminatory policies has further added to the evidence of environmental racism. As Bullard has commented: "There is a growing movement to turn the current model of environmental protection on its head. It just does not work for many vulnerable populations . . . Government has been too slow in adopting a prevention framework for these groups." (1994b: xvi).

One of the more damaging revelations from investigations into U.S. environmental injustice was the widespread non-enforcement of laws and regulations (e.g., GAO, 1983; Kratch et al, 1995; and Lavelle and Coyle, 1992). This failure of governance amounted to a political sanctioning of environmental injustice. Race was shown to be a particularly accurate indicator of enforcement failure; with communities of color found to endure disproportionately higher non-enforcement of laws intended to control industrial pollution. Clearly, the explanation lay within the routine practice of social institutions: "Racism plays a key factor in environmental planning and decisionmaking. Indeed, environmental racism is reinforced by government, legal, economic, political, and military institutions." (Bullard, 1993: 17). As Bullard (1993) described, environmental racism is a consequence of people of color being excluded from decision-making by a system of state-corporate relations that extends from boardrooms of multinational corporations to local zoning boards. Accordingly, the affected communities who responded to these problems were motivated to seek political solutions: "What do grass-roots leaders want? These leaders are demanding a shared role in the decision-making processes that affect their communities. They want participatory democracy to work for them" (Bullard, 1994b: xvii).

However, of all the social groups concerned with environmental justice, indigenous peoples may have the most at stake. Unless solutions to conflicts involving 'commons' resources of land, air, and water use explicitly address their needs, indigenous ways of life are irrevocably harmed. North American resource politics, for example, involves decisions over sovereignty and control of Indian lands and, therewith, cultural survival of Indian peoples. As Churchill (1993; Churchill and LaDuke, 1992), Deloria (1997), and others describe, the U.S. political economy depends on American Indian tribal lands for mining uranium and coal, testing nuclear weapons, and impounding rivers for hydroelectric power. The expropriation of Indian lands and resources has left a trail of toxic threats to Indian communities. But most significantly, it has blocked Indian self-determination.

Grassroots environmental protests have forced American society to recognize the conjunction of race, gender, indigenous culture, and class in contesting the landscapes and workscapes of environmental inequality. From this point onward, political economy must focus on this conjunction in order to explain the unequal pattern of environmental harm and risk. In this way, the critique of 'environmental justice' has emerged as a potent challenge for political economy.

Environment—Globalization Nexus

As the environmental justice movement gathered momentum and support in the industrial world, there was growing recognition that environmental inequality and racism was advancing around the world. Injustices could not be relegated to local failures in wealthy nations, but were symptomatic of systemic tendencies of globalization. The demand for environmental justice at an international scale became a concurrent concern of those interested in environmental dimensions of the global political economy.

Examination of the international patterns of environmental injustice was propelled by activists and scholars from the Third World, in particular, Bello (1992, 2000; Bello et al, 1982; and Bello and Rosenfeld, 1990), Escobar (1988, 1995, and 1996), Khor (1993), and Shiva (1991, 1994a, b, c, and 1998). This work revealed the roles of multinational corporations and international financial institutions in a sustained process of shifting environmental pollution from industrial to Third World countries. This has affected the fate of indigenous peoples in the exploitation of vast pools of commons resources in the Third World, and has reinforced imperialist tendencies of modern science and technology (e.g., Alvares, 1991; Nandy, 1992). Women and families have been shown to be particularly disadvantaged by environmental injustices in the developing world, despite much-heralded reforms of the sustainable development movement (Shiva, 1991, 1994a, 1998). Agarwal (1991) and Jain (1991), for example, have respectively described the ways in which women are affected by changes in fuel wood systems in rural south Asia. The famous "Chipko" protest movement, led by Indian women, to protect the traditional uses and ecological values of their forests is a prominent example of women-led environmental justice struggles.

Established environmental organizations became prominent in environmental justice issues and were particularly important in highlighting international themes. NGOs, such as Greenpeace, No-Nukes Asia Forum, Friends of the Earth, and the Third World Network, brought attention to nuclear energy risks, international waste trade, and the activities of multinational corporations in the developing world, and other issues.

A key concern in this new phase of inquiry has been the impacts of economic globalization on Third World communities and environments. Global production and consumption has been found to lengthen commodity chains, with the developing world supplying much of the raw materials. Globalization has also fostered greater capital mobility with multinational corporations shifting manufacturing locations to reduce production costs. For example, destruction and social crisis in Central America have been linked to that area's relationship with foreign economic interests, as shown by Faber (1993). As an integrated feature of globalization, smokestack industries with histories of heavy pollution and rapid resource depletion have migrated to the Third World, along with trails of industrial wastes sent on journeys to the South for disposal.

Environmental problems such as stratospheric ozone loss, climate change, and declining biodiversity have also underscored the international dimension of issues of environmental justice. While global environmental degradation has been the result of historic patterns of exploitative practices by the industrial elite, in most instances the consequences are or will be borne most heavily by poorer communities. Developing countries are especially vulnerable to environmental change because they have fewer resources to respond to these problems. But more importantly, community livelihoods in the South depend to a greater extent on the health of natural environments than the technological enclaves of the North. Environmental degradation for these communities is not subject to repair in the manner of Northern solutions to remediate pollution problems.

Evidence on all these fronts point to the need to cast environmental justice in a global context, in addition to the community and national contexts that have already been established. The movement has now made it a priority to examine international structures of social and environmental exploitation for systemic linkages to patterns of injustice.

Environmental Colonialism

Research in political economy has long demonstrated the interrelation of the social and economic conditions of developing nations with the operations of the global economy. The Third World largely receives foreign investment when it can furnish cost advantages of cheap labor, land and raw materials. Corporate investment in the developing world is typically directed towards imitative industrialization, which can serve Northern needs for lucrative export markets. Carried with these patterns of development, however, has been a set of environmental structures that favor certain ecologies over others. While less investigated before the 1970s than the social effects of globalization, the *nature* of international political economy is nevertheless a core attribute of expanding networks of technology and markets.

Particularly affected by the industrialization of the developing nations are indigenous peoples, whose lives are closely tied to access to commons resources. Development activities, such as converting indigenous ecologies to pasture and crops, timber lands and mineral mines, and privatizing water, land and other ubiquitous resources, have dramatically shrunk available commons areas. In turn, this has greatly compromised the capacities for self-determination and independence of indigenous peoples.

Industrial development in developing countries has also mirrored the production of hazardous environments that occurred in the industrial world. Modernization in the Third World has frequently brought forward threats to workers, communities, and the urban environment that were widespread in industrial nations throughout much of the 20th century.

Degradation and even disappearance of global commons resources is one of the forecasted effects of expanding modernization. Global environmental crises nearly always concern global commons resources such as the atmosphere, biodiversity, the water cycle, etc. Yet, their resolution often invokes global management regimes based on an appropriation of these resources. Such a project also carries forward the broader agenda of 'development,' as Sachs (1999: 55) observes: "Certainly, interpreting the sate of the world chiefly in terms of 'resources,' 'management' and 'efficiency' may appeal to planners and economists. But it continues to promote development as a cultural mission and to shape the world in the image of the West." Environmental agreements have been, and are being, developed to transform commons areas into international properties subject to the principles of modern organization and business management. Developing nations are at risk in many of these international negotiations of losing autonomy still further to the interests of the North, as ecosystems in and beyond the political borders of the South are secured for long-term 'protection' (see e.g., Sachs 1993, 1994, and 1996; and Byrne and Glover, 2000).

Several researchers identify a consistent thread of environmental injustice in the manner in which nations and peoples are being treated over these issues. For example, Agarwal and Narain (1991, 1996) have drawn a parallel between exploitation of societies under colonial regimes and the contemporary environmental relationships between industrial and developing nations, charging that the latter are now being subjugated by forms of 'environmental colonialism.' In this expansion of the original idea of environmental justice, global economic development is seen as attempting to colonize not only the labor and resources of societies, but whole cultures and ways of life through an appropriation of the environmental conditions upon which communities depend.

Ecological Imperialism

Modification of the natural landscape is clearly evident throughout human history. However, human modification of ecology prior to the industrial era appears to have differed in geographical and temporal scale, with pre-industrial ecological transformation limited to local areas and cumulative effects evolving slowly and taking long stretches of time to be realized. By contrast, ecological change in the industrial era appears to affect much larger geographical scales and cumulative effects are surfacing in very short periods of time (e.g., the thinning of the atmosphere in 40 years due to the use of chlorofluorocarbons).

With the advent of worldwide exploration by the European powers and the accompanying era of global colonialism, the planet's ecology underwent a series of profound changes. Human modification of ecology resulted in continent-wide transformations, and human impacts on evolution were unprecedented. Much of this change occurred in the New World, where indigenous peoples and ecosystems were frequently devastated.

Colonization is typically considered as the appropriation of a people, nation, or region by another for the purposes of economic exploitation. It imposes an external culture, social structure, laws and institutions, technology, systems of production, and even social relations on the colonized society. In the era of European colonization, an ecological transformation also took place, so that the ecology of colonized places was altered by the introduction of new species, land uses and land management—unleashing an 'ecological imperialism' (Crosby 1988). Deliberate ecological changes included clearing of native forests to create pastures and plantations, damming of watercourses, planting of crops and gardens, opening mines, building towns, homes, roads and other infrastructure, systematic harvesting of native species, the introduction of exotic species to shape the landscape according to European preferences, and so on. Much of what resulted from the introduction of exotic species into the

New World was unexpected. Yet of all the effects, the most pernicious were those resulting from diseases and pests introduced by Europeans, which cumulatively caused enormous loss of indigenous human life and the extinction of entire plant and animal species.

New frontiers of ecological imperialism are now being forged through modern science with the advent of genetic research and genetically modified organisms (Shiva, 1997). The ecological consequences of this work are not only unknown, but by definition, unprecedented. Because of the commercial value to agricultural and pharmaceutical corporations of genetic resources from developing nations, especially those with diverse flora, a new era of trade involving 'biopiracy' has appeared (Shiva, 1997; Martínez-Alier, 2000a).

Not only are these ecological initiatives made in order to allow Western colonizers to undertake modern forms of production, but often they are a part of deliberate strategies to dispossess, displace, or eliminate indigenous occupants. An example of one such intervention into the fabric of existing society-ecology relations by scientific 'advances' is the Green Revolution, in which a rationale of development and progress has covered the imposition of a system that is ecologically unsustainable, socially destructive, and economically exploitative of traditional land users (Shiva, 1991).

In this regard, society *and* ecology have been and continue to be fundamentally altered in the drive to industrialize social relations. Ecological imperialism offers a deconstructed picture of the biological implications of international industrialization that underscores the linkage between structures of social inequality and ecological transformation. In brief, contemporary political economy requires not only attention to particular structures of social relations, but to changes in ecological structure as well. Together, these structures produce evolving patterns of social and environmental inequality.

The Rise of Ecological Justice

Insights from ecological imperialism and environmental colonialism add a critical dimension to the issues raised by the movement to address issues of environmental injustice. Outlines of a systemic relation between society and ecology are evident with the theoretical innovations underlying the eco-imperialist and colonialist critiques. These approaches suggest that society-ecology relations are at once local and global/systemic in their formation and evolution. On the question of action, environmental justice can likewise be conceived as requiring direct action at the grassroots level and in need of cooperative civil action on larger scales (e.g., see Martínez-Alier, 2000b). In this emerging framework, local efforts to resolve unequal environmental and social risk can be gauged by immediate results *and* systemic reactions. Because one community can 'win' by shifting their hazard onto others, and today's hazards can be transferred into risks for future generations, we need a framework cognizant of eco-imperialist tendencies. Such a framework can provide a more thoughtful understanding of the challenges of environmental justice.

As Low and Gleeson (1998) expound in *Justice, Society, and Nature*, ecological justice applies not only to the living generations and general environmental values, but also embraces future generations, non-human species, and ecosystem processes. Environmentalism becomes, therefore, a framework that can critically assess the local and systematic expressions of social and natural processes. Awareness that social and ecological structures are mutually determined in some degree likewise promotes an understanding of our challenge as engaging the 'ethics' of immediate conditions while also being mindful of the systemic implications for cultures embedded in nature, for the diversity of cultures and species and environments, and for the viability of nature and society 'in common' (the idea of a *lifeworld*, a *commons of life*).

Global environmental problems underscore our need to understand the political economy of society-ecology relations. Human activity is shaping local and global ecologies in definable ways that likewise structure social and environmental justice. Thus, the world's ecological future will almost certainly reflect processes of economic and cultural globalization. At the same time, local environmental and social conditions will continue to reflect the economic and political axes of power that typically organize and manage localities. It is at the intersection of society, ecology and geography that we can examine and act on the challenges of *ecological justice* (taken to include social *and* environmental expressions).

Conclusion

Too often, political economy has conceived its concerns in sociocentric rhetoric that ignored or ineffectively addressed ecological justice. That time is past. Political economy now must grapple with the implications of modernity and industrialization for society and for ecology at all scales. The fate of indigenous peoples and traditional cultures, and the viability of natural commons areas and their associated institutions are being decided in contests with the forces of globalization. These struggles for political influence, self-determination, and restitution center on the quest for justice. In this way, justice is becoming a central concept for environmentalism and vice versa.

The variety of discourses on ecological justice and the different theoretical frameworks that enlighten them offer hope for a political economy that is better grounded in the full range of conflicts embedded in the contemporary era. Contests for justice across geographies and timescales will define core problems of society, ecology, and, finally, political economy. Ecological justice has become a palimpsest on which contemporary struggles for understanding and change are being written.

References

Agarwal, Anil and Sunita Narain. 1996. "Pirates in the Garden of India." *New Scientist*. Volume 152, Number 2053, (October 26): 14-15.
_____. 1991. *Global Warming in an Unequal World: A Case of Environmental Racism*. New Delhi: Centre for Science and Environment.
Agarwal, Bina. 1991. "Under the Cooking Pot: The Political Economy of the Domestic Fuel Crisis in Rural South Asia." In Sally Sontheimer (ed). *Women and the Environment: A Reader. Crisis and Development in the Third World*. New York: Monthly Review Press. pp. 93-116.
Alvares, Claude. 1995. *Science, Development and Violence: The Revolt against Modernity*. New York: Oxford University Press.
_____. 1991. *Decolonising History: Technology and History India, China and the West from 1492 to the Present Day*. New York: The Apex Press.
Bello, Walden. 2000. "The Iron Cage: The World Trade Organization, the Bretton Woods Institutions, and the South." *Capitalism, Nature, Socialism*. Volume 11, Number 1: 3-32.
_____. 1992. *People & Power in the Pacific: The Struggle for the Post-Cold War Order*. San Francisco, CA: Food First Books.
Bello, Walden and Stephanie Rosenfeld. 1990. *Dragons in Distress: Asia's Economic Miracle in Crisis*. San Francisco, CA: Food First Books.
Bello, Walden; David Kinley; and Elaine Elinson. 1982. *Development Debacle: The World Bank in the Philippines*. San Francisco, CA: Institute for Food and Development Policy.
Bryant, Bunyan (ed). 1995. *Environmental Justice: Issues, Policies, and Solutions*. Covelo, CA: Island Press.
Bryant, Bunyan and Paul Mohai (eds). 1993. *Race and the Incidence of Environmental Hazards: A Time for Discourse*. Boulder, CO: Westview Press.
Bullard, Robert D. 1995. "Residential Segregation and the Urban Quality of Life." In Bunyan Bryant (ed). 1995. *Environmental Justice: Issues, Policies, and Solutions*. Covelo, CA: Island Press. pp. 76-85.
_____. (ed). 1994a. *Unequal Protection: Environmental Justice and Communities of Color*. San Francisco, CA: Sierra Club Books.

_____. 1994b. "Introduction." In Robert D. Bullard (ed). 1994b. *Unequal Protection: Environmental Justice and Communities of Color*. San Francisco, CA: Sierra Club Books. pp. xv-xxiii.

_____. 1993. "Anatomy of Environmental Racism and the Environmental Justice Movement." In Robert D. Bullard (ed). *Confronting Environmental Racism: Voices from the Grassroots*. Boston, MA: South End Press. pp. 15-39.

_____. 1990. *Dumping in Dixie: Race, Class, and Environmental Quality*. Boulder, CO: Westview Press.

_____. 1983. "Solid Waste Sites and the Black Houston Community." *Sociological Inquiry*. Volume 53, Numbers 2-3 (Spring): 273-288.

Bullard, Robert D. and Beverly H. Wright. 1987. "Environmentalism and the Politics of Equity: Emergent Trends in the Black Community." *Mid-American Review of Sociology*. Volume 12: 21-37.

Byrne, John and Leigh Glover. 2000. *Climate Shopping: Putting the Climate Up for Sale*. Melbourne, Australia: TELA Publications Series, The Australian Conservation Foundation.

Churchill, Ward. 1993. *Struggle for the Land: Indigenous Resistance to Genocide, Ecocide and Expropriation in Contemporary North America*. Monroe, ME: Common Courage Press.

Churchill, Ward and Winona LaDuke. 1992. "The Political Economy of Radioactive Colonialism." In M. Annette Jaimes (ed). *The State of Native America: Genocide, Colonialism, and Resistance*. Boston, MA: South End Press.

Crosby, Alfred W. 1988. *Ecological Imperialism: The Biological Expansion of Europe, 900-1900*. New York, NY: Canto. (Originally, Cambridge: Cambridge University Press, 1986).

Deloria, Jr. Vine. 1997. *Red Earth, White Lies. Native Americans and the Myth of Scientific Fact*. Golden, CO: Fulcrum Publishing.

Escobar, Arturo. 1996. "Constructing Nature: Elements for a Poststructural Political Ecology." In Richard Peet and Michael Watts (eds). *Liberation Ecologies: Environment, Development, Social Movement*. London and New York: Routledge. pp. 46-68.

_____. 1995. *Encountering Development: The Making and Unmaking of the Third World*. Princeton, NJ: Princeton University Press.

_____. 1988. "Power and Visibility: Development and the Invention and Management of the Third World." *Cultural Anthropology*. Volume 3, Number 4: 428-443.

Esteva, Gustavo. 1992. "Development." In Wolfgang Sachs (ed). *The Development Dictionary: A Guide to Knowledge as Power*. London, UK and New Jersey: Zed Books. pp. 6-25.

Faber, Daniel (ed). 1998. *The Struggle for Ecological Democracy: Environmental Justice Movements in the United States*. New York, UK: Guildford Press.

_____. 1993. *Environment Under Fire: Ecological Crisis in Central America*. New York, NY: Monthly Review Press.

Foster, John Bellamy. 1994. *The Vulnerable Planet: A Short Economic History*. New York, NY: Monthly Review Press.

Gibbs, Lois Marie. 1982. *Love Canal: My Story*. Albany, NY: State University of New York Press.

Goldman, Benjamin. 1993. *Not Just Prosperity: Achieving Sustainability with Environmental Justice*. Washington, D.C.: National Wildlife Federation.

_____. 1991. *The Truth about Where You Live: An Atlas for Action on Toxins and Mortality*. New York, NY: Times Books/ Random House.

Goldman, Benjamin A. and Laura Fitton. 1994. *Toxic Wastes and Race Revisited: An Update of the 1987 Report on the Racial and Socioeconomic Characteristics of*

Communities with Hazardous Waste Sites. Washington, DC: The Center for Policy
Alternatives, National Association for the Advancement of Colored People, United
Church of Christ.

Gottlieb, Robert. 1993. *Forcing the Spring: Transformation of the American Environmental Movement.* Washington, D.C.: Island Press.

Hamilton, Cynthia. 1993. "Coping with Industrial Exploitation." In Robert D. Bullard (ed).
Confronting Environmental Racism: Voices from the Grassroots. Boston, MA: South
End Press. pp. 63-75.

Hofricher, Richard (ed.). 1993. *Toxic Struggles: The Theory and Practice of Environmental Justice.* Philadelphia, PA: New Society Publishers.

Jain, Shobita. 1991. "Standing up for the Trees: Women's Role in the Chipko Movement." In Sally Sontheimer (ed). *Women and the Environment: A Reader. Crisis
and Development in the Third World.* New York, NY: Monthly Review Press. pp.
163-178.

Khor, Martin. 1993. "Economics and Environmental Justice: Rethinking North-South
Relations." In Richard Hofricher (ed). 1993. *Toxic Struggles: The Theory and Practice
of Environmental Justice.* Philadelphia, PA: New Society Publishers. pp. 219-225.

Kratch, Kellye et al. 1995. "Special Report on Environmental Justice: Grassroots Reach
the White House Lawn." *Environmental Solutions.* Volume 8, Number 5: 68-77.

Krause, Celene. 1994. "Women of Color on the Front Line." In Robert D. Bullard (ed).
Unequal Protection: Environmental Justice and Communities of Color. San Francisco:
Sierra Club Books. pp. 256-271.

_____. 1993. "Blue-Collar Women and Toxic-Waste Protests: The Process of
Politicization." In Richard Hofricher (ed). *Toxic Struggles: The Theory and Practice of
Environmental Justice.* Philadelphia, PA: New Society Publishers. pp.107-117.

Lavelle, Marianne and Marcia Coyle. 1992. "Unequal Protection: The Racial Divide in
Environmental Law." *The National Law Journal.* September 21: S1-S2.

Lee, Charles. 1993. "Beyond Toxic Wastes and Race." In Robert D. Bullard (ed). *Confronting Environmental Racism: Voices from the Grassroots.* Boston, MA: South End
Press. pp. 41-52.

_____. 1987. *Toxic Wastes and Race in the United States: A National Study of
the Racial and Socioeconomic Characteristics of Communities with Hazardous
Waste Sites.* New York, NY: United Church of Christ Commission on Racial
Justice.

Low, Nicholas and Brendan Gleeson. 1998. *Justice, Society and Nature: An Exploration of
Political Ecology.* London, UK and New York, NY: Routledge.

Mann, Eric. 1993. "Labor's Environmental Agenda in the New Corporate Climate." In
Richard Hofricher (ed). *Toxic Struggles: The Theory and Practice of Environmental
Justice.* Philadelphia, PA: New Society Publishers. pp. 179-185.

Martínez-Alier, Joan. 2000a. International Biopiracy Versus the Value of Local Knowledge." *Capitalism, Nature, Socialism.* Volume 11, Number 2: 59-77.

_____. 2000b. "Retrospective Environmentalism and Environmental Justice Move-
ments Today." *Capitalism, Nature, Socialism.* Volume 11, Number 4: 45-50.

Moses, Marion. 1993. "Farmworkers and Pesticides." In Robert D. Bullard (ed). *Confronting Environmental Racism: Voices from the Grassroots.* Boston, MA: South End
Press. pp.161-178.

Nandy, Ashis. 1992. "Introduction: Science as a Reason of State." In Ashis Nandy (ed).
Science, Hegemony and Violence: A Requiem for Modernity. Delhi: Oxford India
Paperback, Oxford University Press. pp. 1-23.

Pulido, Laura. 1996. *Environmentalism and Economic Justice: Two Chicano Struggles in
the Southwest.* Tucson, AZ: University of Arizona Press.

Sachs, Wolfgang. 1999. *Planet Dialectic: Explorations in Environment and Development*. London UK, New York, NY: Zed Books.

_____. 1996. "Neo-development: Global Ecological Management." In Jerry Mander and Edward Goldsmith (eds). *The Case Against the Global Economy*. San Francisco, CA: Sierra Club Books. pp. 239-252.

_____. 1994. "The Blue Planet: An Ambiguous Modern Icon." *The Ecologist*. Volume 24, Number 5: 170-175.

_____. (ed). 1993. *Global Ecology: A New Arena of Political Conflict*. Atlantic Highlands, NJ: Zed Books.

Shiva, Vandana. 1998. *Staying Alive: Women, Ecology, and Development*. London; Atlantic Highlands, NJ: Zed Books.

_____. 1997. *Biopiracy: The Plunder of Nature and Knowledge*. Boston, MA: South End Press.

_____. (ed). 1994a. *Close to Home: Women Reconnect Ecology, Health, and Development Worldwide*. Philadelphia, PA: New Society Publishers.

_____. 1994b. "Conflicts of Global Ecology: Environmental Activism in a Period of Global Reach." *Alternatives*. Volume 19, Number 2 (Spring): 195-207.

_____. 1994c. "The Seed and the Earth: Biotechnology and the Colonization of Regeneration." In Vandana Shiva (ed). *Close to Home: Women Reconnect Ecology, Health, and Development Worldwide*. Philadelphia, PA: New Society Publishers. pp. 128-143.

_____. 1991. *The Violence of the Green Revolution: Third World Agriculture, Ecology and Politics*. London; Atlantic Highlands, NJ: Zed Books.

Szasz, Andrew. 1994. *Ecopopulism: Toxic Waste and the Movement for Environmental Justice*. Minneapolis, MN: University of Minnesota Press.

Third World Network 1989. "Toxic Waste Dumping in the Third World." *Race and Class*. Volume 30, Number 3: 47-56.

(US) EPA (United States Environment Protection Agency). 1992. *Environmental Equity: Reducing Risk for all Communities*. Volumes 1 and 2. Office of Policy Planning and Evaluation. Washington, D.C.: U.S. Government Printing Office.

(US) GAO (United States General Accounting Office). 1983. *Siting of Hazardous Waste Landfills and their Correlation with Racial and Economic Status of Surrounding Communities*. Washington, D.C.: GAO/RCED.

Wright, Beverly. 1995. "Environmental Justice Centers: A Response to Inequity. In Bunyan Bryant (ed). *Environmental Justice: Issues, Policies, and Solutions*. Covelo, CA: Island Press. pp. 57-65.

Wright, Beverly H. and Robert D. Bullard. 1990. "Hazardous in the Workplace and Black Health." *National Journal of Sociology*. Volume 4: 45-62.

2

Ecology, Justice, and the End of Development

Wolfgang Sachs

Nearly 15 years have passed since the *World Commission on Environment and Development*, chaired by Gro Harlem Brundtland, offered its famous formula of how nature could be preserved and development nevertheless continued: sustainable development is development "that meets the needs of the present without compromising the ability of future generations to meet their own needs" (WCED, 1987: 8). After the golden post-war decades with their explosion of world economic output, the bitter insight had thus received an official blessing that conventional development, like a fire, burns off resources which are essential for generations to come. All of the sudden the future changed its tone; it was not any longer a bright period when the fruits of development could be harvested, but appeared as a potentially gloomy period when finally the bill for the party would have to be paid. Against this background, the Brundtland Commission pleaded with governments to consider the time dimension in all their decisions and to weigh benefits in the present against losses in the future. For politicians are not just accountable to their contemporaries, but also bear responsibility for posterity. They are consequently supposed to systematically consider the effects of action taken today upon the conditions of life in the future. The commission called for justice between generations, a concept that had gradually come to the fore since the 1972 United Nations Conference on the Environment in Stockholm.

In light of this concept, the essence of sustainability is to be found in a particular relationship between people and people rather than between people and nature. In fact, the concept can serve as the cornerstone for a new ethical framework; it extends the principle of equity among the human community along the axis of time.

Another anniversary is equally unlikely to shed more light on the issue of justice. At least not in an environmentally reasonable sense. Because in 1992, the United Nations Conference on Environment and Development (UNCED) in Rio de Janeiro was as ambiguous about equity within generations as the Brundtland Commission 15 years ago. It is true, the conference would probably not even have taken place, if the demands of the Southern countries that inequality should be addressed had not been accommodated. But the concern for equity was couched in the language of "development," circumventing again the question: whose development and of what? In fact, the Rio Declaration first reiterates the "right to development" before it proceeds to state the need for environmental protection—which was the motive for convening the conference in the first place. Although during the conference Southern governments countered demands for environmental restrictions with calls for a better balance in North-South relations, they entered an unholy alliance with the North in their praise of development. Both South and North continued to perceive themselves as moving along one single track, each country hoping for redemption in economic growth, albeit starting from different levels. Feeling compelled to mobilize the ever-scarce resources to that end, they converged in assigning sustainability a back seat in the vehicle called economic development. While thus the South entertained its mimetic desire to follow the well-to-do nations, the North could feel free to indulge in its competitive compulsion to keep on rushing ahead. This way, overdevelopment was scarcely an issue, and the fact that it produces both poverty and bio-spherical risk was off the agenda. As the quest for justice was firmly wedded to the idea of development, nobody had to profoundly change and all parties could turn to business as usual—a result amply borne out in recent years.

Point of Departure

The expectation that justice will be brought about through development is deeply engrained in the post-war political discourse. To be sure, its roots reach back to the European Enlightenment, when the people of the globe were recognized as mankind, unified by common dignity and destined to move towards the reign of reason and progress. But it was only after the war that the perception of the world as a site where in a few decades equality could be engineered took hold. For instance, the United Nations (UN) solemnly announced their determination in the Preamble to the UN Charter "to promote social progress and better standards of life in larger freedom . . . and to employ international machinery for the promotion of the economic and social advancement of all people."

Politically, two historical shifts converged in creating a global consensus around this idea. On the one hand, the United States, after the terrors of war, was in search of a new world order which would guarantee peace. In their view, the outbreak of war in Europe had been due to the economic upheaval following the Great Depression. Remembering their own successful management of economic crisis during the New Deal, when Keynes had advised to stabilize the economy through state action, they projected the need for economic growth—steered along through public intervention—upon the globe. The Four Point Program of technical assistance, according to President Truman in his *Memoirs*, "aimed at enabling millions of people in underdeveloped areas to raise themselves from the level of colonialism to self-support and ultimate prosperity" (Truman, 1956: 252). Economic development had to be launched globally in order to lay the base for peace. On the other hand, with the definite downfall of England and France as colonial powers, decolonization set in and new nation-states emerged. With independence achieved, most of these states saw their *raison d'être* in economic development. They secured the support of their citizens by holding out the promise of greater economic output. After extended periods of humiliation during colonialism, they longed for recognition and rushed to join the modern world. For that purpose, they were even ready to turn their societies upside down in order to remake them in the image of the West. Rising income levels and increasing export earnings seemed to be the obvious road to attain a standing equal to the industrial countries. As a result of historical shifts, a global consensus emerged around "development" (Sachs, 1992; Lummis, 1992) as the supreme aspiration which bound North and South together. Social justice, on the level of international politics, was therefore recast as catching up with the rich. Both the hegemonial needs of the North and the emancipatory needs of the South were nicely taken care of in this perspective.

Landslide

The Short Twentieth Century, according to British historian Eric Hobsbawm, lasted from 1914 till 1991, bridging from the breakdown of 19th century civilization in World War I to the collapse of the

Soviet Union after the demise of the Cold War. During most of this period governments felt entitled to intervene in economic affairs for reasons of social welfare. In particular in the decades after World War II, with the disastrous consequences of massive unemployment in Europe in the early 1930s still at hand and communist destabilization looming, nation-states claimed an active role in guiding their economies for, as they saw it, the benefit of all citizens. However, the rapport between territory, wealth creation and governance, which provided the basis for the welfare state, began to disintegrate in the 1980s and 1990s. Hobsbawm calls it a landslide: "As the transnational economy established its grip over the world, it undermined a major, and since 1945, virtually universal, institution: the territorial nation-state, since such a state could no longer control more than a diminishing part of its affairs" (1994: 424).

Before this landslide, states had been the centers of gravity, nationally and internationally. They were therefore in the position to forge a social contract between the wealthy and the poor and to redistribute resources accordingly. In the North, the welfare pact was based on an economy producing jobs, a state redistributing surplus, and on workers purchasing goods and paying taxes. In the South, the developmentalist state mobilized productive resources of all kinds, claiming to cater to the needs of its population. And internationally, the development consensus was in effect a social contract which promoted a system of bilateral and multilateral cooperation that was supposed to close the gulf between the haves and the have-nots. But the social contract was in all of these cases made possible by a certain congruence between the polity and the economy as both were to a large extent bounded by territory. Inasmuch, however, as the power of territories diminishes in the age of globalization, such social contracts are bound to unravel.

Indeed, the power of territories is on the decline and not just in the economic arena. Also satellite television, jobs abroad, cyberspace, and air travel converge in delinking place from community. A transnational sphere of reality has taken shape, which is oblivious of boundaries and cuts across national territories. Nevertheless, the emergence of the globe as an economic arena where capital, goods and services are able to move without much consideration for local and national communities has delivered the most serious blow to the idea of a polity which is built of reciprocal rights and duties among citizens. As corporations attempt to take off for gaining foreign markets, they feel held back by the weight of domestic calls on their responsibility. The same holds true for the elites.

As they aspire to catch up with the vanguards of the international consumer class, their old-style sense of responsibility for the disadvantaged sections of their own society withers away, because they themselves, instead of feeling superior with respect to their countrymen, feel now to be inferior with respect to their global reference groups. Globalization thus undercuts social solidarity. Through transnationalization, capital is in the position to escape any links of loyalty to a particular society. It by far prefers not to be bothered by things like paying taxes, creating jobs, reinvesting surplus, keeping to collective rules, or educating the young, because it considers them mere obstacles to global competition. As the transnational arena becomes the frame of reference, the national community loses in relevance. As a result, in many societies a split opens up between the globally oriented middle class on the one side and—in terms of the world market—superfluous populations on the other. While globalization removes barriers between nations, it thus erects new barriers within nations.

Under the impact of that shift, the basis of the developmentalist state is cracking. More often than not, the states ally themselves with the globalizing forces and increasingly show disregard for the majority of their citizens who live outside the global circuit (Kothari, 1993). They are ever more committed to promoting the insertion of their industries and middle classes into global markets and consider the non-competitive social majority a liability rather than a boon. While "development" still contained the hope of redistribution of wealth and power in favor of the poor, "globalization" redirects state action to providing better opportunities to the well-to-do in their scramble for international standing. As a consequence, the promise of development for all, which was once the glue keeping states together across social and ethnic groups, crumbles and leaves the state with less legitimacy. In the wake of this shift, not the needs of people but the rights of corporations are the focus of politics in the era of globalization. Governments, therefore, are backing out from the development consensus; they increasingly consider the quest for justice outside their competence.

Furthermore, the landslide undermined not just the domestic but the international development consensus as well. For decades it was taken for granted that governments of the North, either directly or indirectly, would extend assistance to Southern countries in order to steer them along the path of development. With the rise of the neo-liberal world view this understanding has withered away, and the claims of the South for more equity remain largely without echo. Particularly the notion—upon which the UN was built—that "the social advancement of peoples" would be a matter of international public responsibility has lost acceptance; private investors are hailed as benefactors of mankind instead. While in the development discourse the state was supposed to be the engine of transformation, this role is taken over by transnational corporations in the globalization discourse. Therefore, international agencies focus their attention on creating a worldwide "level playing field" for companies, whereas redistributive action between governments falls by the wayside. In the neo-liberal view, greater equity—if it matters at all—is seen as expanding the reign of the law of demand and supply across the globe. Not more development cooperation but more investment opportunities seem to offer the prospect of catching up with the North. Whenever, therefore, the "right to development" is invoked today, it is likely to be a call of national elites to be more fully admitted to the global circuit of capital and goods, and not a call for greater solidarity with the majority world beyond the hustle and bustle of the world market.

Impasse

However, the more serious blow to the post-war idea of merging justice and development comes not from changing political but from changing environmental conditions. Because the future, in the image of "development," is constructed as an infinite process of continuous improvement. Tomorrow's conditions, so the story goes, will always surpass today's conditions, if society is put in motion and managed in a rational way. "Development," during the decades after World War II, was nothing else than a reincarnation of the late 18th century idea of material progress, now only projected worldwide and considered attainable through planning and engineering within a few decades. Like progress, also development is open-ended; it knows no point of arrival. Within such a framework, it became possible, domestically as well as internationally, to conceive of justice as an ever-increasing participation of ever more people in an ever growing surplus. The famous metaphor of the growing cake which offers larger pieces for everyone without imposing smaller pieces on anybody illustrates nicely how justice is understood when mankind is perceived as a net-gain community. The quest for justice, in this view, is best satisfied by the incorporation of ever more people in an open-ended global growth process. Given that the overall size of the cake is growing, everybody will be absolutely better off, even if the relative size of the pieces remains the same. Easy to see that this notion of justice has prevailed for at least half a century, not only on the international level but also on the level of national welfare politics. And equally easy to see that it derives its attraction from the promise to achieve justice without redistribution. In other words, the dedication to growth has always been fuelled by the desire to sidestep the hard questions of justice.

Such an open-ended conception of justice and growth rests on a fundamental assumption, however, which has become increasingly shaky in the last quarter of this century. For the long march to greater justice through expanding growth can only continue without getting stuck as long as growth generates more advantages than costs. Indeed, this expectation about the benign nature of growth has dominated Western thought ever since around 1800 (Brunner et al, 1984). It was largely taken for granted that the economic process will turn out to be a positive sum game, i.e., that the benefits accumulated will by far outweigh all the burdens caused in the process. If this was not the case, and growth uncertain in its overall outcome, society would have been foolish to opt for an unfettered pursuit of growth. What is looming behind this expectation, to be sure, is modernity's notorious optimism about the consequences of human action. After all, the moderns believe that the consequences of their action will on balance always be positive, while non-modern cultures tend to have a greater awareness of the fragility of human action, judging the outcome of such action as fundamentally uncertain. Such skepticism in the power of human action has been left behind by the moderns; the belief that economic growth, on the whole, will eventually result in a higher state of welfare for everybody follows from this rosy outlook.

But this optimism about the future—after it had already been shaken by the catastrophic events of the 20th century in the heartlands of Europe—has been finally shattered by what is somewhat euphemistically called the ecological crisis. Far from being just a transitory phenomenon, the emergence of bio-physical limits to economic growth redefines the conditions of wealth creation for the century to come. The open-ended nature of growth cannot be taken for granted any longer; on the contrary, it appears that growth itself is undercutting its own prospects to a point that its finite nature becomes obvious. From the local up to the global level, it has become evident in many instances that the sources (water, timber, oil, minerals etc.), sites (land for mines, settlements, infrastructure), and sinks (soils, oceans, atmosphere) for the natural inputs of economic growth are becoming scarce or being put in turbulence. From now on, material progress has to operate under multi-layered constraints. Even though economic growth has lasted just for several generations and has been limited to a minority of the world population, its finiteness has already become apparent.

The principal ecological constraints are by now well known (e.g., UNDP, 1998: 65-68). On the side of fossil inputs for economic growth it is less the availability of resources in the earth which is presently threatened but the availability of biospherical sinks for absorbing gases which are released while these resources are burned. As the greenhouse effect gathers momentum, climatic turbulences are likely to appear which, among other things, will cause crop failures, flooding, hurricanes, droughts, and an increased rate of losses in biodiversity. On the side of biological resources for growth it is rather the long-range availability which is at stake. In the course of the last fifty years, for example, one third of arable land has been seriously degraded worldwide, and one third of tropical forests, one fourth of the available freshwater, one fourth of the fish reserves have disappeared, not to mention the extinction of plant and animal species. As it stands, a change in these trends is not in sight, on the contrary, in most dimensions the pressures on nature are bound to increase.

However, ecological constraints represent only half the story. They are exacerbated by the fact that the rule of the thumb according to which 20% of world population consumes 80% of the world's resources holds still true. In the global context, the industrialized countries have already overshot their limit by far; they are living well beyond their means. The "ecological footprint" (Wackernagel and Rees, 1996) they produce is larger—and in some cases much larger—than their own territories; they have to tap into the resources available for other countries. In fact, the OECD countries surpass the permissible average size of such a footprint by a magnitude of about 75-85%, while only nine out of 52 analyzed countries remain below this permissible average altogether. As matters stand today, the wealthy 25% of humanity occupy a footprint as large as the entire biologically productive surface area of the earth (Wackernagel, 1997). Surely, such a level of resource consumption cannot be imitated by the rest of the world; any emerging country is well-advised to remain considerably below that level in their industrial development.

Consider, for instance, the greenhouse effect. Oceans and terrestrial biomass are capable of absorbing 13-14 billion tons of carbon dioxide each year, a volume which therefore the world could afford to release without harmful consequences through the burning of wood and fossil energies. If one divided this admissible budget by today's world population of 5.8 billion, everybody were allowed to emit 2.3 tons of CO_2. However, the average German citizen at present accumulates nearly 12 tons (and the average U.S. citizen 20 tons) of carbon dioxide emissions every year. It follows that a country like Germany under present circumstances has overdrawn its carbon budget by a factor of five. Still, this rough calculation is rather favorable for developed countries as it considers only present greenhouse gas emissions and not their increase over the past two hundred years, of which more than 80% have been produced by industrial countries (Sachs et al, 1998: 72). In any case, the German level of 12 tons, short of major climate disruptions, will not be attainable by developing countries. For if all countries followed the German pattern of production and consumption, the world would annually release 67 billion tons in the atmosphere. Given that only 13-14 billion tons are tolerable, mankind would be in need of five planets to have sufficient sinks for CO_2—but it has got just one. A similar argument holds true for living resources, like fish, as well. Despite the fact that fish is essential for the food supply in poorer countries, Japan, Europe, USA and Russia account for more than 40% of the catch, although they comprise just a little more than 20% of the world population (Sachs et al, 1998: 75). This way, a global commons, like ocean fishing grounds— a quarter of which is already exhausted and nearly half of which is already exploited up to the biological limit—is excessively appropriated by the rich, and patterns of fish consumption (including animal feed) are sustained which could spread to the rest of the world only at the price of eliminating any fish from the seas altogether.

Climate change is the most obvious example, and other emerging limits tell a similar story: global equality on the level of the highly industrialized countries would seriously undermine the biosphere's hospitality for humans. Given these historically new circumstances, the message implied in the metaphor of the growing cake has become dangerously misleading. The prospect of greater equity cannot lie any longer in the perspective of ongoing growth. To be sure, there is no eternally fixed relationship between the monetary and the physical size of an economy, but up to the arrival of the post-industrial society economic growth has always implied correspondingly higher inputs of energy and materials, while this connection weakens under post-industrialism, albeit on very high absolute levels of resource consumption. Assuming for the time being a close link between monetary and physical growth, it is therefore not exaggerating to say that, beyond a certain threshold, conventional economic wealth is intrinsically oligarchic; it could be democratized across the globe only at the price of biospherical disruption. Moreover, in a closed space with finite resources is the underconsumption of one party the necessary condition for the overconsumption of the other party. From this angle, it is erroneous to assume that economic growth evolves like a positive sum game; on the contrary, growth is accumulating adverse side effects at such a scale that it is heuristically useful to regard it rather as a zero-sum game. Or to refer to another metaphor dear to the protagonists of growth: the rising tide, before lifting all boats, is likely to burst through the banks.

The illusion that growth can be relied on as a positive-sum game could be sustained because the costs associated with it remained invisible for a long time. What rendered them largely invisible is the fact that the have been successfully shifted elsewhere. Indeed, the novelty brought home by the environmental crisis is not the recognition that growth injures nature but the experience that unpleasant consequences can no longer be kept at a distance. After all, the creation of economic value has always been the art of internalizing benefits and externalizing costs. How benefits and costs are separated out, and who is able of retaining the first while shifting the latter elsewhere is obviously a matter of power; it is for this reason that power has always been an essential ingredient of value creation. Reaping value is made much easier when—mediated through power—a gradient can be established which makes the benefits accrue to the center and the costs slide off to the periphery. Above all during the industrial age, fossil materials and energies could increase the power of money only in as much as the social and environmental costs involved didn't have to be accounted for by economic actors. What appeared as value in official accounts showed up, so to say, as disvalue in the imaginary accounts of future generations, distant countries or humble people.

Because in the history of progress, time, space, and social class have been the major dimensions along which costs have been shifted out of sight and out of mind. As to the dimension of time, it was unrecognized practice for more than a century to move some of the bitter effects of economic progress along the axis of time to future generations. As a consequence, there is by now little doubt that the depletion of fossil reserves, the degradation of soils, the loss in biodiversity, and the change in climate will in all likelihood diminish the chances of posterity to lead flourishing lives, at least in the sense of today's aspirations. As to the dimension of space, the rise of Western nations was greatly facilitated by their power to concentrate the social and environmental costs of resource mobilization in geographically remote areas. Large distances protected the centers from feeling the bitter effects of mining, monoculture, and deforestation, effects that had mainly to be carried by colonized peoples around the world. And finally with regard to social class, the consumer classes often succeeded in passing on environmental burdens to less advantaged groups, leaving them the noise, the dirt, and the ugliness of the industrial hinterland in front of their doorsteps. Particularly hit are those groups—as can be observed in many Southern countries today—which derive their livelihood directly from the free access to land, water, and forests. Building dams and extracting ore, drilling groundwater wells and capitalizing agriculture for the benefit of the urban classes often degrade the ecosystems they live from. More often than not, small peasants, artisans, and tribals are displaced and subsequently marginalized in order to step up the resource provision for the dominating middle class (Gadgil and Guha, 1995).

However, nowadays the distances shrink which once safely separated places of accumulation from places of exploitation, and winners from victims. Costs shifted to the future spill already into the present, geographically there are few frontiers of exploitation left, and socially the powerless come closer, be it through television or migration. As with globalization in general, the world has become a smaller place, not only for goodies but also for troubles. Costs of economic growth, which once accumulated in a fragmentary, dispersed and small-scale manner, and had in addition been shifted to distant points in time and space, now coagulate more and more into limits. It is as if the latency period of industrial affliction were finally over, making the illness break out in many places and instances simultaneously. The old thermodynamic truth that production generates both wealth and waste is looming large, as with the globalization of wealth production also the waste production is closing in upon the planet. For that reason, the notion of the "world risk society" (Beck, 1985) adequately captures the present historical constellation. For with economic growth the manufactured risks seem to grow at a faster rate than the riches produced. Justice at the beginning of the 21st century, therefore, will be more concerned with the reduction of risks than with the redistribution of riches.

The New Colour of Justice

In a world risk society it has become obsolete to turn the desire for justice into a demand for more and accelerated economic development. As the environmental space available for humanity is finite and in some respects already overstretched, conventional growth of enormous physical scale is bound to heighten the various threats. And these threats, there is no doubt, will make everybody, but particularly the poorer countries, worse off. This shift towards a world risk society profoundly modifies the background conditions for the relationship between rich and poor, between Northern and Southern countries. Previously, at the time of President Truman, the worldwide development project could still appear as a global positive sum game where all could be expected to eventually gain; there was no suspicion that the journey towards modernization could at some point be overtaken by a rising flood of risks. Under the new historical constellation, this certainty has vanished, turning the unfettered pursuit of conventional development into a doomed adventure. As a consequence, the demand for justice and dignity on behalf of Southern countries threatens to accelerate the rush towards biospherical disruption, as long as the idea of justice is firmly linked to the idea of development. Delinking the aspiration for justice from the pursuit of conventional development therefore becomes vital for both rescuing the ideal of justice, as "development' falters, and for inventing paths of social improvement which do not systematically overstep the limits of nature.

Certainly, "development" contains a noble hope whose roots reach back to the first half of the 19th century, the founding period of socialist thinking. Impressed by the rapid advances of technology, it was the socialist intuition that there is a floor of minimal technological progress below which equity could never be achieved. With all the advances in agriculture and industrial technology before their eyes, progressives of all shades believed that this floor was reached, and that from now on nobody would have to go hungry anymore. As a consequence, they have worked for rationalizing society and spreading technical progress in order to uplift the poor, first in Europe and then in the rest of the world. Although, however, the assumption that a certain level of technology is indispensable for overcoming chronic scarcity contains more than a kernel of truth, it is about to reveal itself as dangerously one-sided. For the emerging biophysical limits suggest that there is also a ceiling to nature-intensive development beyond which equity cannot be achieved any longer. Chemical agriculture, the automobile society or meat-based nutrition are cases in point. These levels of development are structurally oligarchic; they cannot be generalized across the world without putting life chances of everybody in jeopardy. Given the fact that the 20% who enjoy the highest income of the world population lay claim to 85% of the world's timber, 75% of its metals, and 70% of its energy (UNRISD, 1995), there is no way—even taking a considerable saving potential into account—that their lifestyle can serve as the imagined standard of equity. For this reason, the socialist intuition of the 19th century today has to be complemented by the environmentalist insight of the late 20th century that justice calls for an upper limit to material-intensive development. It appears that this insight is making some headway into official circles, given that the *1998 Human Development Report* of UNDP affirms that "the poor countries have to accelerate their consumption growth, but they must not follow the road taken by the rich and rapidly growing economies in the past half a century." (UNDP, 1998: 8).

It is, however, often overlooked that environmental consumption on the part of the rich, globally and nationally, has an enormous bearing on the possibilities for achieving greater social justice. One reason for that is the confusion which is often made between cleanliness and sustainability. It is true, for 25 years environmental policy has largely focused on cleaning and protecting air, water, and soils. Regulators concentrated on reducing the flow of harmful substances into nature, and filter technologies were mounted at the end of the pipe in order to control emissions at the tail end of production. If the environmental crisis is defined in terms of too much pollution, the issue of justice enters only when the social distribution of harmful impacts—who gets polluted more than others?—is considered. The environmental justice movement in the U.S., for instance, has mobilized protest around the frequent siting of polluting industries in non-white areas. But the issue of justice acquires a different and probably more fundamental relevance if the environmental crisis is defined in terms of excessive resource use. Such a shift in

attention from the tail end to the front end of the economic cycle, however, is in the first place overdue for ecological reasons. For even a clean
economy could cheerfully continue eroding soils, cutting down forests,
degrading biodiversity, and heating the atmosphere. What really matters
is the sheer volume of material input, not so much the pollutants in the
output (Schmidt-Bleek, 1994). After all, the average German consumes
about 80 tons of energy and materials annually and the average Dutch or
American even 3-7 tons more (Adriaanse et al, 1997: 12). These mega-
tons of materials and energy have to be mobilized, at home or in distant
countries, for keeping the entire volume of goods and services on offer.
It is this voracity of the industrial system which puts pressure on
biospherical sources and sinks including the people connected to them.
For this reason, not a clean but a lean economy is the implicit utopia of
sustainability. It means to make the systems of wealth creation less dependent on resource use. Seen in this light, the issue of justice does not
in the first place concern the social distribution of pollution but rather
the social distribution of resource consumption.

The resource perspective, of course, becomes particularly significant
when the overall availability of sources and sinks is limited. Under such
circumstances the question of "Who takes how much?" acquires utmost
political importance. This question, however, does not arise in a pollution perspective which moves developing areas into the focus of attention since pollution tends to be more intense there. It arises only in a
resource perspective where overconsumption is defined as the critical
problem that industrialized countries are put on the spot. For rich countries may be relatively clean, but they remain, at the present state of
affairs, always omnivores. One way to conceptualize the resource perspective in a context of finiteness is the notion of environmental space.
It signifies the total amount of energy and materials which can be utilized by a given society without hurting neither the principle of ecology
nor the principle of equity (FOE, 1995; Carley-Spapens, 1998; and Sachs
et al, 1998). According to the principle of ecology this amount is limited
by the earth's carrying capacity, like the availability and renewability of
resources or the absorptive capacity of natural systems. And the principle of equity confines this amount to a size which can be reconciled with the equal claims of other countries on the patrimony of
resources in the world. In this sense, a society can be called sustainable
when its demands on nature do not exceed the environmental space it is
entitled to use. Fusing an ecological and a social notion of space, the

concept of environmental space therefore captures the two central concerns of sustainability at once, the concern for ecology and the concern for equity. It allows rephrasing of the crucial question of environmental justice as follows: are the rich countries capable of living without the surplus of environmental space they appropriate today?

However, conventional development thinking continues to implicitly define equity as a problem of the poor. Facing the gap which separates the rich from the poor, developmentalists perceive this gap in the first place as a deficit of the powerless and not as a fault of the powerful. They see a lack of credit, education or tools and advocate remedies for bringing the poor up to the task. They launch themselves into raising the living standards of the poor towards the level of the rich. In short, it was the poor who had to be developed in order to achieve greater equity. But designing strategies for the poor, developmentalists work for lifting the bottom—rather than lowering the top (Haavelmo-Hansen, 1991; Goodland and Daly, 1993). The wealthy and their way of producing and consuming remain entirely outside the spotlight as always in the development discourse where the burden of change is solely heaped upon the poor. However, with the emergence of bio-physical limits to growth the classical notions of justice, which were devised in a perspective of finitude and not in a perspective of infinity, acquire new relevance: justice is about changing the rich and not about changing the poor. It was only after the enlightenment, as optimism in progress had firmly settled in, that justice was discussed in terms of promoting the poor rather than of converting the rich. In a world of environmental finitude this tradition of thought is bound to surface again. Today, any debate on equity will have to focus in the first place on lowering or at least transforming the top instead of lifting the bottom. Against the backdrop of drastic global inequality in resource use, it is the North (along with its outlets in the South) which needs structural adjustment. Over and above redistributing riches, the North is called upon to shape its patterns of production and consumption in a way that Southern countries are not deprived of what they are entitled to use.

Given that the Northern consumer class occupies the available environmental space—the patrimony of nature on the planet—to an excessive extent, a systematic retreat from using other people's land and share of the global commons, like the atmosphere and the oceans, is the most important step to be done in the spirit of global responsibility. Northern economies weigh heavily on nature and other peoples; it is this weight which has to be reduced. The environmental space (Opschoor, 1992; Spangenberg et al, 1995) which can be legitimately claimed by a society is delimited by environmental constraints on the one side and by the rights of other societies on the other. In a way, both criterias can be seen as expressing different dimensions of justice. The first speaks about equity between generations, and the second about equity within one generation. While the first criterion has been widely celebrated after the Brundtland Report, the second one remains the object of hot debate. Some argue that rights to resources are to be distributed according to historical achievement, others point to varying degrees of responsibility for resource consumption in the past, while again others invoke different resource needs in different climate zones. Yet the only morally defensible rule is that all citizens of the globe should have an equal right to the world's natural resources. However, such a rule should not be mistaken as a planning objective for planetary redistribution; it is rather a moral principle guiding one's own behavior. Loosely improvising the Kantian imperative, it makes sense to say that a society can only be called sustainable if the maxim of its action is such that this maxim can be the maxim of every other society. Justice above all requires circumspection and self-critical conduct; the principle of equal right of all people to the world's resources is a yardstick to make one's own society a fair global player.

Industrialized countries, as recent research has shown (Factor 10 Club, 1995; Sachs et al, 1998; and MacLaren, 1998), if they aspire to become good global neighbors, will have to bring down their throughput of energy and materials by a factor of 10 within the next fifty years. In other words, if they intend to take sustainability seriously, they will have to reduce their resource weight by 80-90% with respect to the year1990. No doubt, this enormous challenge will amount to a civilizational transition of sorts, bringing both technological talents and new public virtues to bear. It will amount to both an efficiency revolution, giving a new shape to technical progress, and a sufficiency revolution giving rise to a certain disinterest for monetary and material growth. But sufficiency had been the hallmark of justice before the dreams of infinity have taken over; sufficiency in resource consumption is now bound to become the axis around which any post-developmentalist notion of justice will revolve. In future, for industrialized countries and classes, justice will be about learning how to take less rather than how to give more. Whoever calls for equity will have to speak about sufficiency. The anniversaries of both the Brundtland Report and the Earth Summit will remain luke-warm events, if this truism continues to be kept in diplomatic disregard.

References

Adriannse, Albert et al. 1997. *Resource Flows: The Material Basis of Industrial Econo-mies.* Washington, D.C.: World Resources Institute.

Beck, Ulrich. 1985. *Die Risikogesellschaft.* Frankfurt: Suhrkamp.

Carley, Michael and Philippe Spapens. 1998. *Sharing the World: Sustainable Living and Global Equity in the 21st Century.* London: Earthscan.

Friends of the Earth (FOE) 1995. "Action Plan Sustainable Netherlands." In J. Spangenberg et al. *Towards Sustainable Europe: A Study from the Wuppertal Institute for Friends of the Earth Europe.* Lutton: Friends of the Earth.

Gadgil, Madhev and Ramachandra Guha. 1995. *Ecology and Equity.* London: Routledge.

Goodland, Robert and Herman E. Daly. 1993. "Why Northern Income Growth is Not the Solution to Southern Poverty." *Ecological Economics.* Number 8: 85-101.

Haavelmo, T. and S. Hansen. 1991. "On the Strategy of Trying to Reduce Economic Inequality by Expanding the Scale of Human Activity." In Robert J. A. Goodland; Herman E. Daly; and Salah El Serafy (eds). *Environmentally Sustainable Economic Development: Building on Bruntland.* World Bank Working Paper Number 46, July, Washington, D.C.: World Bank.

Hobsbawm, Eric. 1994. *The Age of Extremes: A History of the World, 1914-1991.* New York: Pantheon.

Kothari, Ranji. 1993. *Growing Amnesia: An Essay on Poverty and Human Conscious-ness.* New Delhi: Penguin.

Lummis, D. 1992. "Equality." In Wolfgang Sachs (ed). *The Development Directory: A Guide to Knowledge as Power.* London: Zed Books.

McLaren, D. et al. 1997. *Tomorrow's World: Britain's Share in a Sustainable Future.* London: Earthscan.

Opschoor, Johannes B. et al. 1992. Environment, Economics and Sustainable Develop-ment. Gronigen.

Sachs, Wolfgang (ed). 1992. *The Development Directory: A Guide to Knowledge as Power.* London: Zed Books.

Sachs, Wolfgang et al. 1998. *Greening the North: A Postindustrial Blueprint for Ecology and Equity.* London: Zed Books.

Schmidt-Bleek, F. 1994. Wieviel Umwelt braucht der Mensch? Berlin and Basel: Birkhauser.

Spangenberg, J. et al. 1995. *Towards Sustainable Europe. A Study from the Wuppertal Institute for Friends of the Earth Europe.* Wuppertal: Wuppertal Institute.

Factor 10 Club. 1995. *Carnoules Declaration.* Carnoules.

Truman, Harry. 1956. *Memoirs, Volume 2: Years of Trial and Hope.* New York: Doubleday.

UNDP (United Nations Development Programme). 1998. *Human Development Report 1998.* Oxford and New York: Oxford University Press.

UNRISD (United Nations Research Institute for Social Development). 1995. *States of Disarray: The Social Effects of Globalization.* Geneva: UNRISD.

Wackernagel, Mathias and William E. Rees 1997. "Perceptual and Structural Barriers to Investing in Natural Capital: Economics from an Ecological Footprint Perspective." *Ecological Economics.* Number 20: 3-24.

Wackernagel, Mathias and William E. Rees. 1996. *Our Ecological Footprint: Reducing Human Impact on the Earth.* New Society Publishers: Gabriola Island, British Co-lumbia.

WCED (World Commission on Environment and Development). *Our Common Future*. Oxford and New York: Oxford University Press.

Part II

Case Studies

3

A Revolution in Environmental Justice and Sustainable Development: The Political Ecology of Nicaragua

Daniel Faber

> Not only humans desired liberation.
> The entire ecology cried for it.
> The revolution
> Is also for lakes, rivers, trees and animals.

Father Ernesto Cardenal
Nicaraguan Minister of Culture, 1986

Introduction

On July 19, 1979, the Sandinista National Liberation Front (FSLN) assumed power over the Nicaraguan government after a popular insurrection toppled the brutal dictatorship of Anastasio Somoza Debayle. Recognizing the interlinkages between the conditions of poverty, social injustice, and environmental degradation which gave birth to the revolution, the Sandinista government immediately launched an array of ambitious social and environmental programs designed to revitalize the country. Initiated in concert with ecologists, trade unionists, peasant organizations, community associations, and other mass-based movements in a popular-class political alliance, these programs would quickly emerge as among the most comprehensive governmental efforts to simultaneously protect nature and raise the quality of life for its people ever seen in Latin America, if not the entire Third World.

Over the course of the 1980s, the ecological successes in Nicaragua would draw widespread acclaim and support from the U.S. and international environmental movements. For codified within these programs was a radically new approach to Third World environmentalism. Ecological concerns were not subordinated to other governmental initiatives, as had been the case with so many previous "progressive nationalist" and socialist Third World states. Rather, *la liberación del medio ambiente*, or the liberation of the environment, became fundamental to the process of revolutionary social transformation.

Under the banner of *revolutionary ecology*, the new Nicaraguan government aimed to create policies, projects, and programs which would: (1) promote *social* and *environmental justice* by resolving the dialectically related economic *and* ecological burdens which *Somocismo* had unequally displaced onto Nicaragua's popular classes, especially the masses of poor peasants and workers; (2) promote *national sovereignty* and *control* over the country's natural resources by establishing greater autonomy vis-a-vis the more exploitive features of the world capitalist system in general, and U.S. neo-colonialism in particular; (3) promote a model of *sustainable development* dedicated to meeting the needs of all present and future generations of Nicaraguans by overcoming the interrelated "free" market-based economic irrationalities and ecological contradictions which had continuously plagued the country since the beginning of the Alliance for Progress in the 1960s; and (4) to promote *ecological democracy* by building popular democratic forms of social governance and economic planning in which the people themselves (and the movements which represented their interests) would share the responsibility of designing and implementing environmental programs in their own communities.

These four mutually reinforcing principles: (1) social and environmental justice; (2) national sovereignty and self-determination; (3) sustainable development; and (4) ecological democracy; embodied the essence of what would become the single most important national experiment in radical ecology the world has ever seen. For in order to build a viable and lasting alternative to the destructive tendencies of dependent capitalist development, on the one hand, and bureaucratic state socialism, on the other hand, required the realization of these four basic goals. Without a viable revolutionary ecology, Nicaraguan society would inevitably fail to overcome the massive problems inherited from the past, or to resolve the internal and external pressures to be encountered in the future. The revolution would ultimately collapse under the weight of its own unfulfilled promises.

In this chapter, I will illustrate the manner in which this unique experiment with revolutionary ecology initially proved to be so successful. I also examine the forces responsible for its eventual failure, emphasizing the devastating impacts of U.S.-sponsored economic and military aggression. It is a painful review, for the optimism so abundantly expressed by ecologists and Left-progressive movements with regard to the potentialities of the Nicaraguan revolution in the early 1980s has been superceded by a pessimism grounded in the desperate realities of the country's current crisis—a condition magnified by the devastation wrought by Hurricane Mitch in November of 1998. This socially-created "natural" disaster, which killed over 3,000 Nicaraguans, damaged or destroyed over 500,000 homes, and wiped out twenty-five years of investment in infrastructure, was somewhat inevitable given the dismantling of the environmental programs established under the Sandinista government during the 1980s. Nicaragua, like so much of the Central American region, now sits on the verge of economic collapse. Until the political, economic, and ecological conditions which allowed Hurricane Mitch to become such a cataclysm are transformed, more disasters will occur. This is one of many critically important lessons to be learned from this revisit of history. For despite the downfall of the Nicaraguan revolution in the late 1990s, it still remains a powerful example of the emancipatory possibilities which exist when the democratic masses of the Third World assume control over their own destiny, as well as the tragic consequences which occur when such control is lost.

Prelude to an Ecological Revolution: The Social and Environmental Crisis of Nicaragua under Somoza

The roots of the Sandinista revolution lay in the legacy of widespread poverty and repression experienced by Nicaragua's popular classes, the products of a United States-promoted model of dependent capitalist development. Under the Alliance for Progress beginning in the early 1960s [and before], the U.S. and Somoza governments initiated policies designed to integrate Nicaragua more fully into the world economy as a cheap supplier of agricultural commodities and raw materials. This was accomplished by promoting the modernization and expansion of large agricultural estates under the control of a small class of large landowners, or *latifundistas*, allied with the Somoza dictatorship. By the time of the insurrection in 1979, large landholders representing a mere 1% of the population controlled half of the land in Nicaragua. Somoza himself owned 20% of the nation's prime farmland. Export commodity crops—cotton, coffee, sugar, tobacco, and cattle—dominated the agricultural landscape. The Somoza family and allied agrarian elites received the bulk of foreign development aid and financial credit to generate these cheap export commodities for the United States and other first world countries.

Laboring in service of this capitalist agricultural export system, but receiving few of its benefits, Nicaragua's majority, the poor peasant farmers and workers who made up the subsistence sector, struggled to survive. Over 60% of rural people were deprived of the land they needed to feed themselves. Over half of Nicaragua's children were undernourished under Somoza. Impoverished Nicaraguan peasants compelled to work on the large export estates during the short harvest season received wages as low as a dollar a day. Malnutrition, disease and illiteracy were rampant.

Moved off their traditional lands by the rapid expansion of the capitalist export sector over the previous two decades (often with the use of brutal military force by the U.S.-backed National Guard), tens of thousands of peasant families had migrated into steep surrounding hillsides and interior rainforests, clearing the trees and vegetation in order to plant food crops. However, most of these fragile lands were of marginal quality and ill-suited for agriculture. As a result, massive soil erosion, habitat destruction, watershed deterioration, mudslides and flash flooding soon ravaged the countryside. Land degradation was so severe, for instance, that the arable layer of soil had been eliminated on hillsides covering thousands of miles, particularly in the Matagalpa, Estelí, and Ocatal regions. Soil erosion was also quite severe on the steep slopes south of Managua.

Forced to overexploit their smallholdings in order to survive, much of the peasant subsistence sector had reached a point of severe ecological degradation and collapse. Tens of thousands more family members were forced to give up their farms, and move into Managua and other urban areas to populate the growing slums. Lacking such basic services as water and electricity, these shantytowns would often locate along riverbanks and floodplains, steep barren hillsides, and other ecologically precarious areas. Many remain to this day. In Honduras as well as Nicaragua, most of the over 10,000 people swept away by the flood waters and landslides of Hurricane Mitch in early November of 1998 (such as the massive Casitas volcano mudslide in Nicaragua, which buried numerous villages and killed 2,000 people) were the poor who resided in these environmentally degraded and dangerous areas. The flooding, avalanches and resulting deaths were the products of widespread poverty and environmental degradation, which were in turn the creation of the region's exploitive political-economic structures. The legacy of *Somocismo* in Nicaragua (and *Caudillismo* in Honduras) were as much responsible for the devastation as were the rains of the hurricane itself.

After the overthrow of Somoza in 1979, the new Sandinista government immediately faced the monumental task of not only rebuilding and transforming a society crippled by the 1972 earthquake, which had killed up to 20,000 people and caused a minimum of $772 million in damage, including the destruction of 75% of Managua's housing and 90% of its commercial capacity; but also with revitalizing a society devastated by civil war. Some 50,000 Nicaraguans lost their lives in the 1978-79 revolution against the U.S.-backed regime, with material damage estimated at an additional $480 million by the United Nations, a huge sum for such a small economy. To make matters worse, Somoza had sacked the national treasury before fleeing to Miami, leaving the country with a $1.6 billion foreign debt, the highest in Central America.

In addition to an economically devastated society, Somoza left behind something else. The Sandinistas discovered a national environmental crisis of massive proportions. Most of Nicaragua's Pacific coastal plain suffered serious pesticide contamination, including subterranean water resources. In 1977 alone, a United Nations report estimated that insecticide-caused environmental and social damage amounted to $200 million a year (a figure greater than the total foreign exchange earnings of the cotton crop on which the vast bulk of the pesticides were used). The country held the dubious distinction of being a world leader in pesticide poisonings; nearly 400 pesticide-related deaths were reported annually. Pesticide runoff from cotton agriculture, toxic chemical pollution from lakeside industries and untreated sewage dumped from the capital city had virtually killed Lake Managua; a body of water equivalent in size to California's Lake Tahoe had become the "Lake Erie" of Central America. The World Health Organization found that polluted water led to 17% of all Nicaraguan deaths. Deforestation had caused widespread soil erosion, dust storms and flash floods. In the eastern half of the country, cattle ranching was eating into Nicaragua's extensive tropical rainforests, 30% of which disappeared in the 1970s. Many species of wildlife teetered on the brink of extinction, the result of habitat destruction and unregulated sale in local and world markets. These environmental problems merged with poverty and the lack of social services to give the Nicaraguan people the lowest life expectancy in all of Central America.

For forty-five years the Somoza family utilized its control of the National Guard and U.S. financial and military support to pillage the country's natural resources, often for direct personal gain. Profits derived from the exploitation of nature were seldom used to serve the majority of the population by building broad-based educational or health systems, but rather flowed into the bank accounts of the *Somocistas* and growing agrarian bourgeoisie. Foreign and domestic companies had access to the country's resources, as long as they paid the necessary "concessions" to the dictatorship. For example, the U.S.-owned Nicaraguan Long Leaf Pine Company (NIPCO) directly paid the Somoza family a percentage of the company's multimillion-dollar timber business from 1945-60 in exchange for favorable terms of trade, such as not having to reforest clearcut areas. Thus, by 1961, NIPCO had cut all of the commercially valuable coastal pines (*Pinus caribea*) in northeast Nicaragua, leaving over 1,160 square miles denuded.

Although there were a few United Nations sponsored environmental projects in Nicaragua, most attempts by environmentalists, trade unions, and other popular organizations seeking a more equitable distribution and rational management of the country's social and natural resources were seen as a threat to the regime. The social and environmental crisis had reached the point where more and more Nicaraguans recognized that only a fundamental transformation in the country's power structure could open the door to ecologically sound and socially beneficial development policies. Many environmentalists even took to the hills and streets to join the Sandinista guerrillas who were waging war against the Somoza regime. Some, such as Ivan Montenegro Baez and Edguard Munguia Alvarez, lost their lives. As limnologist Salvador Montenegro, one of the proponents of the Ministry of Natural Resources told me, "revolutionary struggle and environmentalism became one."

La Liberación del Medio Ambiente: Guiding Principles for the Establishment of Revolutionary Ecology

With the triumph of the Sandinista revolution over the dictatorship, Nicaragua's environmental movement was presented an opportunity for reorienting the country on a socially just and sustainable development path. On August 24, 1979, the new Sandinista government responded by creating the Nicaraguan Institute of Natural Resources and the Environment (Instituto Nicaragüense de Recursos Naturales y del Ambiente - IRENA)—the country's first environmental agency, stating:

> The environment and natural resources are considered to have a great impact on society; they deserve the attention of the State, which aspires to socio-economic change based on national sovereignty, self-determination, and the participation of the population . . . The preservation of natural resources is not a goal for its own sake, but must be directed toward elevating the quality of life!

With the creation of IRENA, there developed within an important sectors of the Nicaraguan government a "revolutionary ecology" perspective [of both socialist and nationalist stripes] which recognized that comprehensive environmental programs and policies were absolutely essential for addressing the country's social and economic crisis, just as comprehensive social and economic reform of the existing model of dependent capitalist development was essential for addressing the country's ecological crisis. In fact, IRENA immediately assumed a powerful and central role in the process of social transformation, taking responsibility for all of the country's renewable and non-renewable resources, including the nationalized mining, fishery, forestry, and wildlife sectors. This political tendency toward revolutionary ecology came to be reflected in IRENA's programs, including reforestation, watershed management, pollution control, wildlife conservation, national parks, environmental education and the conservation of genetic diversity. Other government agencies and non-governmental organizations (NGOs) worked with IRENA, as well as mass-based organizations, on pesticide control and regulation, energy conservation, agrarian reform, appropriate technology, and community/worker health and safety.

Supported by a variety of foreign aid sources, especially from the Scandinavian countries, as well as by multilateral aid agencies like the United Nations Food and Agriculture Organization (FAO) and the Organization of American States (OAS), these programs were guided by principles which sought the achievement of four mutually reinforcing goals: (1) social and environmental justice; (2) national sovereignty and self-determination; (3) sustainable development; and (4) ecological democracy. As such, these environmental programs were seen as essential to the process of social[ist] transformation and national liberation, which had as its goal a new model of "mixed" economic development devoted to the needs of the "popular classes."

(1) Social and Environmental Justice

In pre-revolutionary Nicaragua, the poorest and the least politically powerful segments of the popular classes—industrial and agricultural workers, small family farmers (or peasants) and villagers, poor rural women and children, indigenous peoples, poor families in the informal sector, and even some sectors of the middle class—were impacted to the greatest degree by the ecological crisis. Lacking the same level of protection afforded by environmental regulations and movements in the United States, multinational corporations, nationally based industries, and the *Somocista* bourgeoisie displaced extraneous costs of production in the form of toxic pollution and other hazards onto the Nicaraguan people and their environment.

For instance, some thirty-seven industrial plants located on the shores of Lake Managua freely dumped their waste for years, including the U.S. corporation Pennwalt, Inc., which released an estimated 40 tons of mercury (which causes a series of neurologically-related health problems ranging from birth defects to severe brain damage) into the lake between 1968-81. An investigation by the Sandinista government and Pan American Health Organization found gross mercury contamination at the plant site, including mercury levels in the air of the facility six times higher than deemed permissible by the U.S. Occupational Safety and Health Administration (OSHA). As a result, fifty six (37%) of the plant's 152 workers were found to have damaged central nervous systems—the result of mercury intoxication. By the time of the insurrection, 50% of the country's water sources were seriously polluted by sewage, 75% by agricultural residues, and 25% by highly toxic industrial contaminants. Thousands of people died each year from pesticide poisonings and polluted waterways.

One of the most immediate missions of the new Sandinista government was to correct the multiple, local, historically, and culturally specific manifestations of social and environmental injustice. Only by adopting an "environmentalism of the poor" could the political and economic mechanisms which inequitably *produced* and *displaced* social and environmental problems onto the popular classes, particularly those segments of the working class and peasantry living at the fringe of survival, be effectively dismantled. A central goal of the new Nicaraguan government was to engage in processes of social planning and development which not only eliminated the *discriminatory* or *unequal distribution* of social and ecological hazards among the population, i.e, distributional environmental justice. It was also dedicated to eliminating the root causes which *produced* such hazards in the first place, i.e., productive environmental justice. The politics of productive environmental justice in Nicaragua focused not on distributing ecological risks equally but instead devoted the necessary social resources and reoriented the character of the development model as to *prevent* such hazards from being produced in the first place so that no one is harmed at all. As we shall soon see, the government's agrarian reform measures, which aimed to reestablish the social and ecological vitality of the peasant subsistence sector, would play one of the most fundamental roles for achieving environmental justice.

(2) National Sovereignty and Self-Determination

Prior to the revolution, Nicaragua was integrated into the world economy as a supplier of cheap agricultural commodities and raw materials. Cotton and coffee alone generated between roughly 40 and 60 percent of Nicaragua's total export earnings during the 1960s and 1970s. Neither backward linkages—industries that produce commodities (producer goods or inputs) necessary for raw material and agricultural production (such as farming equipment)—nor forward linkages—industries that process agricultural products and raw materials into another commodity form (e.g., hemp into rope)—had been developed. Despite the creation of the Central American Common Market (CACM), and some industrial expansion, these new enterprises were not well integrated into the domestic economy. As a result, the capitalist export sector remained highly dependent on imported capital goods and highly vulnerable to trade and credit fluctuations in the international market. Thus, the country was *sectorally disarticulated*.

Nicaragua was also *socially disarticulated* in that poverty was so pervasive that the national economy possessed little consumption capacity for commodities produced by the capitalist export sector. Foreign markets, rather than the nation's peasantry and poor working classes, were the primary sources of aggregate consumer demand. As a result, the region's economy was again extremely vulnerable to world market conditions in the form of falling prices for major exports and declining terms of trade, protectionism, overproduction, and economic slumps in the First World.

This condition was magnified by the extremely small size and openness of the Nicaraguan (and Central American) economy. It was more like a small corporation in a highly competitive world market than a truly independent national economy, with contractions or expansions in the local supply of leading agricultural exports having little impact on the international prices for its major export commodities. Hence, the volume of Nicaragua's exports was determined by domestic production costs compared to costs elsewhere and the margin between world prices and production costs. With the primary market located abroad, both the production and consumption capacities of Nicaragua's capitalist export sector were increased by minimizing costs, especially workers' wages and benefits and "unproductive" expenditures related to workplace health and safety and environmental protection. Unburdened by effective environmental and community health and safety regulations that would impose greater production costs on capital, drain profits and damage competitiveness, a host of Nicaraguan industries freely damaged the environment and public health.

Thus, the Nicaraguan struggle to build genuine ecological socialism in "one country" was immediately confronted with a fundamental challenge—namely to break the shackles of foreign economic dependency and build a new development model based on greater national sovereignty vis-a-vis the world capitalist system. Given the history of the Monroe Doctrine, the Sandinistas were painfully aware that any nation seeking to liberate its people and environment from U.S. neo-colonialism was destined to experience severe repercussions. This hostility assumed a variety of political, economic, and military forms— ranging from declining terms of trade to trade embargoes; elimination of badly needed credit, international aid, and development assistance; diplomatic isolation; covert operations aimed at creating social and political destabilization; and indirect or even direct military intervention.

Without greater autonomy from exploitive world economic trade arrangements, the Nicaraguan revolution would undoubtedly experience growing pressures to over-exploit natural resources in order to boost exports, while at the same time having to cut social services and environmental protection, and weaken other programs which did not generate foreign exchange. Lacking other options, a type of self-imposed "structural adjustment" policy would likely occur. Any revolution which is overly dependent upon external inputs for its financial stability would be in an extremely vulnerable situation.

In order to further the process of social transformation and reduce their susceptibility to international economic pressures, the Sandinista government pursued policies aimed at promoting a non-aligned foreign policy; economic and agricultural diversification of both domestic and export products; socialization of the country's renewable and non-renewable resources; greater self-reliance for the domestic production of basic essentials, including food and energy self-sufficiency; increased domestic processing of agricultural and raw material products; and expansion of social planning by the state in order to place strict controls over trade (import and exchange controls), banking (which was nationalized), and other key industries. As we shall soon see, revolutionary ecology became essential in the pursuit of these aims, providing the scientific and technological basis for promoting greater self-sufficiency.

(3) Sustainable Development

Third, the Nicaraguan revolution sought to pursue an alternative economic model which fused the principles of environmental justice and national sovereignty with that of sustainable development, or what Lorenzo Cardenal, former Director of National Parks under the Sandinista government, termed "productive conservation." Such an approach emphasized not only the scientific and cultural value of nature preservation. It also sought to overturn the irrationalities of previous political-economic processes which resulted in the periodic eruptions of ecological instability and crisis.

Under Somoza, disarticulated capitalist development had resulted in the severe degradation and widespread destruction of the material conditions of both subsistence and export production. Encouraged by international trade pressures and a lack of democratic accountability, large growers and businesses ruthlessly overexploited the nation's natural resources. While these economic practices maximized the profits of individual capital in the short-run, the long-run results were the severe degradation and/or collapse of the social and ecological conditions of production for capital as-a-whole (especially cotton growers), culminating in the severe economic/ecological crisis of the late 1970s which helped catalyze the Sandinista revolution. By integrating principles of sustainable development and productive conservation into the many new programs for national recovery, the Sandinista government hoped to identify and arrest such eco-economic irrationalities and contradictions. Leading officials recognized that any program for meeting the needs of the popular classes and promoting national independence, which was not environmentally sustainable in the long run, would become politically and economically destabilizing to the revolutionary project

Unfortunately, for the Sandinista government, very few alternative development models existed elsewhere in the world for them to imitate. At the time of the revolution, existing state-socialist societies proved themselves capable of duplicating the worst ecological irrationalities and contradictions. Much of the problem in these states resided in the "modernist" or "developmentalist" approach to building socialism embraced by Communist Party/bureaucratic elites. Such an approach uncritically imitated the form and substance of capitalist science and technology as being most "advanced." To achieve sustainable development, the Sandinistas faced the challenge of developing new productive forces and processes which treated nature as an ally rather than an adversary—of developing a new science of socialist ecology.

(4) Ecological Democracy

Fourth, in order to build a new society committed to the principles of social and environmental justice, national sovereignty, and sustainable development, the Sandinista government expanded the role of state authority in regulating the economic system. Although Nicaragua was far from being a wholly state-run socialist economy, the Sandinista project did place a heavy emphasis on reconstructing a more expansive state apparatus which would intervene more directly into the economy on behalf of the popular classes. This would include the assumption of state ownership and/or control over key economic sectors, such as banking and credit services, insurance, marketing and commercial exports, natural resources, and the large agricultural estates once owned by the *Somocistas*. For instance, with the passage the "Program of Economic Reactivation to Benefit the People" in January of 1980 (known as Plan 80), the Sandinista government initiated new economic programs and agrarian reform measures with [as we shall soon see] the specific long-run objectives of reactivating industrial and agricultural production and distribution with the aim of satisfying the "basic needs" of the population; as well as to build and maintain a level of "national unity" among various popular sectors (specifically, as the programs saw them, wage and salary workers, small producers and artisans, professionals and technicians, and "patriotic entrepreneurs").

Within Nicaraguan society, however, a public debate emerged as to what forms of state planning and intervention were most appropriate. One of the lessons provided by the legacy of the former Soviet Union and other Eastern European countries is that any socialist society which institutes social *ownership* of the means of production without establishing systems of genuine democratic social *control* by the people is doomed to be a political and ecological failure. Characterized by top-down systems of Party/bureaucratic rule which sever links with both people and nature, really-existing state socialist societies resorted to a rightist politics of commandism. In light of such abuses of power, there was a realization among environmentalists and key sectors of the Sandinista government that an alternative model of democratic state planning would have to be invented. Given the inadequate bureaucratic infrastructure, scarcity of material resources, and the lack of human skills and experience needed to efficiently administer the state planning process, such a state structure of commandism would not be possible in Nicaragua anyway (even if it were desirable). Rather, the Nicaraguan revolution would have to promote new forms of democratic state planning and administration which increased the power of the people themselves to exercise control over the major political, social, and economic institutions in society.

To promote "social governance of the means of production," the Nicaraguan revolution introduced new experiments in what I term *ecological democracy*, based on the sublation of workplace and local direct democracy, liberal democratic procedures and constitutional guarantees, participatory state planning at the neighborhood, regional, and national levels, and the initiatives by popular-based social and environmental movements. Working in conjunction with mass-based organizations, campesino trade unions, international non-governmental organizations (NGOs), producers associations, environmentalists, women's groups, indigenous peoples, and volunteers from all over the world, the new Nicaraguan government would mobilize and coordinate new forms of participatory democracy. These Left experiments in democracy would counteract the tendency towards Sandinista Party commandism by encouraging the empowerment of grassroots organizations and networks which could more effectively identify and implement solutions to the country's social and environmental problems.

In this respect, the Sandinista revolution created a political environment where non-governmental groups like the Nicaraguan Association of Biologists and Ecologists (ABEN), and later the Nicaraguan Environmental Movement (MAN) had access to the highest levels of government and were free to work without fear of reprisal (in contrast to environmental work in Honduras, El Salvador, and Guatemala, where repression is common). Plagued by the Somoza dictatorship's legacy of underdevelopment, a lack of trained personnel; insufficient knowledge and information about tropical ecosystems and ecological processes; inadequate legislation and environmental education; and absence of economic resources necessary to manage many of the proposed programs for the ecological recovery of the country, IRENA and other governmental agencies would in fact, come to rely on the support and participation of both national and international environmental NGOs for the implementation of governmental policy.

For this reason, innovative environmental policies were more efficiently implemented from the "bottom up." Sandinista Party members, elected officials, and state bureaucrats on all levels would often share environmental decision-making power with those movements and mass-based organizations representing the interests of the popular classes not only as workers and producers, but also as consumers, women, community residents, and citizens in a type of broad-based ecological democracy. However, as we shall see, as U.S. economic and military pressures upon Nicaragua multiplied during the 1980s, the politics of commandism would eventually prevail, undermining those democratic forces necessary to the survival of the revolutionary process.

In Defense of Nature, 1979-1986 Agrarian Reform: Social and Ecological Reconstruction of the Countryside

Central to the process of revolutionary social transformation in Nicaragua was the pursuit of a non-aligned foreign policy, economic diversification, democratization of the state and social planning, and agrarian reform. As part of the move toward a "mixed economy" (and eventually democratic socialism), key industries and agricultural estates controlled by the *Somocista* agrarian bourgeoisie, including the one-fifth of the nation's farmland owned by the Somoza family, were confiscated and placed under the direct control of the government. Workers on the new state farms and peasant farmers were encouraged to join unions, grassroots organizations and other participatory structures. The aim of the state was to continue agricultural export production for the world market, but then utilize foreign exchange earnings to fund social and environmental programs.

The establishment of state farms was seen by many Nicaraguans as inadequate, however, and soon landless and land-poor peasants began organizing land confiscations and demanding more comprehensive agrarian reform measures. By the beginning of 1980, increased political pressure by the Association of Rural Workers (Associación de Trabajadores del Campo, or ATC) and National Union of Farmers and Cattle Ranchers (Unión Nacional de Agricultores y Ganaderos, or UNAG), as well as the stagnation of domestic grain production, finally led the government to begin providing campesinos with better credit services, guaranteed prices, technical assistance and agricultural inputs. But campesino impatience continued to grow, and on July 19, 1981, President Daniel Ortega announced the proposed Agrarian Reform Law to the applause of half a million Nicaraguans gathered to celebrate the second anniversary of the triumph. With the enactment of the law and land redistribution in August, the government initiated the first comprehensive program in the country's history for reversing the social impoverishment of the Nicaraguan peasantry and promoting domestic food production. By July 1984, the government had given some 45,000 beneficiaries as family farm owners or members of farm cooperatives free titles to some 2.4 million acres—over one-fifth of the nation's farmland—more than ten times all the land owned by poor peasants before the revolution.

Under the reformulated Law of Agrarian Reform in January 1986, land redistribution of "underutilized" farms (including smaller holdings) to both cooperatives and individual families continued, while state marketing schemes attempted to improve terms of trade and consumer goods distribution for peasant producers. Eventually, the government would give private and cooperative land titles covering nearly 5.2 million acres (over one third of Nicaragua's farmland) to about 120,000 peasant families—more than half of the country's peasant population. In addition, the revolutionary government prevented the new land titles from being held as collateral on bank loans, removing the primary "legal" means by which land had been appropriated from small farmers in the past. This stability meant that peasants took a greater interest in the long-term potential and productivity of their own lands and laid the groundwork for the implementation of soil conservation and other small-scale projects with clear environmental benefits.

As part of this larger process of agrarian and economic reform, the Sandinista government also launched a series of projects designed to reverse the ecological impoverishment of the peasantry. In coordination with many other government agencies and the agrarian reform, IRENA initiated a series of projects designed to restore, protect, and more rationally manage the ecological conditions of peasant *minifundio* production. Between 1982-85, the Western Erosion Control Project provided peasant communities with the education, technical assistance, and supplies needed to address problems of deforestation, erosion, and fertility loss. Some 6,670 acres of achote, pine, and eucalyptus were planted by the program to protect watersheds and provide windbreaks for crops, as well as the construction of 4,220 torrent-regulating dykes to control erosion and flooding. In Managua, the Council of Environmental Quality promoted the cultivation of appropriate crops for soil conservation in the denuded Southern Managua Watershed, a project begun by IRENA in coordination with the area's small farmers. These efforts were extended in 1988, when the FAO and Dutch government supported a grassroots environmental education and restoration project (including reforestation and wildlife protection) called "Heroes and Martyrs of Veracruz," that continued the work with peasant farmers to preserve some 500,000 acres of tropical dry forest and farmland in the degraded Pacific highlands, including the uppermost reaches of the rugged Maribios watershed.

Programs to reverse years of impoverishment and revitalize the subsistence sector were accompanied by a variety of national campaigns. By 1984, because of a massive vaccination campaign in which 70,000 Nicaraguan volunteer health workers participated, polio had been eliminated, cases of malaria decreased 40%, and cases of measles dropped from 3,784 to 104. By 1986, Nicaragua was allocating 14% of the national budget to health care, up from 3% in the days of Somoza. As a result, Nicaragua's infant mortality rate dropped from 120 per 1,000 live births in 1979 to 65 per 1,000 births by 1988, while the average life span increased from 53 to 60 years of age, despite the Contra war. Improvements in health were so dramatic that Nicaragua won the 1982 World Health Organization prize for greatest achievement by a third-world country. Literacy campaigns reduced illiteracy from 58% to 12.9%. As part of the National Literacy Campaign of 1980, workers and peasants were also educated about the country's natural resources and environmental issues such as erosion and deforestation.

Through the "Campesino to Campesino" community-based project supported by UNAG, small farmers also initiated a process of environmental self-education, teaching communities throughout the country about soil conservation, biological control of agricultural pests, organic agriculture, and appropriate technology. The project's objective was to promote and expand a campesino-led sustainable agricultural movement with its own vision of development, capable for forming national alternatives for food production and environmental preservation. This project was initiated in the context of numerous other projects in reforestation, solar ovens and more efficient wood stoves, soy and organic coffee, crop rotation and intercropping, tree planting, composting, landfills and improved latrines, agro-forestry, flood control, and windmills—all designed to restore the ecological conditions of subsistence production and promote a new model of sustainable peasant agriculture.

Wilderness and Wildlife Protection

The implementation of comprehensive agrarian reform in the early years of the revolution had an immediate impact of Nicaragua's rich tropical rainforests. By re-distributing land to peasant families so that they could grow their own crops, the Ministry of Agriculture (MIDINRA) halted migrations from the Pacific coast to the agricultural frontier on the Atlantic side. By 1983 the government had stopped all peasant colonization projects, and removed state repression as a vehicle for cattle ranchers to displace peasants and destroy the forests. As a result, the rate of deforestation of Nicaragua's humid tropical rainforests had been cut in half—from 386 square miles per year in the late 1970s (the highest in the region)—to 194 square miles by 1985 (among the region's lowest). This dramatic reduction in rainforest destruction was unprecedented in the Third World.

To restore watersheds and prevent erosion, IRENA also launched four major reforestation projects. The Western Erosion Control Project in the Pacific region of León planted some 3,000 trees a day over a two-year period to build 745 miles of windbreaks in cotton-growing areas. In the watersheds surrounding both León and Managua, IRENA built thousands of mini-dams for erosion control, reforesting and promoting permanent crop cultivation in order to stop mudslides that continued to damage low-lying areas. In the north-central Estelí region IRENA replanted thousands of acres in an effort to restore the ocote pines (*Pinus oocarpa*) which were decimated by transnational companies in the 1970s. The Northeast Forestry project did the same for the coastal pines that were clear-cut by the U.S. company NIPCO in the 1950s. Nurseries throughout the country grew 2 million trees annually for use in reforestation projects.

Despite Nicaragua's successes in preserving rainforests, tensions did exist between national park plans and indigenous land rights. In 1980 for instance, Lorenzo Cardenal, IRENA's Director of National Parks declared Bosawas, the Western Hemisphere's largest tropical rainforest north of the Amazon Basin, a national reserve and began to make plans for national parks, wildlife refuges, biological reserves and sustained yield forestry within Bosawas' 4,250 square mile boundaries. The Bosawas reserve, according to Native American activists John Mohawk and Denis Shelton, was established with "the intent of benefiting indigenous communities and protecting the environment." Yet Miskito and Sumo Indians living there saw IRENA's park plans as an attempt to "nationalize" their lands. Aggravated by cultural insensitivity on the part of the Nicaraguan government, as well the contra war and political manipulations by the United States, military conflicts soon developed which foreclosed opportunities for establishing IRENA's plan for wilderness and cultural conservation—a clash which would eventually give birth to a unique government supported autonomy project for the entire Atlantic coast.

Regarding wildlife, in spite of the fact that the Somoza government signed the CITES Convention on International Trade in Flora and Fauna in 1973, Nicaragua was a Central American leader in the hunting and export of rare and endangered species during the 1970s. After 1979 the Sandinista government moved vigorously to protect Nicaragua's diverse fauna population which includes 750 bird species, 600 reptile and amphibian species, 200 mammal species, and 100 species of freshwater fish. When the Sandinistas nationalized the import/export banks, IRENA was able to ban the export of endangered species. By 1982 the environmental agency had established seasonal hunting bans for 26 endangered species of mammals, 19 bird species and 4 reptile species, making Nicaragua one of the region's most rigid compliers with the norms of CITIES. Most exemplary of IRENA's wildlife initiatives was the Sea Turtle Conservation Campaign, in which local communities democratically participated in the sustainable management of their own marine resources. This program quickly received worldwide attention for its innovation and success.

Energy and Appropriate Technology

In Nicaragua, problems of deforestation, habitat destruction, and poverty were intimately connected to the peasantry's lack of access to alternative energy sources and appropriate technologies, as well as land, credit, and related social services. Wood accounted for one-half of Nicaragua's energy, and over 90% of all household fuel. With the triumph of the revolution, the Nicaraguan Energy Institute (Instituto Nicaragüense de Energia, or INE) worked with IRENA to promote alternative renewable energy technologies and other "appropriate" productive forces which would foster more democratic and equitable forms of sustainable rural development. Small innovative programs in biomass, solar, wind, and micro-hydroelectricty were soon launched, including the development of three small hydroelectric plants in El Cua and San Jose de Bocay. Designed in coordination with the Nicaragua Appropriate Technology Project (1984-89) to generate electricity for the local town (including the health clinic and school) and reduce a locally serious deforestation problem, it was on the Cua-Bocay Project that the U.S. engineer Ben Linder was assassinated (executed at point-blank range) in April 1987 by the contras, an act which served to further outrage and galvanize the international environmental movement against U.S. policy in Nicaragua.

In coordination with the Center for Appropriate Technology Research (Centro de Investigacion de Tecnologia Apropiada, or CITA-INRA), a branch of the agricultural ministry, a series of other renewable energy projects were also initiated, including development of windmills, hand pumps, biogas and vehicle fuels, new agricultural equipment, and new cattle feeding methods. Working with the Center for Popular Education (CEPA), campesino communities would send elected representatives to the center outside of Estelí to work with technical advisors in the development and distribution of more appropriate technologies. A number of projects supporting the use of more efficient Lorena, Chula, Singer, and Block designed woodstoves made of local materials were also initiated, reducing wood consumption by 19%. Implemented in coordination with the women's organizations and Save the Children, the programs were important for reducing the hardships of rural women and children, for they were often not only charged with the task of traveling great distances to search and haul firewood, but also experienced many health problems related to the smoke from the older "open" stoves.

The Sandinistas also began exploring national energy conservation measures and experimenting with large-scale energy substitutes. In 1984, INE announced a goal of electricity self-sufficiency by the year 2000. As part of a larger sustainable energy program designed to promote the social and ecological reconstruction of the country, the aim of these "revolutionary energy programs" was to liberate the nation from its dangerous dependency on expensive international oil imports and technological inputs (which would help free up foreign exchange for the purchase of more essential items such as medicines, etc.). One such experiment with more economically and environmentally friendly productive forces concerned the construction of the 35 MW Momotombo geothermal plant on the shores of Lake Managua, completed in August of 1983. The first such plant in Nicaragua, the facility used steam heated by the magma underlying Momotombo Volcano to power its generators, a potentially limitless supply of cheap energy.

Blessed with an extensive system of lakes and rivers, the Sandinistas also initiated a series of large-scale hydro projects, including the construction of a pumping station at Asturias with a loan from the Inter-American Development Bank. By the mid-1980s, renewable energy sources in the form of hydroelectric and geothermal power provided 42% of the country's total electricity. But perhaps the most innovative project concerned the construction of the controversial Tipitapa-Malacatoya (Timal) sugar complex, the largest in Central America. As part of a sustainable energy project, eucalyptus and leucace trees were planted in between the circular sugar fields, where they would be harvested and burned along with cane wastes in the mill's boilers to generate electricity for both the plant and the national energy grid. Biomass energy projects, or the use of crop wastes as solid fuel and fertilizer, were also developed in the cotton, coffee, livestock, and other agricultural sectors.

Getting Off of Pesticide Treadmill

Pesticide abuse probably represented the most serious environmental pollution problem that the Sandinista government inherited from the Somoza dictatorship. In the 1970s, Nicaragua consistently led the region in the sheer volume of pesticide applied, and was one of the world's leading users of the dangerous organochlorine chemical DDT. Pesticides drenched virtually the entire area along the fertile Pacific coast, entering the densely populated region's water table and food chain. A 1977 study revealed that mothers living in the city of León had 45 times more DDT in their breast milk than the World Health Organization deemed "safe." Hundreds of workers died each year of pesticide poisoning.

The Sandinista government immediately established some of the most innovative regulations to control pesticide abuse of any country in Latin America. By nationalizing the banking and export/import systems, the government found itself with an effective means to regulate pesticides entering the country. Between 1979 and 1981 the Sandinista government banned the use of eight of the world's twelve most dangerous ("dirty dozen") pesticides, including DDT, BHC, endrin, dieldrin, Phosvel, and DBCP, replacing these chemicals with more expensive, but less harmful synthetic pyrethroids. A product registration law was also established to prevent abuses, eliminating more than 1,400 undesirable products from the market. For cotton alone, the number of imported products was reduced 75% by 1982.

The Labor Ministry (MITRAB) also established a department of worker security, which initiated a workplace safety program to protect agricultural laborers from injury and pesticide-related hazards. More than 4,000 training classes were conducted in cooperation with the Rural Workers Association. Growers and unions such as the Rural Workers' Association (Associación de Trabajadores del Campo, or ATC) were also closely involved in responding to health code and safety problems discovered by the Labor Ministry's worksite inspection program. Furthermore, the Health Ministry (MINSA) and CARE International extended testing across the countryside and provided advice on protective measures to workers. In addition, the government also created the National Pesticide Commission (CNP). Composed of members from the public and private sectors, including environmentalists and union representatives, the CNP developed an innovative set of pesticide regulations to oversee imports and guard workers' health and safety. The commission developed a new system that, for the first time in Nicaragua's history, labeled warnings and instructions on pesticide products in Spanish and color-coded them for those who could not read.

Despite the increased regulation of pesticides, cotton pest problems on both state and privately owned farms continued to increase. In 1981-82, foreign exchange losses to the boll weevil amounted to $42 million, or 16% of the total foreign exchange earnings in agriculture for that year. At the same time, the costs of pesticides applied to cotton increased dramatically to as much as $779 per acre, exceeding 26% of total production costs. As a result, average cotton yields were not enough to pay for expanded production expenses. The ecological crisis of cotton was dealing a severe blow to the revolutionary process, since it was the foreign exchange earned from agricultural exports such as cotton which funded the reconstruction and social transformation of the country.

The Nicaraguan government began looking urgently for more effective alternatives to the pesticide treadmill. In 1980 the Ministry of Agriculture (MIDINRA) resumed and strengthened what was formerly a United Nations' test program in Integrated Pest Management (IPM)—an agricultural science which seeks to minimize the use of damaging pesticides by maximizing the use of more environmentally benign but economically effective naturally-occurring insect controls. Under the Sandinista government, the IPM proved initially to be a huge success. During the first two years of testing in pilot projects, IPM reduced insecticide use to a record low 16-17 applications per season, saving $2.02 million in 1982-83. In fact, IPM's success in 1982 combined with government pesticide regulations to lower the volume of pesticide imports by 45%, lessening the environmental impact of insecticide use, while simultaneously bolstering the economic value of the country's cotton crop. By 1985, the IPM program had expanded to cover about 45% of the nation's cotton crop, the largest such enterprise in Central America, and quite possibly in Latin America.

In summary, Nicaragua's IPM program became exemplary of the integral role performed by revolutionary ecology in the process of social transformation. First, IPM promoted greater national independence. Since the science was "home grown," the IPM program dramatically lessened the country's dependency on millions of dollars in expensive chemical imports from multinational corporations, thereby freeing up scarce foreign exchange for the building of schools, health clinics, environmental restoration, and other programs designed to improve the lives of the popular classes. Secondly, IPM promoted social and environmental justice by improving environmental quality and worker/public health. Thirdly, IPM contributed to a new sustainable development model. By overcoming the dynamics of the pesticide tread-mill the IPM program better enabled Nicaragua to overcome many of the major ecological and economic contradictions which periodically plague export agriculture in the Third World. Finally, IPM technology promoted greater ecological democracy in that the successful applica-tion of the science required democratic state planning, including the close cooperation of coalitions between the Labor Ministry, workers associations and unions, the Health Ministry, environmentalists, na-tional and international scientists and doctors, the Agricultural Min-istry and growers association, and other non-governmental organi-zations. As such, these efforts to safeguard environmental and human health while increasing economic productivity made the Sandinista government's pesticide policy a model for "productive conservation" for the entire Third World.

The U.S. War to Defeat an Ecological Revolution

Despite impressive social and environmental gains in the early years of the Nicaraguan revolution, the Sandinista government experienced increased hostility from the United States. By December 1982, the Reagan administration had organized a counterrevolutiony (contra) military force made up of Somoza's ex-National Guardsmen, and were carrying out their first major attacks from bases in Honduras and Costa Rica which targeted Nicaragua's teachers, doctors, agricultural technicians, small farm-ers, and key economic installations. Over the next seven years, the United States would spend nearly $1 billion and cause as much as $4 billion in damage in its cruel war against Nicaragua—a contra war that would claim the lives of some 60,000 people—almost 2% of the country's entire popu-lation.

The Reagan administration's policy of "rolling back" the Nicara-guan revolution through the contra war of terror was accompanied by a series of economic reprisals as well. This included a finan-cial blockade, which suspended U.S. bilateral aid in 1981, along with the pressuring of Latin American and Western European gov-ernments and international lending agencies like the World Bank and Inter-American Development Bank (IDB) to stop all loans to Nicaragua. On May 1, 1985, President Reagan announced a full commercial embargo, suspending all trade between the two nations. By 1988, the International Court of Justice, ruling in favor of Nicaragua's claims against military and economic U.S. aggression, calculated that the U.S. war had cost Nicaragua $15 billion.

Recognizing the centrality of environmentalism to the revolutionary project, the contras attacked natural resource projects. More than 75 ecologists were killed or kidnapped. In 1983, retreating contras disabled all of the Northeast Forestry Project's fire-detecting and fire-fighting equipment, and set fire to a reforested pine plantation which burned out of control for a month in the North Atlantic Autonomous Region, destroying more than 155 square miles. The contra war damaged the government's pesticide programs as well. In 1983, a CIA-coordinated attack on the port at Corinto destroyed $7 million of methyl parathion that had just been unloaded on the docks. The attack occurred during a critical moment in the pest cycle, forcing the government to remove impounded organochlorine insecticides from warehouses, and dealing Nicaraguan pesticide programs a serious setback. The following year, a daring attack destroyed the main seed storage warehouses. The contras realized that the government's program for agricultural self-sufficiency depended on the recovery and development of indigenous seed varieties, many of which were under the exclusive control of the U.S. Department of Agriculture's global seed bank in Fort Collins, Colorado.

The war also sapped human resources from environmental projects. Technicians and inspectors trained for environmental and human health programs were constantly being mobilized for the military. In 1983, for instance, nearly half of the 40 workplace inspectors were mobilized for the war, greatly impeding MITRAB programs in worker health and safety. Often the targets of contra attacks, more than 100 workplace technicians and a dozen inspectors would be killed. Spare parts, vehicles and machinery were also in critically short supply. Environmentalists often had no means of getting out into the field. The trade embargo and credit crunch also heightened the problem by cutting off access to an array of goods and replacement parts in the agricultural sector, including IPM technologies and less dangerous chemicals. By 1987, cotton production had declined to its lowest point since the revolution, as the difficulties of continuing mass-based IPM programs escalated. At the same time, the number of pesticide poisonings in basic grain production (particularly among small farmers) increased dramatically.

Another equally severe ecological impact of the contra war involved the displacement of the population. Over 250,000 peasants were displaced by the contra war, moved out of zones of conflict to towns or cities (particularly Managua) with insufficient infrastructure or services necessary to guard their health and well-being. As a result, pressures on resources in ecologically fragile areas of nearby cities, especially along the already degraded Pacific coast, increased dramatically.

As Nicaragua's social fabric deteriorated under the weight of U.S. aggression, and as the Sandinista government looked to increase economic production and export revenues in order to survive, programs concerning the social and ecological reconstruction of the country suffered. An opinion gradually developed within the FSLN leadership that there was increasingly less room to experiment with "revolutionary ecology." As a result, IRENA steadily lost its direct regulatory control over natural resource sectors considered the most economically important to the war effort. Between 1980 and 1982, responsibilities for the fishery sector had already been completely transferred into a newly created but separate institute INPESCA (Instituto Nicaragüense de la Pesca); all mining activities had been centralized in another institute, CONDEMINA (Corporación Nicaragüense de Desarrollo Minero); duties concerning the "exploitation" and processing of forest resources had been transferred to the Ministry of Industry; and oversight of *cuencas* (drainage basins) was transferred to the agricultural ministry MIDINRA.

By 1985, the contra war, economic embargo and actions by the Reagan/ Bush administration to block Nicaraguan access to international loans and lines of credit had plunged the country into a deep economic crisis and forced the Sandinistas to revise their development priorities by emphasizing increased short-term production over long-term environmentally sound development models. As part of a more general reorganization aimed at "compacting" the national government and cutting expenses, IRENA became a department within the Ministry of Agriculture and received a new director, Julio Castillo. In addition to the loss of institutional autonomy, IRENA's budget was slashed by 40% (an additional 10% was cut the following year in 1986). Most of its comprehensive development strategies were abandoned, unless supported by external funding. Within a few brief years, IRENA had been transformed from an ambitious independent agency intimately linked to economically important sectors, such as mining and fishery, into a subsidiary of the Ministry of Agriculture, with tasks limited to control, regulation and supporting research.

The Collapse of the Revolution

By the late 1980s, the U.S. siege, compounded by falling international prices for leading exports as well as a mounting foreign debt, had created the worst economic crisis in Nicaragua's history. More than 60% of the national budget went for defense, crippling the government's economic, social, and environmental programs. Between 1987-1990, the gross domestic product declined 11.7%, a per capita drop of 21.5%; while the trade balance showed a deficit of $1.2 billion and the balance of payments was a negative $2 billion. In 1989, despite the implementation of drastic austerity measures by the government, the foreign debt amounted to over $7.5 billion ($2,300 per capita). Although hyperinflation was brought down from 33,000% in 1988 to around 1,700% in 1989, nearly 35% of the population was unemployed or underemployed. As agricultural production stalled and real wages tumbled, per capita food consumption dropped between 15% to 30% and family incomes by a third, resulting in dramatic increases in infant mortality rates and poverty. Illiteracy, which had been reduced from 50% to 12.5%, jumped back up to 22%.

When one calculates the almost unbelievable economic destruction inflicted on this poor country over the past twenty years, it seems miraculous that the revolution could benefit the people at all while standing up to the most powerful nation on earth—the U.S. In 1979, the Sandinista government inherited a country decimated by over $950 million in damage from the 1972 earthquake and 1978-79 revolution, as well as over $4 billion in economic losses (equivalent to two full years of the country's GDP) stemming from capital flight, lost income and export revenues, assumed foreign debt, and a looted national treasury. Between 1982-89, the U.S.-sponsored contra war cost the Nicaraguan economy as much as $4 billion in direct and indirect losses, equivalent to almost 20 years of exports. At the same time, the country suffered from declining terms of trade in the world market and the U.S. sponsored trade embargo. Between 1981-83, the prices Nicaragua received for exports fell by 11.9%, while import prices increased 35%. The 1985 trade embargo cost Nicaragua an additional $50 million in lost exports, as well as additional losses resulting from production problems associated with spare parts shortages. In 1987, a severe drought-affected 80% of basic grain production and caused losses of more than $100 million, while the 1982 drought caused $357 million in damage. Time after time, the nation suffered economic blow after blow, lapsing the process of revolutionary social transformation into coma.

Foreign aggression and natural disaster alone, however, did not fully account for the creation of Nicaragua's economic problems. The Sandinista government also contributed to the severity of the economic crisis, making a number of critical policy errors and strategic mistakes. One of the most important elements of the revolutionary project was to encourage and promote popular participation and grassroots organizing through mass organizations—the basis for a revolutionary democracy. But despite well-intentioned efforts to support and include the peasantry and agricultural workers as part of the revolutionary alliance, many of the structural problems and class privileges which gave birth to the revolution were not adequately addressed. In particular, the agrarian reform and related marketing and support services did not go far enough. Instead, the Sandinistas demonstrated a bias for large-scale investments in state agriculture in place of a comprehensive, long-term approach to the revitalization and transformation of the subsistence sector. As a result, the peasantry was never fully integrated into the FSLN's development strategy, giving the contras opportunities for making inroads into the country, especially in the north.

This situation was also related to the FSLN's trust and "over-reliance" on the so-called patriotic sectors of the agricultural bourgeoisie in the export sector, which among other practices, utilized massive government financial support and assistance in "unproductive" fashions (instead of increasing production, as was hoped for by the FSLN). The financial costs of maintaining the political alliance with the wealthy agrarian bourgeoisie—who would gladly throw them out of power—was also a principal reason for the severe economic crisis. Subsidies to these growers resulted in massive state budget deficits, declining production and decapitalization of export operations, and capital flight—all at a heavy cost to other government programs. The Sandinistas financed these deficits primarily by printing money, substantially contributing to the outrageous inflation rates of the late 1980s.

In some ways, Sandinista government policy served to recreate many of the more destructive aspects of the old model of disarticulated capitalist development by not only subsidizing capital flight by the agricultural bourgeoisie (their political adversaries) at the expense of poor peasants and workers (their political allies), but also by wasting scarce economic resources on unwise large-scale projects. Sometimes the product of lower-level corruption, many of these projects actually increased the country's vulnerability in the world market, particularly in terms of deepening dependencies on expensive inputs and imports. As a result, short-term pressures for increased export production won out over the long-term sustainable development policies. Whether or not these errors were instrumental in preventing the Sandinistas from withstanding U.S. aggression is unclear. But what is clear is these mistakes were a reflection of the need for even greater popular participation in the government's decision-making and planning processes.

By the late 1980s, the harsh austerity programs adopted by the Sandinista government had severely undermined their ability to implement a broad agenda of social and environmental reform, leading to dramatic declines in the living standards of the people. As a result, the FSLN suffered diminished popular support in the months preceding the 1990 national elections. To many political observers, the election was a referendum on whether or not the Nicaraguan people were ready, as Reagan and Bush had long desired, to "cry uncle" in order to stop the death, social destruction, and severe economic deprivation caused by the U.S.-supported contra war. In speeches during the weeks before the election, President Bush and Secretary of State Baker made the choice clear by stating that an Ortega victory would result in a continuation of the war. The FSLN also reinforced the view that the U.S. sponsored war was responsible for the country's growing economic crisis. Many Nicaraguans clearly saw a vote for Chamorro as a vote to end the war and economic hardship. On February 25, 1990, the U.S.-backed conservative National Opposition Union (UNO) won an unexpected victory with 54.7% of the vote for presidential candidate Violeta Chamorro, compared to 40.8% for FSLN incumbent Daniel Ortega. The revolution had come to an end.

Although having adopted the rhetoric of environmentalism, successive former Presidents Violeta Chamorro and Arnoldo Alemán showed a willingness to sacrifice environmental quality, worker health and safety, and decent wages and social services in favor of "structural adjustment" and neo-liberal economic policy. Private investment in resource extraction is being encouraged. In 1996, the Ministry of Environmental and Natural Resources (MARENA) and President Alemán granted Solcarsa, a subsidiary of the giant Korean-based multinational corporation Kumkyung, a 30-year timber concession covering 62,000 hectares in the Autonomous North Atlantic Coast Region (RAAN)—the largest and longest ever granted in Nicaragua's history. The logging inflicted enormous damage on indigenous communities and the second largest rainforest in the Americas, and was a clear violation of Nicaragua's laws against mahogany exports and the right of the region's indigenous peoples to determine the use of local resources under the 1987 Autonomy Law (the logging concession was later declared unconstitutional in February of 1997 by the Supreme Count of Nicaragua on the grounds that it violated Article 181 of the Constitution). Although the concession was revoked in late February 1998 because of local and international protests, another concession was granted to a "new company" PRADA two months later.

Government-owned industry and natural resources have been privatized, and new laws allow foreign interests 100 percent ownership of Nicaraguan companies. As a result, Canadian companies practicing open-pit gold and copper mining (which uses cyanide leaching to remove the precious metals from ore), are now creating severe environmental and human health problems throughout the country. Although some environmental programs will be maintained, it appears likely that the more comprehensive environmental programs initiated under the Sandinista government (and which do not receive external funding) will continue to be dismantled until there is a change in power. And in the wake of the devastation wrought by Hurricane Mitch, there will undoubtedly be increased exploitation of natural resources to generate foreign exchange and rebuild the collapsed economy. This is very likely to further deepen the vicious downward spiral of poverty and environmental deterioration which contributed to the disaster in the first place.

Conclusion

Under the Sandinistas in the 1980s, the Nicaraguan government initiated one of the most comprehensive efforts to restore and protect the environment and improve the quality of life for its people of any country in Latin America, and perhaps the Third World. Yet, by the end of the decade, United States intervention ended this unique experiment in revolutionary ecology and social transformation, pushing the country to the brink of social and economic collapse—conditions which contributed to the downfall of the Sandinistas and the process of social transformation.

But U.S. intervention alone was not solely responsible for the fall of the revolution. Rather, the Sandinistas also committed egregious acts which allowed the specific forms of economic and military aggression practiced by the United States to succeed in sabotaging the revolution. Ultimately, the Sandinistas failed to fully integrate the country's popular forces into the structures of power and governmental decision-making processes. Instead, ministerial "feudalism," corruption, and inter-governmental rivalry undermined the creation of more open and inclusive state structures at the very top (ecological democracy thrived more at the bottom on a project by project basis). As a result of a Leninist approach to Party politics, Sandinista economic policy blundered by placing too great an emphasis on export agriculture and the needs of the state sector and agricultural bourgeoisie over the peasant subsistence sector and workers. This resulted in making Nicaragua's economy vulnerable to private sector sabotage and external market pressures, including: declining labor productivity in the state enterprises, which in turn damaged the ability of the government to generate foreign exchange from the sale of export commodities in the world market; continued foreign dependency on extremely variable and fluctuating international markets; capital flight, including the massive decapitalization of productive assets by the agrarian bourgeoisie (despite massive government subsidies); growing external and internal imbalances, worsened by the state's weak extractive capacity, and so on. And because the Nicaraguan economy remained heavily dependent on imported technology and raw materials, the accomplishments of governmental environmental policy not withstanding, the industrial sector remained vulnerable to external crisis.

Although the Sandinistas did implement significant agrarian reforms measures, these measures were ultimately flawed and deeply inadequate. The Sandinistas needed to shift much more profoundly to a nationally-centered development model which would have given greater priority to domestic self-sufficiency, the needs of the peasantry, local-level planning, and mass participation in economic decisions. The emphasis on export agriculture reinforced many of the more detrimental aspects of the old development model, and eventually eroded the social base of the revolution. In short, the state was unable to create a viable development strategy which would sustain improvements in the quality of life for the majority of all Nicaraguans, and increasingly reverted to policies of simple survival as the weight of U.S. aggression and "natural" disaster after disaster piled on during the course of the 1980s. Revolutionary ecology did not go too far, it failed to go far enough.

Today, having achieved its primary goal of "rolling back" the Sandinista revolution, the United States has largely abandoned Nicaragua, showing little interest in fulfilling its promise to provide the financial assistance necessary to reconstruct the country. The money so far offered as humanitarian relief for hurricane victims and infrastructure repair cannot be equated with the hundreds of millions (perhaps billions) of dollars required to truly reconstruct the country. Lacking popular support, as well as a viable development strategy, it is likely that the current Nicaraguan government will be unable to improve the quality of life for most of the people or reverse the continued ecological decline of the country. More "natural" disasters such as Hurricane Mitch are bound to occur. Furthermore, if hard-line factions are successful in utilizing U.S./international hurricane relief assistance and aid programs to further dismantle those remaining achievements of the revolution (particularly the agrarian reform) in an effort to reinforce the old model of disarticulated capitalist development under the hegemony of U.S. neo-colonialism, civil war will very likely return to Nicaragua. One fact remains clear. The desperate state of the Nicaraguan economy and ecology requires drastic action. Whether the FSLN will become more democratic, open, and inclusive so as to continue the revolutionary struggle "from below," or follow a path of political moderation in order to gain U.S. acceptance, remains to be seen.

In the meantime, the need for a democratic eco-socialist alternative in the South has never been more pressing. As witnessed in the Global Forum during the United Nations Conference on Environment and Development (UNCED) in Brazil in the summer of 1992, broad-based movements seeking social and environmental justice for the popular classes are now rising in every corner of the globe. Made of up environmentalists, urban and rural women, indigenous peoples, workers and trade unionists, health officials, peasants, and other popular forces, this new international ecology movement is showing signs of adopting a self-consciously radical (even socialist) perspective. In this regard, experiments in radical ecology as practiced in Nicaragua, Cuba, and other countries will provide many important examples and lessons on which these movements may draw for many years to come.

Given the state of the Third World ecological crisis, struggles over environmental protection and the reconstruction of nature are obviously crucial. Only with the adoption of a radically new political-economic system can the door to ecologically sound and socially beneficial development policies be opened. Such a system is called democratic ecological socialism. But a comprehensive conception of how such a society would work has yet to be articulated. Left theorists and activists must not only present a vision of such an eco-socialist society, we must also work out the reason by which revolutionary ecology is essential to the revival of the socialist project itself.

Selected Bibliography

Arrighi, Giovanni. 1994. *The Long Twentieth Century: Money, Power, and the Origins of Our Times.* New York, NY: Verso.

de Janvry, Alain. 1981. *The Agrarian Question and Reformism in Latin America.* Baltimore, MD: John Hopkins Press.

Faber, Daniel. 1999. *"La Liberacion del Medio Ambiente*: The Rise and Fall of Revolutionary Ecology in Nicaragua, 1979-1999." *Capitalism, Nature, Socialism.* Volume 10:45-80.

Faber, Daniel (ed). 1998. *The Struggle for Ecological Democracy: Environmental Justice Movements in the United States.* New York, NY: Guilford Press.

Faber, Daniel. 1993. *Environment Under Fire: Imperialism and the Ecological Crisis in Central America.* New York, NY: Monthly Review Press.

Karliner, Joshua. 1997. *The Corporate Planet: Ecology and Politics in the Age of Globalization.* San Francisco, CA: Sierra Club Books.

Mueller, Gerald R. 2002. *Canary for the World: Political Ecology in Nicaragua.* Washington, DC. Nicaragua Network Environmental Fund.

Murray, Douglas L. 1984. "Social Problem-Solving in a Revolutionary Setting: Nicaragua's Pesticide Policy Reforms." *Policy Studies Review.* Volume 4: 219-229.

Pfeiffer, Egbert W. 1986. "Nicaragua's Environmental Problems, Policies, and Programmes," *Environmental Conservation.* Vol.13, No.2: 137-142.

Swezey, Sean and Daniel Faber. 1988. "Disarticulated Accumulation, Agroexport, and Ecological Crisis in Nicaragua: The Case of Cotton."

4

The Long March for Livelihoods: Struggle Against the Narmada Dam in India

Subodh Wagle

Introduction

Mass movements for environmental justice in developing countries are always concerned with the livelihoods of people and communities in rural areas. This is primarily because the lives and livelihoods of rural people are heavily dependent on the local natural resources and yet are vulnerable to disruption from external economic, social, political, and technological influences. The relationship between rural natural resources and rural people is mediated primarily through the activities undertaken by these people to satisfy their livelihood needs. This relationship provides a distinctive standpoint for grassroots environmental movements, furnishing not only the substantive character of the movements but also acts, on practical on a plane, as a source of strength. Further, this standpoint influences the substantive demands and strategies of these movements, and even helps to shape their strengths and weaknesses. In addition to these 'internal' factors, what also affects the fate of these movements are the 'external' macro-political factors. This chapter provides some understanding and insights into these diverse factors, while examining one of the most celebrated environmental justice movements in developing countries—the protest against what is popularly known as the Narmada Dam, in India.

The Narmada Project

The struggle against the building of the massive Sardar Sarovar Dam and associated infrastructure on the Narmada River has acquired international fame in the decades since its inception. The Narmada is the largest

71

westward flowing river in India, coursing through forests and one of the country's richest areas of agricultural land in three states in central and western India: Madhya Pradesh, Maharashtra, and Gujarat. The original proposal for the Sardar Sarovar Dam was a 139-meter high dam wall, which would submerge some 37,000 hectares (ha.) of land. Of these lands to be lost, some 13,400 ha. are forests and another 11,300 ha. cultivated. An equally ambitious aspect of the project is the main canal, which is expected to carry water across the state of Gujarat crossing in its course the valleys of nine major rivers. The main canal is to be connected with a large distribution system submerging an equally large area.

At this time, although greatly delayed and interrupted, the Sardar Sarovar Dam has been constructed to a height of 85 meters. A further increase in height will occur in the near future. While filling of the Dam has only begun and will take several years, already existing villages, tribal lands, and agricultural areas have been submerged, their occupants displaced and agricultural production lost.

The project has been portrayed as the "life-line of Gujarat" as it is supposed to deliver precious water to the drought-ridden areas of North Gujarat, Saurashtra, and the Kutch region in its north and west. Along with irrigation and drinking water benefits, the project also involves the generation of electricity. With these benefits comes an array of costs. The construction-related costs alone were estimated at US$10 billion by the World Bank in 1994, although environment groups consider this an underestimate. What has yet to be accurately reckoned are the costs of environmental destruction and human suffering from displacement of a large number of communities, whose number may exceed a quarter of million people (see Table 1). According to the protest groups, the actual number of those displaced could be three or four times as high. In fact, the Narmada controversy has gained celebrity status because of the enormity, complexity, and distribution of these costs. The accompanying Table 1 depicts some salient details of the project.

There is a sharp distinction in the distribution of the costs and benefits between the three states involved. Most of the Narmada flows through Madhya Pradesh; a small portion flows along the northern border of Maharashtra, before a stretch of about 200 kilometers passes through Gujarat, reaching the Arabian Sea. Land lost to inundation would be 20,800 ha. in Madhya Pradesh, compared with 9,600 ha. in Maharashtra and 7112 ha. in Gujarat. However, most of the proposed 1.8 million ha. irrigation areas created by the Sardar Sarovar Project would be in Gujarat.

Outside observers could mistakenly believe the controversy to only involve one Dam; however the Sardar Sarovar Dam and its related works are one part of a mega-project for the Narmada River and its tributaries. If ever completed, the Narmada Valley project would comprise the largest river valley development scheme in history. Under the ambitious Narmada River Valley Development Plan there are proposals for 30 "major," 135 "medium" (moderately-sized), and about 3000 "minor" (small size) dams. In this Plan, the Sardar Sarovar Dam is the largest water storage unit and

Table 1
Narmada Controversy: Background Information

The River and Valley	
Length (kilometers)	1,312
Width (kilometers, average)	75
Drainage area (square kilometers)	98,796
Rainfall (centimeters, mean)	112
The Dam	
Height (meters, full reservoir level)	138.7
Reservoir length (kilometers)	200
Irrigation System	
Main canal: length (kilometers)	450
Main canal: max. width (meters)	250
Distribution system	1 main & 31 branch canals
Length (kilometers)	75,000
Submergence	
Due to reservoir (hectares)	37,000
Due to canal system (hectares)	80,000
Displacement	
People in submerged area	100,000 in 245 villages
People in command area	140,000
People on downstream side	Many thousands
Claimed Benefits	
Irrigation (million hectares)	1.8
Drinking water in Gujarat	40 million people
Firm power (megawatts)	440 (initial), 50 (final)
Cost Estimates	
Original plan (1981-82 prices) US$	1.44 billion
World Bank (1994) US$	10 billion
Grassroots initiative (1995) US$	13 billion

the centerpiece of the planned transformation of the Narmada River Valley, with the second-largest dam being the planned Narmada Sagar in Madhya Pradesh.

The Substantive Issues Related to Environmental Justice

Development projects are known to affect large numbers of people by displacing communities and destroying habitats. These costs are justified in the name of "development" and/or "national interests." In India, there is no central or state law that gives detailed guidelines for the resettlement and rehabilitation of those displaced or whose lives or livelihoods are affected by development, i.e., the victims of the development process. Nor are there central policy guidelines in this regard. In the absence of such guidelines, resettlement and rehabilitation is, predictably, neglected in the design and planning of development projects—leaving those who are adversely affected at the mercy of project authorities.

The debate over the resettlement and rehabilitation aspects of the SSP is centered on the following: (a) who is affected; (b) what is fair, full, and appropriate compensation; and (c) whether fair, full, and appropriate compensation will occur? Regarding the issue of "Who is affected?" in the initial stages, the victims were defined only as the "land-owning" families to be affected by reservoir construction. Later, in response to grassroots protests and with the intervention of the World Bank, the definition was expanded to include the "encroachers," "landless," and "major sons" category.[1] However, the fact that resettlement and rehabilitation policies in the states of Maharashtra and Madhya Pradesh differed on this matter was not acknowledged in this expanded definition.

The issue of what constitutes full and fair compensation is rooted in a widely accepted resettlement and rehabilitation policy principle that no one should experience a fall in living standard due to the development project. However, there are serious flaws in the understanding of government policy makers in the state and central governments and in the other decision-making agencies about how people in rural, and especially tribal, areas earn their livelihoods and maintain their standards of living.

It has been established that there are hardly any "landless" families in these areas, at least from the perspective of tribals who have farmed these lands for centuries. Almost all families in these communities have been tilling the lands in surrounding areas for several generations. After the British arrived, some of these lands were appropriated as "public" lands by the British colonial government, while some were allotted to private individuals. As a result, some families have legal title to the lands they till, whereas some do not. Thus, the categories of "land-owning," "landless," and "encroachers" are creatures of colonial administration that were maintained by the post-independence central and state governments for their own convenience. Naturally, local peoples' understanding of land access is totally different from that of the government.

It has also already been established that the entire population in the area satisfies a significant portion of its livelihood needs from activities other than agriculture. These communities depend upon a wide range of resources, including grass for grazing, forest products for family consumption as well as for market sale, and river products including water and fish, (caught mainly as a food supplement). Loss of these livelihood opportunities is not addressed in typical resettlement and rehabilitation packages offered by the government which provide land and cash only to those who own the land, without regard to family livelihood needs and desires.

Doubts about fairness of resettlement and rehabilitation policies were rooted in the central and state governments' poor track records and callous attitudes towards families displaced by other development projects in the past. The Narmada project was handled from the outset in a manner that only heightened suspicion. For example, the state governments failed to complete studies about the nature and extent of impacts of the dam on the threatened communities in a timely manner. These studies were to be completed before 1981. Yet, the first master plan for resettlement and rehabilitation was hurriedly prepared by the Government of Maharashtra (GOM) in 1992 only when an Independent Review was commissioned by the World Bank (Patkar, 1995: 167). The World Bank's Independent Review found that implementation of a resettlement and rehabilitation program would, in all likelihood, fail in the states of Maharashtra and Madhya Pradesh due to policy deficiencies, lack of available irrigable land, inadequate institutional commitment, continuous failure to consult with local people and other factors. Further, in the opinion of the Independent Review, despite its claims to the contrary, Gujarat, for similar reasons, would probably not be able to resettle a large proportion of those ousted from Maharashtra and Madhya Pradesh (Morse and Berger, 1995: 373).

Along with the above objections about the resettlement and rehabilitation of the oustees (i.e., those forced off the land by the project), several fundamental issues were raised by the grassroots group leading the opposition movement against the Dam and its supporters, which question the paradigmatic assumptions underlying the project. The agenda put forth by the grassroots struggle was comprised mainly of two elements: total opposition to the dam and demand for *paryayi vikas-neetee*. As an alternative development paradigm, *paryayi vikas-neetee* is essentially a broad framework and a set of norms which allow people to find their own definitions of human progress and work for them in ways that are commensurate with their aspirations, histories, cultures, social norms, and political choices. Accordingly, there cannot be a blueprint of *paryayee vikas-neetee* similar to that of orthodox development practice.

Paryayi vikas-neetee is certainly not a well-articulated, comprehensive, and detailed alternative to orthodox development practice evolved over the last five decades. Also, it has not been tested anywhere in its comprehensive form. *Paryayee vikas-neetee* today exists, at best, in the form of alternatives at sectoral levels, as well as some technical and social experiments. On the one hand, the macro-system institutions have refused to take these ideas and suggestions seriously, perhaps because they found them subversive. On the other hand, very few activists and researchers have been able to carry out detailed and systematic work on techno-economic, managerial, financial, institutional, and other aspects of *paryayee vikas-neetee*. As a result, many proponents of the orthodox model tend to dismiss these arguments for this alternative outright.

The supporters of *paryayee vikas-neetee* have two counter-arguments. Firstly, they argue that *paryayee vikas-neetee* is forced by the 'Orthodoxers' into a trap. Because it is not yet in a comprehensive and articulated form, the Orthodoxers refuse to implement it. Yet it not been tested anywhere because they refuse to recognize its potential and importance and do not allow macro-system institutions and experts to work on it. Secondly, it is also argued that *paryayee vikas-neetee* is not supposed to be a well-articulated, compact, and unique prescription to be applied universally like orthodox development practice. Therefore, the only way *paryayee vikas-neetee* could evolve is through economic, social, institutional, and other experiments conducted by groups of people, communities, villages, and towns. In a way, these two sides are diametrically opposite in not only process and method, but also in the substantive content and goals of development. In this situation, many protagonists of *paryayee vikas-neetee* suggest that the orthodox development theory and practice should, at least, give up its exclusionist approach and stop their "neo-colonial" invasion—encroaching on the rights and resources of people and communities who wish to abstain. Further, the orthodox practice should also allow some space for people and communities who want to chart their own path to progress without encroaching upon other peoples' rights and resources.

The demand to terminate the dam was based on questions about the fundamental assumptions of the project that have direct implications for the development standpoint underlying the project. The grassroots groups questioned the viability of the project in terms of its actual, immediate, and tangible costs versus the claimed and theoretical benefits. In particular, the grassroots group pointed out that the loss of livelihoods by the destruction of habitat and the dispersal of local communities is a real, undeniable, and significant impact of the project, whereas supposed benefits (including irrigation, the provision of drinking water, and electric power) exist, at best, as promises. Furthermore, these promises must be implemented by those very agencies which have historically failed to meet the needs and concerns of the affected communities. Pledges of transitional assistance (resettlement and rehabilitation) were regarded similarly by the affected communities—namely as speculative, future benefits that will incur inescapable and immediate costs. Despite persistent demands on the part of the grassroots group, government agencies failed to provide satisfactory answers to these questions. Hence, the group concluded that the human and environmental costs of the project were too high and the local communities would have to bear the brunt of the burdens and damages.

Beyond the issue of appropriateness of the project, the grassroots group also raised fundamental questions about the orthodox development model: Was the cause ("development") for which the poor tribals and their environments were being sacrificed, justifiable? And, if the "development" in its present form is, as its history suggests, inherently harmful to a the large number of communities while benefiting only an influential few, then why not make fundamental changes in the goals and design of "development" itself? The second part of the agenda of the grassroots group—the struggle for *paryayi vikas-neetee*—is rooted in these questions.

The grassroots group fighting in the Narmada struggle raised fundamental issues, elaborated the interconnections among them, and wove them together into a comprehensive critique of the orthodox development standpoint. The critique based on grassroots concerns of livelihoods was not allowed to remain at an intellectual level or a matter of theoretical discussion. The comprehensive critique and the concomitant demand for *paryayi vikas-neetee* (alternative development paradigm) formed a political agenda around which grassroots struggle in the Narmada Valley was organized. Further, the Narmada struggle and other similar struggles for environmental justice have now joined hands to evolve a nationwide campaign around this agenda. To this end, the group leading the Narmada struggle and the other major grassroots movements created the National Alliance of Peoples' Movements (NAPM).

Emergence of the Grassroots Initiative[2]

In 1985, Medha Patkar—a trained social worker by profession and the first outside activist to initiate dialogue with the dam-affected families in Maharashtra—made her initial contacts in the Narmada Valley. In February 1986, a grassroots-level organization of activists and representatives of the threatened communities—Narmada Dharangrast Samiti—was officially founded in the threatened villages in Maharashtra. This was followed by the formation of similar grassroots organizations in Madhya Pradesh and Gujarat under the banners of Narmada Ghati Navnirman and Narmada Asargrast Sangharsha Samiti, respectively. A large public rally was organized in the beginning of 1986 at Dhadagav to air the grievances of the threatened communities (NBA, 1994: 77).

These grassroots organizations started their activity by raising the issue of fair and comprehensive resettlement and rehabilitation policies. In addition, they also put forth many questions about the design of the project and its implications. They knocked at the doors of every conceivable government agency for more than three years while searching for answers to these questions and issues. Even after satisfying all the procedural demands of these agencies, the organizations and activists failed to get satisfactory answers. The government agencies responded largely by stonewalling. Hence, grassroots organizations decided to seek the necessary information using their own sources.

Gradually, instead of taking for granted that displacement was unavoidable, the grassroots communities and the group started raising more fundamental questions rooted in their livelihood-related concerns: Is displacement unavoidable for the development project? Is it possible at all to rehabilitate the displaced people in the true sense? Have the development policies, which require displacement as an integral part of the development project, properly taken into account the massive destruction of livelihood sources (private and common) relied upon by the members of the threatened communities? Can destruction of all these livelihood sources be truly and entirely compensated by any conceivable and practicable resettlement and rehabilitation policy in the prevailing situation? Toward which causes and in whose interest, is this sacrifice imposed on tribal communities? And are these causes and interests just and justifiable? (NBA, 1995: 1).

After a thorough study of the available documents and reports from the World Bank, the Government of Gujrat (GOG), the Government of Maharashtra (GOM), the Government of Madhya Pradesh (GOMP), and the Government of India (GOI), grassroots groups arrived at the following conclusions:

(a) The government agencies had no intention of taking local communities into their confidence;

(b) The government agencies had no proper plans prepared for fair and adequate resettlement and rehabilitation; in fact, they did not even have the preliminary information necessary for chalking out such plans;

(c) The comprehensive resettlement and rehabilitation policy is impossible to implement even with the best intentions on the part of the government because the land required for rehabilitating the threatened communities is simply not available (even the forest land which was identified by the GOM was already encroached, and the private lands which GOG was offering were either unfit for agriculture or already encroached by others);

(d) The mandatory studies necessary for estimating the environmental damage had not been even initiated and the MOEF had not granted its clearance to the project; and

(e) The project itself is flawed on various technical and economic grounds, including the official figure of the cost-benefit ratio which is unrealistic (Patkar, 1995: 160-167).

The above-mentioned conclusions they had reached and, more importantly, the fundamental questions they had raised, prompted a major transformation in the agenda of the grassroots groups. As a result, in May 1988, the grassroots organizations involved in the Narmada struggle and working in Maharashtra and Madhya Pradesh decided to shift focus of their agenda from demanding a comprehensive resettlement and rehabilitation policy to adopting a stance of complete opposition to the dam.

Over the following two to three years, activists involved in the struggles of local communities worked hard to keep up the tempo of the resistance movement by continuously organizing mass-action programs and developing a strong grassroots-based organizational structure in the affected villages in Maharashtra and Madhya Pradesh. Simultaneously, activists organized a network of support groups comprising sympathetic individuals and organizations in major cities in northern and western parts of India, especially in Delhi, Mumbai, and Pune. In November 1988, Narmada Bachao Samiti (Save Narmada Committees) were formed in major cities and towns of Maharashtra including Mumbai, Pune, Nashik, Dhule, and Nagar.

In this way, the grassroots initiative gradually evolved with the three local grassroots organizations at the core and a support structure in the form of a network of a wide cross-section of supporters from all over the country (Patkar, 1995: 163). The initiative was later named "Narmada Bachao Andolan" (NBA)—the Save Narmada Movement. While the NBA formally came into being in 1990, functional collaboration between the nucleus group of activists, grassroots organizations, and the network of supporting organizations and individuals had already been consolidated by 1988.[3]

Consolidation of the Grassroots Initiative

The structure of the Narmada grassroots initiative has several distinguishing characteristics. The initiative is developed and nurtured initially by a small nucleus group of outside activists. Convinced about the commitment of these activists, the young members, women, and elder leaders of the threatened communities rallied around the group through the three grassroots organizations. Further, impressed by the hard work and commitment of the activists and convinced about the genuineness and critical nature of their cause, a large number of supporters from outside the area also rallied around the nucleus group and the local communities, forming the third layer of the initiative supporting the core.

Although it has not restricted its operation only to grassroots participation, the Narmada Bachao Andolan (NBA) exhibits the three salient features of a true grassroots initiative. First, the primary commitment of the NBA has always been the livelihood concerns of the threatened communities. Second, the NBA has always insisted on participation of members of local communities, especially women and youth, in every activity and program in the decade-long struggle, be it the *jal-samarpan dal* (self-drowning team) or receiving prestigious international awards. Third, despite a vast network of outside supporters, the local communities have always remained the main sources of strength for the initiative. Outside activists in the nucleus group, on their part, have been successful in taking utmost care that no direct or indirect influence from the macro-system would be allowed to weaken their commitment to concerns of the local communities and their reliance on the grassroots communities.

Simultaneously, local people and their leaders have been vocal, active, and ready to rise to any challenge during the decade-long struggle. They have played a prime role in shaping both the agenda and the action of the grassroots struggle. Their questioning of the project in particular, and of the development process in general, has been the main factor that prompted the transformation of the initial reformist agenda of the emerging initiative into the grassroots agenda focused on livelihood related concerns.

Without whole-hearted participation, commitment, and sacrifice of local people, political action in the struggle could not have sustained in the face of large-scale mobilization of resources and state machinery by all the state governments and mobilization of public opinion in Gujarat by mainstream political parties. In almost every single action program—be it a hamlet-level picketing or the joint action at dam site—local people participated in large numbers. For example, the rally at Harsud in September 1989 was attended by over 50,000 people, mostly local tribals; the *chakka-jam* agitation in March 1990 saw participation of more than 10,000 local people; and "tens of thousands" of tribals participated in the Long March in January 1991 (Fisher, 1995a: 3; NBA, 1994: 80-81). Representatives of local people have also been part of every indefinite hunger strike that has been one of the most effective strategies used by the initiative.[4] Local people have also borne the brunt of state repression in numerous incidents throughout the valley. This valiant and sustained struggle of local people is yet to be documented properly.

The outside activists in the nucleus group have continuously and consciously tried to maintain the programs, as well as the image of the initiative, as a joint activity of the activists and representatives of local people (Patkar, 1995: 158). In their personal lives, as well as in their organizational activities, these activists have been austere, surrendering all awards, and avoiding attention. Nonetheless, outside activists, and especially Medha Patkar, the NBA leader, have often been accused of misinterpreting facts, dominating the initiative and the struggle in the name of tribals, seeking the international limelight, building up their personal images, and similar claims (Alagh 1991; Dabholkar, 1990; and Gill, 1995). They have also been the focus of charges that the NBA is not a grassroots-based action group as it claims.

However, it must be noted that, especially during the initial years of struggle, these outside activists, in their efforts to build and maintain strong organizational structure, completely immersed themselves in the daily lives of the threatened communities. This exposure and their collaboration with the threatened communities in the struggle helped them to understand and appreciate the grassroots standpoint rooted in the livelihood-related concerns of the communities. This eventually reflected in the transformation of the agenda pursued by the initiative. Clearly, just because they originally came from outside, these activists cannot be barred from representing the grassroots standpoint. Through their "philosophical and political struggle," they seem to have earned the respect and confidence of the threatened communities as their representatives. It cannot be denied that outside activists in the nucleus group have been instrumental in shaping the Narmada struggle. And, hence, the study of this grassroots struggle requires proper acknowledgment and analysis of the contribution made by the group, like any other actor involved in the struggle.

Seven young activists, four men and three women, aged between 25 and 35, formed the nucleus group. Two of the group members were professional social workers, while one came from engineering background and the other from the media. In the initial stages of the struggle, the group was active in the field and every member was directly working on struggle-related or organizational activities. With the evolution of the initiative, and once the grassroots organizational structure was in place, each of these activists assumed certain specific responsibilities, including:

- Organization of field-level activities

- Office, administrative, and related tasks

- Technical aspects, including coordination of legal battles and liaison with support groups and individuals in the country, as well as abroad

- Documentation, publication, rapport and liaison with the media

- Developing a network of supporting individuals and organization from all over the country, and

- Developing an alliance with similar movements and initiatives struggling against development projects.

The activist group bore a major share of the burden in this long struggle. It was successful in building up a strong, effective, and militant organization of the threatened communities on a participatory model. This was accomplished against immense odds. Apart from the problems posed by the difficult and inaccessible terrain, as well as remote and dispersed hamlets, NBA had to grapple with the centuries-old social seclusion, political marginalization, and economic deprivation suffered by tribal people. Organizing tribal communities, which have borne the brunt of oppression and exploitation for centuries, in a militant but peaceful as well as strong movement, and sustaining such a movement for a decade is an exceptional achievement. The activists successfully motivated people from local communities to fight against the repressive and violent tactics of the state apparatus for a decade. In addition to this work at the grassroots level, the activist group successfully handled challenges posed by various macro-system institutions on different fronts, including the technical, economic, legal, and policy-making dimensions. The group, with help from sympathizers and supporters, managed to successfully challenge the World Bank experts in a duel over highly sophisticated technical and policy issues. They even matched political strategy with one of the most astute politicians in contemporary India.[5] Their multi-faceted success has attracted worldwide attention and has also brought criticisms from mainstream and reformist elements in the macro-system.

Establishing Credibility and Authenticity

Initially, when the efforts of the initiative were focused on demands for a comprehensive resettlement and rehabilitation policy, the response of the macro-system was evasion and stonewalling. In the next stage, only after considerable political action on the part of the initiative, was the macro-system ready to grant concessions on the issue of resettlement and rehabilitation. The government agencies wanted the initiative to cooperate with it on implementing the resettlement and rehabilitation policy (Patkar, 1995: 160). However, when the initiative started raising questions and objections against the project itself, the macro-system agencies reacted aggressively, questioning the authenticity of the initiative and its ability to represent the grassroots people (Gill, 1995: 244). When the initiative demanded responses on these questions and objections, the GOG reacted by utilizing provisions of the Official Secrets Act to withhold information (NBA, 1994: 79).

The struggle for credibility by the initiative began in earnest especially after the announcement of their opposition to the dam in the middle of 1988. The activists and grassroots leaders were criticized by the government and other pro-project elements. In addition, many NGOs and others supporting the dam directly raised doubts about the real intentions and integrity of the activists and their supporters. Some even accused the opposition of being puppets of international interests conspiring against India and attempting to thwart India's development (Dabholkar, 1990). The authenticity of the claim of the initiative as the representative of local communities was hotly contested by the governments involved and their supporters (Gill, 1995: 245-246).

To counter charges of the macro-system, the NBA adopted two strategies. First, it continued its campaign to expose shortcomings in project design and call attention to the serious environmental and social impacts of the project. This effort was assisted by the sympathetic elements in the media and the network of supporting groups and individuals. The second strategy was to establish its authenticity as the representative of local communities by organizing a series of mass-action programs in the Narmada Valley as well as in capital cities like Mumbai, Bhopal (the state capital of Madhya Pradesh), and Delhi. The large-scale participation of members of the local communities in these programs provided effective rebuttal to the efforts of the macro-system and its supporters to doubt the authenticity of the initiative as a representative of affected tribals.

Agenda Setting: Two-Pronged Strategy of the Initiative

The struggle for agenda-setting had taken the initiative itself through an evolutionary process from reformist demands to an agenda comprising total opposition to the project and putting forth the alternative of *paryayi vikas-neetee*. As a first step to take charge of the agenda, the initiative put forth a demand for a comprehensive review of the project and outlined a detailed methodology for such an exercise (Patkar, 1995: 170). At the same time, NBA started work on a campaign to create awareness and develop support for its alternative development paradigm, namely *paryayi vikas-neetee*. On September 28, 1989, the initiative organized a rally of sympathetic organizations and supporters on the issue of *paryayi vikas-neetee*. It was attended by about 50,000 tribal and non-tribal activists and their supporters representing more than 150 organizations from around the country. The rally was helpful in creating rapport and cooperation among organizations and movements working for *paryayi vikas-neetee*.

The NBA was successful in pushing its ambitious agenda for three main reasons. First, the governments involved found it difficult to provide effective rejoinders to the sophisticated criticisms leveled by the initiative and its supporters. This allowed the initiative time to develop its agenda in more detail without the need to continually respond to counter-arguments. Second, the effective liaison the initiative maintained with the national and international media assured wide and sustained coverage of its cause. And, finally, the continuous mass political actions and the crude repressive tactics used by the government created a moral and political force, as well as groundswell of goodwill, behind the agenda put forth by the initiative.

Despite the success of the initiative to focus debate on its agenda, the governments sought repeatedly to narrow the agenda down to some limited resettlement and rehabilitation objections. But the strategy of the state government failed as the courts, media, and national as well as international groups became increasingly persuaded that the project had serious problems and involved enormous costs. The first official acceptance of the cause of the protest movement by the macro-system came when the World Bank commissioned an Independent Review of the project in March 1991, headed by Bradford Morse, former head of the United Nations Development Program. In its final report issued in June 1992 (known as the 'Morse Report') (Morse and Berger, 1992), the Independent Review team accepted most of the positions taken by the NBA, forcing the World Bank to withdraw from the project.

It is important to note that, in forcing the macro-system to respond to its own agenda, the initiative did not become trapped by its success. In this regard, a potentially serious "trap" is for members of the initiative, buoyed by their initial triumphs, to seek further expansion of the agenda. This expansion brings forth the issues demanding fundamental changes and is ill suited for debate before the macro-system institutions, such as courts. To avoid this, the initiative followed a limited strategy of arguing before official forums that the project is economically, socially, and environmentally costly, ill conceived, and demanding that the project be abandoned. As a result, the initiative has also been successful in convincing the arbitrating authorities like the Independent Review and the courts.

Another challenge posed often by expansion of the agenda is disagreement within supporting coalitions and even within the ranks of the initiative over issues requiring fundamental changes. The possibility of disagreement among the members of the NBA did not arise because members had undergone a gradual transformation (from being committed to an essentially reformist agenda to one raising fundamental issues) through first-hand exposure to the grassroots situation and their own analysis of project plans and designs. Thus, members had arrived at a grassroots agenda, not through an ideological and intellectual route, but through their own experience and analysis. Further, NBA developed a network of supporters primarily committed to the cause of the local communities and the agenda of the initiative. This is different from the supportive coalitions that emerge in many other grassroots struggles.

These coalitions, typically, are made up of different organizations and groups having diverse ideological and political backgrounds and having different motivations in supporting the initiative. In such cases, there is the possibility of disagreement over expanding the agenda. The initiative made a concerted effort to keep its supporters (from the threatened communities as well as from outside) focused on the fundamental cause of livelihood security. This helped to protect against members becoming alienated from the struggle because of the increasing complexity of the debate. Members of the local communities, as well as outside supporters were kept well informed about the debate and the strategies being pursued by the initiative. Direct and sustained contact with community members and outside supporters was maintained through meetings in the villages in the valley, as well as in the outside towns and cities. The initiative, especially to maintain contact and ensure support from media and outside activists, also produced a series of publications explaining in very simple language the issues, the debate, and the strategies and programs adopted.

Eruption of the Struggle

By the year 1990, the grassroots initiative had established its credibility and authenticity and had been successful inseting the grassroots agenda into the debate. In the words of NBA's leader, Medha Patkar, "when we heard that submergence was likely in 1990 itself, we decided that we must now start going into mass action with a determination to get the answers to the questions, that we should not just raise questions and create wider awareness because now the mass base was created" (Patkar, 1995: 164). With the dam height reaching the level at which submergence was possible—or unavoidable as some saw it, the struggle reached the eruption stage. For the next four years, intense mass action and equally heated debate ensued.

This phase of struggle started with a *chakka jam* (blocking the road) agitation on March 6, 1990, at Khalghat in Madhya Pradesh, where the major national highway crosses the river Narmada. About 10,000 tribal people blocked the highway for about 28 hours, forcing the Chief Minister of Madhya Pradesh to agree to take up NBA's demand for a review of the project with the Prime Minister on behalf of the local communities and people's organizations in the state. This was followed by a *dharana* (sit-in) agitation in Mumbai by about 400 tribals from villages in Maharashtra, with the demand that their villages should not be submerged before their grievances were heard and acted upon.

In order to force this demand, two activists and two representatives of local communities decided to go on an indefinite hunger strike. On the eighth day of their fast, the Chief Minister of Maharashtra promised to visit the dam site and see to it that the villages from Maharashtra would not be submerged until problems in resettlement and rehabilitation policies were sorted out. On April 8, and again on May 14, 1990, mounted police attacked the protesting tribal men and women in two towns in Madhya Pradesh with canes. On May 18, 1990, there was a *dharana* (sit-in) protest in Delhi. These state-level programs were followed up with the *Jan Vikas Sangharsha Yatra* (Struggle for People-Oriented Development March) or the "Long March" beginning on December 25, 1990. The Long March lasted about a month, travelling through the entire area threatened by the dam. According to reports, tens of thousands of people participated (Fisher 1995a: 3). The march was followed by a 22 day long hunger strike by seven members (3 women and 4 men) of the initiative, including activists and local people. These protests were the beginning of the intense struggle that would follow in the next four years.

Local communities demonstrated extraordinary courage, especially during this phase of the struggle, in the face of intimidation, repression, and violent tactics used by the state apparatus. Several incidents of violent repression took place, including one in which two local people were killed in police shootings (NBA, 1994: 45-6). The official position was to downplay these incidents of repression as unfortunate occurrences being used for propaganda by the initiative with the help of its outside supporters and friends in the media (Gill, 1995: 252). However, a report submitted by the retired Justice of the Mumbai High Court, S. M. Daud, confirmed police repression and atrocities. Justice Daud visited the area at the request of the Indian People's Tribunal on Environment and Human Rights. In the report, he concluded that, if indiscriminate arrests, beatings, confinements, and prohibitory orders do not cease, the victims may be tempted to take to arms and add to the troubles faced by an already beleaguered nation.

The struggle erupted to a higher level of intensity when the Independent Review commissioned by the World Bank concluded that the project was unworkable. The June 1992 report of the Independent Review criticized the governments involved and the World Bank for poor project design and implementation and neglect of environmental and human concerns. It observed (Morse and Berger, 1992: xii):

> We think the Sardar Sarovar Projects as they stand are flawed, that resettlement and rehabilitation of all those displaced by the Project is not possible under prevailing circumstances, and that the environmental impacts of the project have not been properly considered or adequately addressed. Moreover, we believe that the (World) Bank shares responsibility with the borrowers (i.e. various governments in India) for the situation that has developed.

The Morse Report changed the situation drastically. It supported the initiative's criticisms on design and implementation of the project, especially its claim that a comprehensive and fair resettlement and rehabilitation was not possible in the given situation. After an effort to salvage some level of support for the project, the World Bank finally succumbed to the pressure created by the coalition of international organizations and grassroots communities and effectively decided to withdraw from the project in March 1993 (Blinkhorn and Smith, 1995: 109).[6] Criticisms from such a prominent institution in the hierarchy of the macro-system undermined the position of those government agencies supporting the project. With the World Bank withdrawing its support, the Indian governments were confronted with numerous problems vis-à-vis other multilateral and bilateral funding agencies. The Japanese Government also canceled the loan it had extended. This loss of international support and funding was a major blow for the governments, which were already short of funds to continue work on such a large project.

The Report had reverberations inside the country also. Its most important impact was the loss of credibility of the government agencies supporting the project in the eyes of general public and arbitrating agencies within the macro-system. It also lent credence to the positions of the initiative and created an opportunity for it to attack the state and central governments' positions during formal arbitration in the macro-system. However, government supporters held their ground and vowed to complete the dam despite all the problems (Fisher, 1995a: 6).

With the 1993 monsoon season approaching, it became clear that the dam wall would cause submergence of some villages in Maharashtra. From December 1992, the GOM started making an organized effort to move out villagers from the immediately threatened areas, including Manibeli, which would be the first village to be submerged. To force people out of the villages the GOM tried, and was partly successful, in clearing the forest around the area (on which villagers depended for their daily needs). In addition, a road was constructed to enable police to reach the area easily and press the local people to leave. On May 29, 1993, according to NBA information, the GOM Police encircled the village of Manibeli, blocked all entry and exit points, and destroyed several houses and the main office of the initiative in order to intimidate people and force them out (NBA, 1994: 83). In protest, one activist and the representative of the local community went on an indefinite hunger strike demanding immediate and comprehensive review of the project. The Manibeli incident and the indefinite fast created immense support for the initiative in the country and compelled the state government to act on the demands of activists. After fourteen days of the fast, the GOI put forth a "concrete" proposal to initiate a review process on June 17, 1993.

However, on July 11, swelling backwaters of the partly constructed dam submerged the first village. The initiative took the position that it was immoral and illegal to submerge villages without completing the review of the dam. The initiative's leaders also decided that the only effective way to protest submergence was to stay in the villages with the local community and expose themselves to drowning in the swelling waters. The *jal-samarpan* (self-drowning) agitation was officially announced on July 17, 1993. On August 3, 1993, bowing to public pressure and embarrassed by the resolve of the activists to drown themselves, the GOI offered to form a "discussion group." However, the offer was rejected by the initiative. Finally, on August 5, 1993, succumbing to grassroots pressure, the GOI announced the appointment of an "expert review panel" to undertake the review of the project. After three years of intense struggle, during which on many occasions activists and local people had to put their lives at stake, the initiative finally forced the government to agree to suspend the dam construction and negotiate a resolution with the initiative.

The Indian Supreme Court and the Quest
for Environmental Justice

While the GOI agreed to appoint an expert panel to undertake a comprehensive review of the project, the Terms of Reference greatly restricted the scope of the review. Nonetheless, the initiative decided to go ahead and participate in the review process. The review panel conducted its hearings between August 1993 and October 1993. It invited participation by all government agencies involved, the grassroots initiative, and other organizations and individuals that were interested in presenting their views. The GOG again refused to cooperate but the GOI, the GOM, and the GOMP all made presentations. The documents and supporting data submitted by the GOI, the GOM, the GOMP, the initiative, and many organizations and individuals were so voluminous that the expert panel was forced to request extension of its term. The Report was finally submitted in July 1994. In the meantime, following a petition from pro-dam elements, the High Court of Gujarat had served an injunction on the panel ordering it not to make its report public.

Simultaneously, in spite of the resolution process initiated by the GOI, the GOG continued its effort to complete the construction of the dam as fast as possible. In December 1993, the Narmada Control Authority ordered the GOG to stop the construction of the dam. In January and February 1994, the Water Conservation Department and MOEF of the GOI passed similar orders. These orders notwithstanding, construction of the dam continued. Reacting to this, the initiative sought and won an injunction from the High Court of Gujarat restricting GOG from carrying out any work that would cause further submergence. However, in February 1994, violating all these orders and restrictions, the GOG went ahead and closed down the sluice gates of the dam creating a permanent submergence in a large area.

In response, the initiative filed a comprehensive writ petition in the Supreme Court of India, covering all issues of the controversy, and especially those pertaining to submergence, and the resultant displacement of the local communities. The Supreme Court decided to join all ongoing legal cases in this matter together and deliberate on them as one case. In July 1994, the review panel submitted its report to the GOI but due to the High Court orders, it was kept secret. As it became clear later, the report had accepted most of the arguments of the initiative and other dam opponents, but had avoided arriving at any firm conclusions mainly because of the restricted Terms of Reference.

Finally, on December 13, 1994, the Supreme Court issued orders instructing the GOI to make the report of the review panel public and removed legal restriction that the award of NWDT cannot be challenged for 45 years.[7] It also directed the expert review panel to evaluate various objections and issues on their merits, complete its report, and arrive at firm and clear conclusions, without considering the NWDT award or the Terms of Reference as constraints. And, the Supreme Court banned further construction at the dam site and the height of the dam was restricted to 80.3 meters until the matter was settled. The second report of the review panel was submitted to the Court in April 1995. The final hearing of the case began finally in November 1995, which went for six days. The next hearing started on March 12, 1996 when serious disagreements between various state governments interrupted the process and the Court ordered the governments to resolve their differences and report back in three months. July 18, 1996 was the next date for hearing.

Until late 1998, the initiative had been successful in convincing the Supreme Court to continue the ban on the construction of the dam despite repeated pleas by the GOG. However, in February 1999, the GOG was successful in convincing the Supreme Court to allow it to construct the dam up to 85 meters of height (plus a 3 meter high hump to facilitate smooth overflow). Reacting to this, the initiative launched another phase of grassroots struggle. Along with the other forms of political action, the initiative announced the *Jal-Samarpan Abhiyan*, which involved voluntary drowning with the rising waters. On two occasions in the monsoon of the year 1999, the water level rose threatening the lives of the group of activists who had decided to stay put in their makeshift office at village Domkhedi, which included Ms. Patkar and members of local communities. These activists threatened that if the Court allowed an incremental increase without looking in the matter in its entirety, they would offer themselves to the rising waters without even informing their sympathizers.

Any remaining hopes that the Indian Supreme Court would side against the course of orthodox development and support a grassroots movement for democracy and ecology were dashed with the release of its judgement on 18 October 2000 after six years of deliberation. In a two-to-one majority, the Supreme Court allowed resumption of construction on the Sardar Sarovar Dam to immediately raise the height by a further five metres to reach 90 metres (Supreme Court of India, 2000a). This decision was made in view of the fact that the Government of Madhya Pradesh announced that it is unable to provide agricultural land for the 156 families (identified in the official estimate, but disputed by activist groups) who would become homeless when the dam reaches 90 metres. An immediate outcome is that the decision of the Supreme Court contradicts the award of the Narmada Control Authority (NCA) in early 1999 in which any affected family must be resettled one year prior to submergence of their land. Therefore in ordering the NCA to resume construction, the Supreme Court is directing to NCA to violate its own award.

Disturbing to Narmada activists and the wider community concerned with justice and the environment is that the Supreme Court's decisions contradicted the mass of expert opinion and common experience on the ecological and social damage caused by large-scale water storage in the developing world. It is the opinion of the Indian Supreme Court that large dams generate economic prosperity, do not cause environmental harm and can lead to improved ecological conditions (whatever that may mean), and that oustees will benefit from relocation. In his Minority Judgement, Justice Bharucha found that the environmental impact studies (EIS) of the project, required under Indian law, have not been undertaken (Supreme Court of India, 2000b). In the absence of the EIS, the Justice stated that the project could not proceed (Supreme Court of India 2000b). Prashant Bhushan, a public interest lawyer at the Supreme Court and advocate for the NBA, surmised of the situation in the *Hindustan Times*: "This judgement is bound to shake the confidence of the people in the ability of the judiciary to protect the rights of the weak from the onslaughts by the State and powerful vested interests." (Bhushan, 2000).

As if to further underscore the contrarian nature of the Supreme Court's judgment, World Commission on Dams released a case study of India in March 2000 with some particularly uncomplimentary conclusions on the nation's large dam projects (WCD, 2000). Its objectives included a review of: the contributions of large dams; the option assessment mechanisms for energy and water resources management and development; and the assessment and mitigation of the economic, social, and environmental impacts of large dams (WCD, 2000: 3). Amongst their findings were:

"Environmental and social considerations remained marginal to the technical process and not integrated in the early planning stages" (WCD, 2000: 7); and "Environmental risks associated with dam projects are not key factors in the decision making process" (WCD, 2000: 13). On social issues, the Report concluded: "Adverse social implication of dam projects is not a factor in the initial economic assessment and therefore does not influence the decisionmaking process to reach least-cost social alternative." (WCD, 2000: 12). Indeed, it is difficult to locate a Report finding or conclusion that does not explicitly support the claims of the NBA regarding the Sardar Sarovar Dam and refute those of the Supreme Court, something the protest movement was quick to point out.

A View to the Future

Despite the blow that the judgment of the Supreme Court has dealt to the cause of environmental justice, the environment, and the futures of hundreds of thousands of potential Narmada victims, we must not underestimate the achievements of the protest movement. The NBA was successful in forcing the GOI to accept the review process and in bringing the matter before the Supreme Court, so the issues of justice and environment came sharply into focus for the GOI and the attentive world community. Furthermore, those findings of the Morse report independently validated the NBA's claims regarding the ecological and social losses that the Sardar Sarovar Dam would incur. Consequently, the World Bank's support for the project was removed, as had been the funding from Japan and from some U.S. and European corporations as a consequence of NBA protest action. As well, the initiative has been successful in convincing the highest court of the land to remove a major constraint to acceptance of their position—the constitutional sanctity granted to the award of NWDT. Overall, the protest movement retarded construction progress on a massive project and made questioning the orthodox development paradigm a legitimate inquiry and carried that challenge to those vested and powerful interests of state and corporations.

A key element of grassroots strategy in the Narmada struggle has been to focus on its demand for cancellation of the project by arguing that: (a) the project is ill-conceived and severely flawed on techno-economic grounds; and (b) it is impossible to satisfy the environmental and resettlement and rehabilitation standards set by various official agencies. This latter point has now been reiterated by the GOM itself. Two advantages of this strategy are clear. First, these arguments are addressable by macro-system arbitrating institutions and, therefore, it was difficult for these institutions to dismiss them easily as "irrational" arguments. Second, while defending their own project design, the project authorities were forced to explain why their design would work whereas scores of other similar designs had been dismal failures in the past. Macro-system agencies were vulnerable in these circumstances because their track record in the areas of resettlement and rehabilitation, environmental impacts, and project implementation were historically poor. In effect, the macro-system had to defend not merely its design of Narmada project, but its full record of development projects. Involving the network of supporting institutions and individuals that included some of the best minds in the country was also an important component of the strategy adopted by the initiative.

The forces of national and state governments, the legal and financial system, and the law enforcement groups have helped to build the mighty structure of the Sardar Sarovar Dam as much as any engineers and construction crews. Given the demonstration of the immense upheaval and social damage that hundreds of communities will now face, it could be possible to overlook the rationale of the Narmada Plan is one based on development. This project drew its funding on the basis that it would help communities in their daily lives. Yet independent assessments of the proposals have supported the grassroots movement's claims that the project is causing immense and irreversible harm and is unleashing social mayhem across the Narmada River valley and the involved states. In attempting to deny these claims, it appears that the Indian Supreme Court has brought itself under scrutiny as an independent body, rather than bringing fresh support for the development project.

Both the natural ecology and the life support systems of the Narmada River are being destroyed by the project. By their heroic struggle, the grassroots movements have pulled away the disguise of alleged development that the Narmada project purports to offer and exposed to all the world its true character, namely that it fails the test of environmental justice. Now the project can only continue in the public knowledge that it leaves the inhabitants and the ecology of the Narmada River Valley worse off by virtue of its existence.

Protests continued throughout the monsoon season of 2000. These occurred within the Narmada Valley and beyond. Narmada *Satyagraha* 2000, which involved occupation of the villages of Jalsindhi and Domkhedi on the banks of the Narmada, concluded on 17 September,

2000, with plans for its resumption next season (Vasave et al, 2000). Given the decision of the Supreme Court in the weeks following *Satyagraha* 2000, next years' protests are likely to assume an even more intense character. As the Sardar Sarovar Dam fills and lands and livelihoods are inundated and displaced, work has now begun on the next water storage projects along the Narmada River, namely the Narmada Sagar and the Maheshwar Dams. And the struggle for environmental justice will continue.

Notes

1.   "Encroachers" are defined as "those residing on and cultivating land to which they do not have legal title" and "major sons" are "sons over the age of eighteen" in the affected families (Fisher, 1995a: 31).
2.   The term 'initiative' is used here to indicate a group of activists leading the movement or struggle with a shared goal and also with articulated processes and structures for making and implementing decisions.
3.   The nucleus group of outside activists has no separate existence and has been working since beginning of the struggle as part of the grassroots organizations. It is identified as a separate entity in this analysis as it has played a critical role in this struggle.
4.   These indefinite hunger strikes lasted for 14 days in June 1993, 22 days in January 1991, and 26 days in November 1994.
5.   This refers to the former Chief Minister of Gujarat, the late Mr. Chimanbhai Patel, who had a very controversial but successful political career. In 1975, he became the first chief minister to be overthrown by a student movement protesting his corrupt government. After two decades of political machination, he became the Chief Minister of the state leading Gujarat in implementing the Narmada project. He died in 1994.
6.   As a face-saving measure, GOI was allowed to withdraw its request to the World Bank for a project loan in March 1993.
7.   This part of the order from the highest court in India was important because the state governments had taken the position that the award (which had constitutional sanctity) was binding on all, and that changes in or review of the project could be made only within the framework of the award. This position effectively made a comprehensive review of the project impossible because the award had stipulated some basic parameters of the project which themselves were the roots of the problems. Even the GOT had restricted the TOR of the 1993 review panel, citing this restriction.

References

Alagh, Y. K. 1991. "Foreword." In Mahesh T. Pathak (ed). *Saradar Sarovar Project: A Promise for Plenty.* New Delhi, India: Oxford and IBH Publishers.
Blinkhorn, Thomas A. and William T. Smith. 1995. "India's Narmada: A River of Hope." In William F. Fisher (ed). *Toward Sustainable Development: Struggling Over India's Narmada River.* Armonk, NY: M. E. Sharpe.
Bhushan, Prashant. 2000. "People be Damned." *The Hindustandu Times Online.* Saturday, 21 October, New Delhi. Available online at: http://www.histandutimes.com

Dabholkar, Dattaprasad. 1990. *Mate Narmade (O, Mother Narmada)*. Pune, India: Rajhansa Prakashan.

Fisher, William F. 1995a. "Development and Resistance in Narmada Valley." In William F. Fisher (ed). *Toward Sustainable Development: Struggling Over India's Narmada River*. Armonk, NY: M. E. Sharpe.

————. 1995b. "Full of Sound and Fury? Struggling Toward Sustainable Development in India's Narmada Valley." In William F. Fisher (ed). *Toward Sustainable Development: Struggling Over India's Narmada River*, Armonk, NY: M. E. Sharpe.

Gill, M. S. 1995. "Resettlement and Rehabilitation in Maharashtra for the Saradar Sarovar Narmada Project." In William F. Fisher (ed). *Toward Sustainable Development: Struggling Over India's Narmada River*, Armonk, NY: M. E. Sharpe.

Morse, Bradford and Thomas Berger. 1995. "Findings and Recommendations of the Independent Review." In William F. Fisher (ed). *Toward Sustainable Development: Struggling Over India's Narmada River*, Armonk, NY: M. E. Sharpe.

Morse, Bradford . 1992. *Saradar Sarovar: Report of the Independent Review*. Ottawa, Canada: Resource Futures International.

Narmada Bachao Andolan (NBA). 1995. *Narmada Ghati Ke Sangharsha Ke Dus Varsha: 1985-95: Sanze Sangharsha Ki Or (Ten Years of Struggle in Narmada Valley: 1985-95: Toward a Common Struggle)*. Bombay, India: NBA, Bombay.

————. 1994. *Hum Ladenge Sathee: Narmada Ghati Ka Jansangharsh (We Will Fight Comrades: Peoples' Struggle in the Narmada Valley)*. Pune, India: NBA, Pune, India.

Patkar, Medha. 1995. "The Struggle for Participation and Justice: A Historical Narrative." In William F. Fisher (ed). *Toward Sustainable Development: Struggling Over India's Narmada River*, Armonk, NY: M. E. Sharpe.

Supreme Court of India. 2000a. Civil Original Jurisdiction, Writ Petition (C) No. 319 of 1994, Narmada Bachao Andolan, Petitioner Versus Union of India & Others, Respondents. *Judgement.* New Delhi, October 18. Available online at: http://www.narmada.org/sardar-sarovar/sc.ruling/majority. judgement. htm

Supreme Court of India. 2000b. Civil Original Jurisdiction, Writ Petition (C) No. 319 of 1994, Narmada Bachao Andolan, Petitioner Versus Union of India & Others, Respondents. *Judgement.* Minority Judge - Justice B. N. Bharuch. New Delhi, October 18. Available online at: http://www.narmada.org/sardar-sarovar/sc.ruling/Bharucha.doc

Vasave, Kewalsingh, Pravinkumar, Rukminikaki, Patkar, Medha, Chavan, Gitanjali, Muhariya, Baba and Mohan Patidar. 2000. *Conclusion of Narmada Satyagraha – September 17, Jalsindi and Domkhedi*. Available online at: www.narmada.org/events / satyag/satyagraha.conclusion.html

WCD (World Commission on Dams). 2000. *WCD Case Studies: India. Executive Summary.* Final Draft 24 March. Cape Town, South Africa: WCD Secretariat.

5

A 'Necessary Sacrifice:' Industrialization and American Indian Lands

John Byrne and Steven M. Hoffman

The understanding of society as autonomous from nature is a distinctive idea of industrialization. It represents a paradigm shift that has utterly altered social relations and, as we are now learning, natural order as well. One writer has summarized the shift in the following manner: "the idea of nature as animate and living, where species seek to realize their own natural ends, has been replaced by the idea of . . . mechanical nature . . . The modern mind has come to view nature as nothing more than matter-in-motion, whether planets, projectiles, or even animals" (Oelschlaeger, 1991: 77). In this construction, society is portrayed as standing outside of, rather than within, nature. The animate character of society is assumed to be self-provided, with nature merely representing the inanimate context of social development. In this regard, industrialization is not only a technological or economic phenomenon, but a cultural and political orientation as well.

The historical requirements of industrialization have institutionalized a development structure in which the physical environment is valued either for its raw materials or for its ability to absorb industrial wastes. Within the logic of industrial society, value derives from the "efficiencies" gained for production and use through the transformation of materials found in nature into items of market exchange. This process is not socially or ecologically neutral, instead producing environmental degradation and social inequality as necessarily functional elements.

It is important to recognize that while the outward form of this process has taken on various guises over time, the underlying needs of the system have remained constant. The earliest phases of the industrial era required mainly the raw 'inputs' of nature, i.e., the deposits of coal, iron ore, petroleum, and other resources available to those societies up to the challenge of acquiring and exploiting them. As industrial society expanded its reach and power, however, individual mines, estuaries, and other discreet 'parts' of nature proved to be insufficient. Instead, the sacrifice of entire landscapes and ecosystems became necessary. Various regions of the world became scrapheaps, serving to remind society that progress entailed certain costs that, while significant, were necessary for the realization of a greater social good. Costs were, of course, not limited to the degradation of water bodies, the atmosphere, or landscapes; social conditions and structures were also included in the calculus of profit and loss.

The appetite of industrial society for development grew from 'resource use' to alteration of what had hitherto been considered permanent processes and structures of nature. In this respect, contemporary industrial transformation both embodies and supersedes its ecological antecedents. Acidification of the rains, for instance, is an outcome of typical industrial processes of extraction and exploitation, i.e., the mining and use of coal, petroleum and other fossil fuels. Yet, it also reflects a scale of industrial activity in which an elemental process upon which all organic life—the evapo-transpiration cycle—is altered to suit industrial needs. While breathtaking in its scope and reach, acid rain, with its attendant possibilities for widespread forest, soil, and freshwater degradation, is simply the latest stage in an historical process of industrial development.

The indigenous cultures of North America offer a point of departure for an analysis of the industrial conception of social and ecological relations. A common view promulgated by European cultures is that indigenous peoples wandered "perpetually in scattered bands, grubbing out marginal subsistence from hunting and gathering without developing serious appreciation of art, science, mathematics, governance, and so on" (Churchill, 1986: 15). In this view, it was the obligation of European culture to civilize the indigenous. This cultural stereotype set in motion European efforts at assimilation, which, in part, centered on the education of indigenous communities regarding the principles and practices of capitalism. Policies of removal and relocation to reservations, allotment, and reorganization are taken to represent variations on one or the other of these efforts.

In North America, the industrialization of the continent involved not only the spread of mechanical modes of production, but also a cultural assault on the nature-society relations that had organized American Indian communities for centuries prior to European invasion. This cultural assault had an explicit ecological strategy—to spoil the free gifts of land, water, fire, and animals to the point where Indian life itself is endangered. The 'civilization' stereotype used by Europeans to justify this cultural assault expresses the racism that informed North American industrialization. But a full understanding of the takeover of the continent by a machine culture and a surplus-based political economy requires parallel attention to the ecological strategy that implemented North American 'civilization.' Indeed, we suggest that the cultural and ecological elements of industrial civilization of the continent are expressions of a common process—the industrialization of society *and* nature. U.S. policies of the last two hundred years toward American Indians and the ecologiesapon which they depended into the contemporary era are used to illustrate a consistent and continuing attempt by an evolving industrial civilization to pursue the logic of its expansion at the expense of Indian culture and ecology. It is our conclusion that U.S. exploitation of Indian communities and the continent's ecology over the last two hundred years are expectable outcomes of essentially two 'faces' of the same phenomenon—the industrialization of reality (physical, social, political, cultural, and ecological).

Mining Indian America

According to Mumford, a machine culture rooted in European tradition and transplanted to the New World, became the foundation for a uniquely modern worldview. Mechanization, capitalism and a carbon power base combined to form a pattern of developmental relations that equated improvement of the human condition with the expanding production and consumption of goods (Mumford, 1934: 105):

> Happiness was the true end of man, and it consisted in achieving the greatest good for the greatest number . . . The quantity of happiness, and ultimately the perfection of human institutions, could be reckoned roughly by the amount of goods a society was capable of producing: expanding wants, expanding markets, or expanding body of consumers. The machine made this possible and guaranteed its success. To cry enough or to call a limit was treason. Happiness and expanding production were one.

In the transformation of the "good life into the *goods* life" (Mumford, 1934: 105, italics in original), both human institutions and the natural environment were reorganized in accordance with the pervasive principle of quantification and the goals of material.

The emerging industrial order that Mumford described in the 1930s was indeed able to produce goods at an unsurpassed rate. But this surplus production exacted a price for its result: a pattern of unequal development accompanied by widespread environmental degradation. In the new social order, society and nature were simultaneously drawn into a process of industrialization in which the ultimate end in all aspects of life was to produce. Indeed, a defining feature of industrial culture is that there can never be enough. As one writer has noted (Daly, 1991), industrial civilization has no rational understanding of an optimal limit for economic growth—it is utterly incapable of stopping industrial expansion. The environment offers a seemingly endless supply of natural resources for industrial growth: land, timber, minerals, metals, and a variety of energy sources all valued for their ability to increase industrial production. As the machine culture spread, the world was divided in two parts, machine areas and non-machine areas, areas of production and areas of supply. According to Mumford, 'advanced' societies were seen as those that were organized in compliance with the quantification principle, exploiting nature's endowments and transforming them into industrial products (1934). But this political economy depended upon the expansion and reproduction of unequal development, such that no place or culture was immune to the central imperative of exploitation.

This beginning of industrialization is dominated by the products and operations of the mine (Mumford, 1961: 158):

> The animus of mining affected the entire economic and social organism: this dominant mode of exploitation became the pattern for subordinate forms of industry. The reckless, get-rich-quick, devil-take-the-hindmost attitude of mining rushes spread everywhere: the bonanza farms of the Middle West in the United States were exploited as if they were mines, and the forests were gutted out and mined in the same fashion as the minerals that lay in their hills ... And the damage to form and civilization through wasteful expenditure remained, whether or not the source of energy disappeared.

The establishment of territorial colonialism over American Indian communities occurred in this earliest stage, as industrial mining— not only of minerals, but timber, soils, and water—propelled the European takeover of the continent. The incompatibility of the machine culture with the land-based tradition of American Indians was readily apparent (Ulysses S. Grant, quoted in Takaki, 1979: 171):

> The building of railroads, and the access thereby given to all the agricultural and mineral regions of the country, is rapidly bringing civilized settlements into contact with all tribes of Indians. No matter what ought to be the relations between such settlements and the aborigines, the fact is they do not harmonize well, and one or the other has to give way in the end.

Initial European relations with American Indians were established through formal treaties between tribes and the U.S. government, the aim of which was to secure land and resources in exchange for both money and social services (education, health, welfare, etc.) The lands left in Indian hands as part of treaty agreements were designated as tribal reservations. The establishment of reservations served dual purposes during this period. On the one hand, Indian tribes were effectively removed from the possibility of controlling any of the continent's vast resources. At the same time, reservations provided the means for U.S. efforts to manage and "educate" Indians in the habits of industrial society. A central feature of Indian policy during this period was assimilation: "[Indians] would be required to learn and practice the arts of industry until at least one generation had been placed on a course of self-improvement" (Takaki, 1979: 187).

The needs of industrial society soon outgrew this mode of Indian/ non-Indian relations. European population and economic growth in the 19th century occurred on an unprecedented scale, creating an insatiable demand for exploitable resources. The pressures of growth combined with other trends to heighten non-Indian demands for land. These complementary trends included burgeoning settlements in eastern urban areas, expansion of the railroad across the continent and the opening of canals and waterways and new developments in agricultural technology, which enabled the cultivation of greater farm acreage. As well, the industrializing economy required ever-greater amounts of timber as both fuel and building material, and access to minerals and energy for increased industrial production. All of these conditions translated into a heightened conflict between the needs of the surplus economy and Indian sovereignty.

Forced migration of eastern Indian tribes was officially instated with the Indian Removal Act of 1830 to address the conflict of industrial and Indian ecology. Indian communities stood in the way of industrial progress and Indian tenure of lands had to be removed. In his analysis of this period, Barsh (1988) suggests that the impetus behind the policy of Indian removal was largely to restart the nation's economic engine during periods of recession. Railroad companies and timber and mining industries were the principal recipients of tribal land cessions. As an official of the Missouri, Kansas and Texas Railroad explained to the U.S. Congress at the time, "[Y]ou, then, Gentlemen must hold the scales fairly and equally between the parties before you—the railroad on the one hand, and the Indians on the other" (quoted in Takaki, 1979: 174). The centrality of the railroad system to the industrializing nation assured the proper response.

By 1840, 420 million acres of land, or 22% of the continental area was secured from Indian tribes for an average of 7.4 cents an acre (Barsh, 1988: 819). The Indian treaties had served their purpose and it was now possible to turn to new strategies of industrialization. As the U.S. Congress unilaterally ended the era of treaty making in 1871, the westward expansion of the industrial political economy ensued. The U.S. government strengthened its assimilationist strategy by instituting an aggressive land and minerals acquisition policy. The General Allotment Act of 1887, also known as the Dawes Act after its sponsor Senator Henry Dawes, furthered the assimilation strategy by dividing sections of communal tribal lands into individual parcels and distributing them as private property to tribal members. Significant parts of the communal lands, which remained after allocation to tribal members, were sold by the federal government. The Dawes Act was publicly justified as an effort to further the Indian cause by instituting a system of private property and individual initiative. As Commissioner of Indian Affairs T. Hartley Crawford stated (quoted in Takaki, 1979: 189):

> Unless some system is marked out by which there shall be a separate allotment of land to each individual ... you will look in vain for any general casting off of savagism. Common property and civilization cannot co-exist.

While civility may have served as the official explanation for the Dawes Act, the result was to transfer 90 million acres of Indian land and its resources to non-Indian holdings for development. By the end of the 19th century, American Indians had lost half of their lands by U.S. policy design (Kelley, 1979: 32). The shrinking of Indian culture through assimilation and a frontal attack Indian ecology through industrial takeover went hand in hand. The ideological passage from a commons idea of nature to a mining idea, and from industrial civilization to Indian ghettoes as official policy—this is the seamless path from industrial culture to industrial ecology in its early expression in the U.S.

As the demands of industrial society continued to grow, policies regarding the disposition of American Indian lands changed. Mineral leasing was inaugurated and presidential executive orders were used to remove certain lands from Indian control (Kelley, 1979: 31-33). Manufacturing was becoming the leading economic sector in the U.S. economy, and correspondingly, the demand for coal, oil, and other minerals was growing rapidly. The mineral abundance that lay on Indian lands was known since the 19th century, and knowledge of its existence influenced the character of subsequent Indian policies.

In 1891, "[b]ecause the minerals were going to waste from the dominant society's perspective, Congress authorized mineral leasing of tribal and allotted lands" (Ambler, 1990: 37). The authorizing or leasing agent was not the tribe itself, but rather responsibility was placed within the federal government through the construction of a trusteeship role. The idea of trusteeship was, of course, extraordinary (and offensive) on a number of levels. The racism embedded in the idea is obvious. But it should be noted that official U.S. policy not only presumed the inferiority of American Indian culture, it also asserted the superiority of European ecological beliefs that justified mining, industrial-scale agriculture, massive canal and dam based redesign of watersheds, and colossus-sized urban agglomerations of people and machines. The repeated complaint of the U.S. government and its industrial elite was not only that Indians were un-European, but that their ideas about the land and its biology contradicted the core conceptual underpinnings of industrialism.

U.S. trustee policy unleashed a flurry of mining activity in Indian country and set the course for development on Indian lands. As early as 1894, the Oklahoma Territory was producing approximately 130 million barrels of oil per year,[1] and 39 corporations were extracting an average of 1.5 million tons of coal per year in the Choctaw Nation alone (Ambler, 1990: 35). Indeed, the wealth of minerals and energy resources, which lay underneath much of existing Indian reservations, and the battle for control of them, became the foundation for what eventually resulted in the separation in U.S. law of land surface rights and mineral rights. The stakes of this conflict did not escape the tribes or the U.S. government: as Interior Secretary Carl Schurz suggested in 1881, "there is nothing more dangerous to an Indian reservation than a rich mine" (quoted in Ambler, 1990: 32).

The Indian Reorganization Act of 1934 formally ended the period of allotment and assimilation. Section I of the Act stipulated that "no land on any Indian reservation . . . shall be allotted in severally to any Indian" (Prucha, 1990: 222). A principal component of the Act was the reorganization of tribal governments, which hereafter were to be the only "officially" recognized governing bodies of American Indian tribes. These newly formed tribal councils would be responsible for "economic planning, mineral lease negotiating and approval and other governmental commitments" (LaDuke, 1983: 10).

The organizational form of these tribal governments was drawn, not from tribal tradition or custom, but by Congressional directive. A primary accomplishment of this reorganization was to standardize American Indian governance structures, and specifically, as Churchill notes, to "replicate corporate directorates" (Churchill, 1986: 16). In addition, the U.S. Department of Interior retained ultimate authority over Indian development policies, ensuring that tribal governments would not interfere with industrial exploitation on shrinking Indian lands.

While the 1934 Indian Reorganization Act is commonly described as heralding an era of self-determination for Indian communities, in fact the impact of the newly dictated economic and technological institutions on Indian tribes was devastating. The authorization of a national Bureau of Indian Affairs (BIA) preempted Indian political development and created the tools for state suppression of Indian dissent, down to the community level. In this phase, Indian ecology and culture were disrupted on a scale that has endangered Indian life itself.

Sensing this result, U.S. policy in the 1950s terminated federal Indian tribal status. This effort continued through the 1960s when termination as a formal policy was rolled back, in part because of growing non-Indian embarrassment. The end of termination, however, has not put a halt to the acquisition of Indian resources. New forms of exploitation continue and involve 'royalty agreements' negotiated by trustee agents of the U.S. government on behalf of tribes and approved by the tribal councils created under the 1934 Act. The grossly deficient level of compensation realized under these agreements is well documented. Between 1959 and 1975, for example, the Navajo Nation received approximately 15 cents per ton on coal sales of approximately 2.6 billion tons. During the same period, more than 300 million barrels of oil were taken out of Navajo lands and sold for $2 billion as crude oil and $100 billion as refined products. For this, the Navajo Nation received approximately $700 million in royalties, bonuses, and rents from the energy companies (Steiner, 1983: 35). The pattern of abusive agreements has changed little since the 1950s. In the mid-1980s, for instance, Indians were receiving 3.4% of market value for their uranium, 6% for oil, 11.3% for natural gas, and about 2%

for coal. These royalty amounts were substantially lower than royalty rates paid to non-Indians for the same minerals (Churchill, 1986: 16).

Across the numerous policy regimes, from assimilation to self-determination to negotiation, a consistent pattern of exploitation has prevailed. American Indian tribes and lands were recognized by Euro-American culture almost exclusively in terms of commodity value. As Gedicks remarks, "[h]istorically, one of the most stable investment areas" for corporate interests "has been Indian lands" (1998: 274).

A Necessary Sacrifice: Indian America versus Nuclear America

The U.S. government's decision to pursue the development of nuclear weapons and, later, to demonstrate a peaceful nuclear alternative through the supply of electricity, signaled a new era for Indian country. With this decision, a large segment of the Indian population was inextricably bound up with a technology capable of disrupting social and ecological relations on an unprecedented scale. As with the era of carbon power, Indian involvement was not a matter of choice, but the result of political geology: Indian communities lived atop the mineral seams of the uranium fuel needed to power the new technology and, therefore, were literally in the way of progress.

Over 60% of all known U.S. domestic deposits of uranium are on Indian lands (Churchill, 1986: 16). Most of these deposits are located on the southern edge of the Colorado Plateau, an area encompassing significant portions of Arizona, Colorado, New Mexico, Utah, and Wyoming. Parts of South Dakota also have significant resources and in 1976, a Bureau of Indian Affairs (BIA) report listed uranium as one of the many "mineral resources" on Wisconsin Indian lands. Since 1948, the mines of the Colorado Plateau have produced over 95% of the nation's uranium, first exclusively for nuclear weapons, and after 1954 for the "Atoms for Peace" commercialization program (Gilles, 1996). Until nuclear plant orders ceased in the late 1970s, 80% of the uranium mining and 100% of uranium processing took place on Indian lands (Allen, 1989: 887).

The advent of uranium mining, milling and enrichment on Indian lands ushered in an era of what Churchill and LaDuke have called "radioactive colonialism" (1986). Whereas the "old colonialism" used territorial conquest and clearance to accomplish industrial culture's aims, the new colonial era sought dominion over Indian lands to facilitate technological advance. The aim of radioactive colonialism had less to do with maximizing the economic value of uranium ore *per se,* than with establishing a technological system of electric generation that would be "too cheap to meter" (Lewis Strauss, quoted in Byrne and Hoffman, 1996: 11). System imperatives for 'efficient' nuclear power-generated electricity would take precedence over everything, including even the survival of Indian families and the inhabitability of Indian lands.

In this stage, the assimilative and regenerative properties of a nuclear power system became paramount and were promoted over those of communities and natural environments. Technological reality needed to supersede social and natural reality. The Indian communities and natural environments originally drawn into the operations of the U.S. nuclear power system would come to depend upon the elaboration of that very system for their safety and future viability.

The first American Indian experience with the disruptive effects of nuclear technology involved the mining of uranium. While the Navajo Nation was opened for the mining of minerals in 1919 under an 1872 law, mining for uranium began in 1948 under the supervision of the U.S. Atomic Energy Commission (Chenowith, 1997: 268). The mining and fabrication of nuclear fuels in the Colorado Plateau produced a variety of hazardous byproducts to which Indian miners and workers in fuel processing plants were exposed. Indian communities adjacent to these operations were put at radioactive risk from exposure to residual ores and radioactive wastewater, which accumulated and was to be stored in mill tailing ponds. Large-scale accidents involving these wastes began to occur in the 1960s and continue to the present, threatening human and biotic life on Indian lands.

On June 11, 1962, 200 tons of radioactive mill tailings washed into the Cheyenne River, an indirect source of potable water for the Pine Ridge Reservation. Eighteen years later, the Indian Health Service announced that as a result of this accident the well water at the reservation community of Slim Buttes contained gross alpha levels at least three times the national safety standard. A new well proposed to replace the old one tested at 14 times the national standard. Federal aid was needed to secure replacement water supplies. However, the BIA stipulated that the replacement water "could only be used for consumption by cattle" (Churchill and LaDuke, 1986: 59).

In July 1979 a dam that formed United Nuclear's uranium mill tailing pond at Church Rock, New Mexico, broke under pressure and released more than 100 million gallons of highly radioactive water into the Rio Puerco River. According to Churchill and LaDuke, "although United

Nuclear had known of cracks within the dam at least two months prior to the break, no repairs were made (or attempted). 1,700 Navajo people were immediately affected, their single water source contaminated beyond any conceivable limit" (1986: 58). The Church Rock spill is the largest leak of radioactive liquid in U.S. history (Gilles et al, 1990: 3).

In 1980, over 140 miles of normally dry washes in the Grants Uranium District of northern New Mexico flowed year-round with radioactive mine wastewater. The wastewater was discharged from the District's mines and milling operations (over 100 of the former and five of the latter) in lieu of containment ponds. Concentrations in this water of uranium, selenium, cadmium, lead, and other toxic materials often exceeded natural levels by 100 times. Drainage from uranium mine waste rock piles in the District included concentrations of these hazardous substances often 200 times greater than natural levels (Gilles et al, 1990: 3).

The accidents endured by these communities were only one legacy of radioactive colonialism. As American Indians have learned, contamination is a necessary and functional part of the ordinary operation of nuclear fuel production. The Kerr-McGee mine at Church Rock routinely discharged 80,000 gallons of radioactive water from its primary shaft per day, contamination that was introduced directly into local and downstream potable water supplies (Churchill and LaDuke, 1986: 58).

Even after operations cease at a specific site, the radioactive threat often continues. Thus, the Lost Orphan Mine in the Grand Canyon continued to emit 26,280 millirems of radiation per year after it closed in 1969. This compares with normal background emissions for the area of 150 millirems per year, which is itself somewhat higher than the national average (Gilles et al, 1990: 4). The nuclear industry has also left in its wake thousands of abandoned mines, tons of unprotected and unsecured mine waste and millions of gallons of waste liquid in largely untreated mill tailing ponds (Gilles, 1991: 3):

> 40 years of mining, milling, and transporting uranium ore on the Colorado Plateau, along with the testing of more than 900 nuclear weapons above and below ground since 1952, have brought radioactive contamination to the Plateau's water, air, and soil. Since the 1950s, thousands of unregulated uranium mines that supplied the mills have been abandoned on federally and privately owned lands, on pueblo lands, and on lands belonging to the Navajo, the Utes, the Paiutes, and the Hopi—along with hundreds of thousands of tons of radioactive uranium mill tailings.

The long-term burden associated with this legacy is now becoming clear. Since as early as 1975, groundwater contamination at numerous

New Mexico mill tailing dumpsites has been evident. Two sites—
Homestake-Milan and United Nuclear's Church Rock—have shown severe enough groundwater damage to merit listing on the U.S. Environmental Protection Agency's (EPA) Superfund National Priority List, a
nationwide list of the most dangerously polluted lands in the country. EPA
investigations near the Homestake-Milan site demonstrated dramatically
increased levels of uranium, radium, chloride, molybdenum, nitrate and
selenium. The 1975 analyses of groundwater in residential drinking water
wells downstream of the mill showed selenium concentrations up to 3.42
mg/l—more than 300 times the maximum recommended for drinking water
(Robinson, 1998). Extensive groundwater contamination at the UNC-
Church Rock was first detected in 1979, soon after the mill reopened
following repair of the dam wall. Significant levels of chloride, sulfate,
nitrate, radium, and thorium were among the many elevated constituents
detected in either alluvial or bedrock aquifer systems. Both sites have
undergone groundwater restoration for at least twenty years, long after
demolition of the mill facilities and closure of surface reclamation of the
tailings piles. It is anticipated that remedial treatment will be required well
into the 21st century (Robinson, 1998).

The health effects of uranium-related activity on local communities have also been substantial, affecting both those who directly
participated in the extractive and milling process and those who did
not. For example, 38 of the 150 Navajo miners who worked in the
Ship Rock shaft between 1952 and 1970 had died of radiation in-
duced lung cancer by 1980. Another 95 had contracted serious res-
piratory ailments and cancers by that year (Churchill, 1986: 27-28).
But the threat to human health spans well beyond the experience of
Indian mine workers. Indian communities throughout the Colorado
Plateau are routinely at risk from the simple, necessary act of drinking water. As Donald Fixico states, "[I]n a cyclic manner, mining
has come back to harm Native Americans yet again, for radiation
from uranium mines has contaminated Indian miners and the drinking water where they live" (1998: 200). The U.S. government has
been slow to act even on the most obvious and direct human harm
from its commitment to nuclear power—the diseases and loss of life
suffered by Indian miners. Despite the fact that in nearly every other
occupation associated with the nuclear cycle, Congress long ago imposed health and safety standards. As Peter Eichstaedt notes, "[N]early
two decades after the mining began and only after deaths began to mount

among the miners did the government impose radiation exposure standards on the uranium mines—in spite of relentless opposition from mining companies" (1994: xvi). Finally, in 1990 Congress recognized the extraordinary threat to Indian miners' lives caused by the national commitment to nuclear power. In passing the Radiation Exposure Compensation Act (RECA) the Congress declared that (U.S. Congress, 1990):

> The Congress finds that . . . radiation released in underground uranium mines that were providing uranium for the sole use and benefit of the nuclear weapons program of the United States Government exposed miners to massive doses of radiation that produced an epidemic of lung cancer and respiratory diseases among the miners . . . Congress recognizes that the lives and the health of uranium miners and of innocent citizens . . . were sacrificed to the national security interests of the United States, and Congress apologizes to these citizens and their families on behalf of the Nation.

Yet, RECA is at best a partial response to the legacy of radioactive colonialism. First, RECA has been selectively applied. While more than 2,700 harmed Navajo miners and their relatives have registered with the tribe's Office of Uranium Workers, only 242 have received compensation under the Act. One reason that less than 10% have received any assistance is the proof-of-employment requirement under the program. Unfortunately 'old timers' among the Navajo miners did not save check stubs or other documents to demonstrate that they had worked in the uranium mines and, as a result, are ineligible for compensation.

Second, the law addresses the loss of miners' lives but not the harmful effects suffered by their children. This is despite the fact that the children in uranium-based Indian communities are experiencing some of the highest levels of birth defects and physical traumas in the U.S. In a study conducted for the period 1969-70, the Navajo communities of Cameron and Grey were found to have rates for several defects and traumas that were five times the national average. A 1981 study, the last population-wide epidemiological research conducted in the uranium mining area of New Mexico, indicated that children growing up near the uranium mining towns of Shiprock, Farmington, and the Grants Uranium Belt had developed ovarian and testicular cancers at 15 times the national average and bone cancers at five times the national average (Gilles, 1991: 6; see also Wones, et al, 1995).

RECA also fails to account for other types of losses that can be associated with uranium activity. For instance, animal studies in the Grants Uranium District conducted throughout the 1980s found an uptake of radionuclides from forage and water was observed in the muscle and organs (e.g., liver, kidney, and bone) of livestock that grazed in Ambrosia Lake and Church Rock areas. As a result, New Mexico health authorities recommended that the meat from animals raised in Ambrosia Lake not be eaten. In addition, cattle and sheep in Church Rock had significantly higher levels of uranium deposits in muscles and in organs than non-contaminated animals grazing in a control area (Lewis et al, 2000).

While American Indians have been long-standing victims of uranium mining and milling operations, evidence is accumulating that adverse health effects from these industrial activities have migrated to populations and areas distant from the immediate extraction or production sites. Thus, Arizona's statewide birth defect rate between 1969 and 1990 was one-third higher than the national average (Gilles, 1991: 5). Regional water supplies have also been adversely affected due to radioactive contamination of the Colorado River. For instance, studies conducted in the 1980s found that many of the beaches in the Grand Canyon were contaminated with radioactive sand as a result of unregulated dumping into the Colorado River's tributaries, including the Animus, the Dolores, and the San Juan Rivers. Farther to the north, the U.S. Department of Interior concluded that contamination in the Madison aquifer, the principal regional water supply for the Dakotas, was "well beyond the safe limit for animals. Escape by infiltration into the water table or by breakout to stream drainages could cause contamination by dangerous levels of radioactivity" (quoted in Churchill and LaDuke, 1986: 60).

The degradation of Indian lands, and increasingly the contamination of adjacent regions, has led to the characterization of radioactive colonialism as the "underside of an industrialism that has no regard for people or the earth" (Johansen and Maestas, 1979: 146). In fact, the national policy debate on this issue has assured that environmental and human casualties are the necessary price for nuclear progress. In 1972, in conjunction with studies of the national energy situation performed by the Trilateral Commission, the U.S. government sought to designate certain parts of the Dakotas, Montana and Wyoming as "National Sacrifice Areas." These areas were to be formally declared uninhabitable as a consequence of uranium mining and processing and the attendant waste produced. Other areas which had not yet been rendered a threat to life were also to be designated as sacrifice areas in the recognition that continuing efficient uranium mining and milling would eventually lead to uninhabitability (Churchill and LaDuke, 1986: 62; Johansen and Maestas, 1979: 141-166). The loss of such lands to the demands of the nuclear technology system were to be treated as a normal cost of doing business. While in law no National Sacrifice Areas have been designated, Indian lands, after being subjected to 30-40 years of uranium mining and milling, have been transformed *de facto* into dangerous and unhealthy places that for non-Indians would be considered uninhabitable.

Long-Lived Injustice

American Indians continue to experience the consequences associated with the front end of the nuclear cycle. Yet even as they attempt to deal with the effects of mining and processing of uranium, the long-lived threats associated with the back end of the nuclear cycle, i.e., the disposal and storage of nuclear waste, promise that Indian communities will endure radioactive risks as far into the future as one can imagine.

The federal government's effort to establish a permanent high-level nuclear waste storage facility has included several policy initiatives intended to respond to ongoing delays at the permanent repository targeted for Yucca Mountain, Nevada. One such response was the establishment of the Office of the Nuclear Waste Negotiator (ONWN). Authorized under the 1987 Nuclear Waste Policy Amendments Act, the Office was directed to find a "State or Indian tribe willing to host a repository or monitored retrievable storage facility at a technically qualified site on reasonable terms" (42 U.S.C. 10242). The site would provide for 'temporary' storage of high-level nuclear waste until a permanent federal repository is available. The Office is empowered to negotiate with states and Indian tribes about the feasibility of a monitored retrievable storage (MRS) facility that would provide for the 'temporary' storage of high-level nuclear waste. While the directive for the ONWN included both state and tribal governments, there is little doubt that the primary target has been tribal governments since public resistance to nuclear waste storage virtually guaranteed that no state political authority would consider such a project. Indeed, researchers have found that the ONWN has focused almost entirely on negotiating with American Indian tribal governments to act as hosts for the nation's high-level nuclear waste (Leonard, 1997; Schrader-Frechette, 1996).

In approaching the tribes, the Office has been careful to present proposals as 'economic development' opportunities of largely impoverished Indian communities. It has also been very careful to downplay the long-term dangers of high-level nuclear waste. Assisting the Office in its efforts has been the U.S. Department of Energy (DOE), which had given the

National Congress of American Indians almost $1 million in grants be-
tween 1986 and 1990 to encourage tribal government participation in
nuclear waste disposal schemes (see United States Senate, 1997). The
Office added to this incentive package by promising $100,000 with "no
strings attached" to any tribe that would agree to consider temporary
waste storage. If a tribe opted to offer a temporary nuclear waste dump,
the waste would be transferred after 40 years to the permanent storage
slated for Yucca Mountain (Hanson, 1995).

By May 1992, the Office had allocated 20 Phase I MRS planning
grants of $100,000 each to Indian communities. Nine tribes then
applied for the $200,000 Phase IIa grant, which involves further site
study and community education. Four applicants received the funds.
These four tribes subsequently applied for the $2.8 million attached to a
Phase IIb grant, at which time final preparations are to be made and
serious decisions are to occur about construction design and location. The
Mescalero Apache tribe, whose reservation lies in southern New Mexico,
was the first to sign up for the MRS program. According to Tribal President Wendell Chino, "The Navajos make rugs, the Pueblos make pottery
and the Mescaleros make money" (quoted in Hanson, 1995). Tribal Council
Vice President Fred Peso went a step further by framing the issue in
terms that evoked traditional values and beliefs, saying that "the Mescaleros
can bear this [waste storage] responsibility because of our strong traditional values that favor protection of the Earth. We can serve as reliable,
trustworthy and responsible guardians of the nation's spent fuel" (quoted
in Hanson, 1995).

Despite such reassurances, the debate over the proposed facility
left the community deeply divided. Following a December 1995
agreement between a 33-member coalition of nuclear utilities and
the Tribal Council, strong community opposition emerged. In an
attempt to placate the opposition, a January 1996 referendum was
held, and in a result that stunned the Council and the nuclear industry, a strong majority of tribal members voted to halt all further negotiations with nuclear utilities over hosting the proposed private
sector temporary nuclear waste storage facility. In response to this
defeat, tribal leaders put forward a second referendum. Through the
use of what some observers, including New Mexico Attorney General Tom Udall, took to be "strong-arm tactics," the initial vote was
overturned and a majority voted in favor of continuing negotiations
with the nuclear utility companies. Subsequent to this public debacle,

the consortium of utilities behind the initiative has gradually disintegrated and opposition in other parts of New Mexico, as well as within the Mescalaro tribe, has brought the project to a standstill. However, the divisions within the community remain—a legacy of injury that cannot have been surprising to the federal government.

The setback in New Mexico has not deterred at least some in the nuclear industry from their pursuit of Indian lands as the solution to the social and ecological risks embedded in the use of their technology. Some have simply re-focused their efforts on the Goshute tribe of Skull Valley, Utah. Even more than the Mescalaro, the Goshute community is emblematic of the sacrifices required by Indian civilization in the name of industrial and nuclear progress.

The Goshutes have inhabited the southwestern part of the continent for thousands of years. While numbering about 20,000 at their peak, today there are less than 500 Goshutes, 124 of whom belong to the Skull Valley Band and reside on the 18,000 acre Skull Valley Goshute Reservation. South of Skull Valley, on traditional Goshute territory, are the Dugway Proving Grounds where the United States government developed and tested chemical and biological weapons. In 1968 chemical agents escaped from Dugway and approximately 6,000 sheep and other animals died. At least 1,600 contaminated sheep were buried on the Reservation by the Government, where they remain today. East of Skull Valley, in the area known as Rush, is a nerve gas storage facility for the United States government, which, in turn, sits astride the world's largest nerve gas incinerator. Only recently constructed, the incinerator is designed to destroy thousands of tons of the most deadly chemicals ever fashioned by humankind. South of Skull Valley lies the Intermountain Power Project that provides coal-fired electrical power primarily for California. Air pollution from the power plant fills the skies of the western desert, deeply impacting the Skull Valley Reservation. Northwest of Skull Valley is the Envirocare Low-Level Radioactive Disposal Site that handles radioactive waste for the entire country. Also within the immediate area of the reservation are two hazardous waste incinerators and one hazardous waste landfill. Finally, north of the Reservation is the Magnesium Corporation plant, a large production facility that has been identified by the US EPA as the most polluting plant of its kind in the United States (www.skullvalleygoshutes.org). Chlorine gas releases from the plant also impact the Skull Valley Reservation. According to tribal leadership, the Skull Valley Tribal Government and people were never once consulted during the siting process for any of these facilities (www.skullvalleygoshutes.org).

Spearheading the MRS effort in Skull Valley is Private Fuel Storage (PFS), the sole purpose of which is to develop a temporary site for the storage of spent nuclear fuel for the utility industry. PFS's members include American Electric Power, Consolidated Edison Company of New York, Dairyland Power Cooperative (Minnesota), Southern California Edison, GPU Nuclear Corporation, Xcel Energy (formerly Northern States Power), Illinois Power Company, and Southern Company. Together, these companies serve over 50 million electricity users.

The history of the Skull Valley facility parallels that of the Mescalaro tribe. According to the project's supporters, from 1992 until 1995, the leaders of the Band carefully accumulated data and traveled to various parts of the United States and the world to examine first hand all aspects of storage of spent nuclear fuel under the MRS Program. In the words of the tribal leadership, "[I]n view of the current hazardous waste facilities and nerve gas incinerators surrounding the Skull Valley Reservation, the Band has carefully considered a variety of economic ventures, including the storage of spent nuclear fuel. After careful consideration, the Skull Valley Band of Goshutes have leased land to a private group of electrical utilities for the temporary storage of 40,000 metric tons of spent nuclear fuel" (www.skullvalleygoshutes.org).

Again, however, opposition to the project has arisen both inside and outside the community. Utah state officials, for instance, have made no secret of their opposition. The Governor's Office has fought to keep the facility out of the state arguing that "[W]e know the citizens of Utah are behind us. We know a majority of the Legislature is behind us. We will not consider the business of this Legislature complete until we have bills to stop nuclear waste from coming to Utah" (*The Salt Lake Tribune*, February 28, 2001). The Governor seems to have been correct in his estimation: in the waning days of the 2001 legislative session, the Utah state legislature passed a bill designed to, in the words of the bill's author, "put roadblocks in the way of the project" (Associated Press, March 1, 2001). Under the bill, PFS would have to put up as much as $150 billion in cash for reparations in case of an accident before the waste could enter the state. The bill was drafted by the Governor's staff and passed in the Legislature by a vote of 60-12 (Associated Press, March 1, 2001).

Significant opposition has also arisen within the Band. In this case, however, the politics has taken on a divisive personal tone. According to LaDuke (1999: 106):

> Tribal politics are tough at Goshute, as on most other reservations. The numbers are small, so it's usually a few families or a family who end up with the most influence. When the tribe voted on whether to consider the PFS dump, half the participants walked out of the meeting. Those who remained voted in favor of the tribe.

The divisions and animosity resulting from the PFS proposal are reflected in the words of one tribal member, who observed, "it is family against family now. [The pro-PFS advocates are] punishing the people who are against them" (quoted in LaDuke, 1999: 106).

The stakes in this phase of challenge to the cultural and ecological identity of Indian communities are profound. Legally sanctioned processes of the U.S. government now target Indian communities for what must be known inescapably—in pursuit of industrial society, governments, industry and the majority community in the U.S. plan to risk Indian life and lands permanently through the insertion of radioactive wastes into the 'everyday' of all the future days of communities who inhabit this region. The only escape is to abandon the land and, possibly, to sacrifice community life itself.

Conclusion

Occupied by technological 'inhabitants' who *normally* pose carastrophic risks (Perrow, 1984), and who threaten life-affirming uses of natural environments, Indian lands have continually been locations of what Jacques Ellul has termed "technological invasion:" "technique can leave nothing untouched in a civilization. Everything is its concern . . . [I]t is a whole civilization in itself" (1964: 125-126). When the Havasupai Tribe of northern Arizona recently saw one of their most sacred sites turned into a uranium mine operated by United Nuclear Corporation (Gilles, 1991: 9), what was inconceivable in one culture-ecology relation became an unexceptional transaction of industrial culture-ecology relations. In this regard Ellul's warning needs to be understood as cultural and ecological: to be modern is to risk natural environments and the human communities living interdependently on them. Non-technical human cultures *and* natural ecologies are being subjected to technical invasion in the modern era.Importantly, the 'technical'has a racial and cultural cast in this case.

Embedded in the conflict between Indian and non-Indian communities over the past two centuries has been the struggle for cultural and ecological identity in the face of industrialization. To a great extent, the demonstrated ability of technological society to threaten Indian cultures by transforming ecologies on which cultural identifies depend offers a concrete case of the nexus between social, environmental and ecological injustice. The historical experience of American Indian communities is a prelude of what can be expected systemically. Rather than a story of local sacrifices of specific landscapes and communities, we may learn through Indian struggles for the land about the historical narrative of "ecological imperialism" (Crosby, 1986) that is a defining feature of contemporary industrialization.

The environmental degradation of American Indian lands and the harms imposed upon Indian people over the last 200 years are best understood as an integral part of the history and politics of U.S. industrial progress. As the ideas and institutions of technological civilization achieve worldwide hegemony, the history of Indian peoples in North America are being reproduced on a global scale (Churchill and LaDuke, 1986: 73):

> Ultimately, the Lagunas, the Shiprocks, Churchrocks, Tuba Cities, Edgemonts and Pine Ridges, which litter the American landscape, are not primarily a moral concern for non-Indian movements (although they should be). Rather, they are pragmatic examples, precursors of situations and conditions, which, within the not-so-distant future, will engulf other populations.

"[I]n the final analysis" argues LaDuke, "the survival of Native America is fundamentally about the collective survival of all human beings. The question of who gets to determine the destiny of the land, and of the people who live on it—those with the money or those who pray on it—is a question that is alive throughout society" (1999: 5). A political economy of society-nature relations that seeks to engage the issues of injustice on cultural and ecological scales will be guided by this question. Indeed, the practical value of political economy will be measured by the actions it informs in light of its consideration of this question.

Notes

1.   The Ambler volume incorrectly reports the Territory's production as 130 *billion* barrels in 1894.

References

Allen, Mark. 1989. "North American Control of Tribal Natural Resource Development in the Context of the Federal Trust and Tribal Self-Determination." *Boston College Environmental Affairs Law Review.* Volume 16: 857-895.

Ambler, Marjane. 1990. *Breaking The Iron Bonds: Indian Control of Energy Development.* Lawrence, Kansas: University of Kansas Press.

Barsh, Russel Lawrence. 1988. "Indian Resources and The National Economy's Business Cycles and Policy Cycles." *Policy Studies Journal.* Volume 16, Number 4 (Summer): 798-825.

Byrne, John and Steven M. Hoffman, (eds). 1996. *Governing the Atom: The Politics of Risk.* New Brunswick, NJ: Transaction Publishers.

Chenowith, William. 1997. "A Summary of Uranium-Vanadium Mining in the Carrizo Mountains, Arizona and New Mexico, 1920 - 1968." New Mexico Geological Society Guidebook, 48th Field Conference, Mesozoic Geology and Paleontology of the Four Corners Region.

Churchill, Ward and Winona LaDuke. 1986. "Native America: the Political Economy of Radioactive Colonialism." *The Insurgent Sociologist.* Spring: 51-78.

Churchill, Ward. 1986. "American Indian Lands: The Native Ethic amid Resource Development." *Environment.* Volume 28, Number 6: 13-33.

Crosby, Alfred. 1986. *Ecological Imperialism: The Biological Expansion of Europe, 900-1900.* Cambridge, UK: Cambridge University Press.

Daly, Herman. 1991. *Steady-State Economics.* Washington, DC: Island Press.

Eichstaedt, Peter. 1994. *If You Poison Us: Uranium and Native Americans.* Santa Fe, NM: Red Crane Books.

Ellul, Jacques. 1964. *The Technological Society.* New York, NY: Vintage Books.

Fixico, Donald. 1998. *The Invasion of Indian Country in the Twentieth Century: American Capitalism and Tribal Resources.* Niwot, Colorado: University Press of Colorado.

Gedicks, Al. 1998. "Racism and Resource Colonization." In Daniel Faber, editor. *The Struggle for Ecological Democracy: Environmental Justice Movements in the United States.* New York, NY: Guilford Press. pp. 272-292.

Gilles, Cate. 1996. "No One Ever Told Us: Native Americans and the Great Uranium Experiment." In John Byrne and Steven M. Hoffman, eds., *Governing the Atom: The Politics of Risk.* New Brunswick, NJ: Transaction Publishers. pp. 103-125.

_____ . 1991. "Uranium Mining at the Grand Canyon: What Costs to Water, Air, and Indigenous People?" *The Workbook.* Southwest Research and Information Center. Albuquerque, NM. Volume 16, Number 1: 2-17.

Gilles, Cate, Marti Reed, and Jacques Seronde. 1990. "Our Uranium Legacy." *Northern Arixzona Environmental Newsletter.* Volume 2, Number 1.

Hanson, Randel D. 1995. "Indian Burial Grounds for Nuclear Waste." *Multinational Monitor.* Volume 16, Number. 9 (September): 21. (web version).

Johansen, Bruce and Roberto Maestas. 1979. *WASI'CHU: The Continuing Indian Wars.* New York, NY: Monthly Review Press.

Kelley, Klara B. 1979. "Federal Indian Land Policy and Economic Development in the United States." In Rosanne Dunbar Ortiz, editor. *Economic Development in American Indian Reservations.* Institute for Native American Studies. Albuquerque, NM: University of New Mexico.

LaDuke, Winona. 1999. *All Our Relations: Native Struggles for Land and Life.* Cambridge, MA: South End Press.

_____ . 1983. "Native America: The Economics of Radioactive Colonialism." *Review of Radical Political Economy.* Fall: 9-19.

Leonard, III, Louis G. 1997. "Sovereignty, Self-Determination and Environmental Justice in the Mescalero Apache's Decision to Store Nuclear Waste." *Boston College Environmental Affairs Review.* Volume 24, Number 3: 651.

Lewis, Johnnye L., Teresa Coons, and Chris Shuey. 2000. *Uranium Research and Education in Navajo Communities.* Project sponsored by the Southwest Research and Information Center. Albuquerque, NM.

Mumford, Lewis. 1961. *The City in History: Its Origins, Its Transformations, and Its Prospects.* New York, NY: Harcourt Brace Jonaovich.

_____. 1934. *Technics and Civilization.* New York, NY: Harcourt Brace.

Oelschlaeger, Max. 1991. *The Idea of Wilderness From Prehistory to the Age of Ecology.* New York, NY: Yale University Press.

Perrow, Charles. 1984. *Normal Accidents: Living with High-Risk Technologies.* New York, NY: Basic Books.

Prucha, Francis Paul. 1990. *Documents of United States Indian Policy.* Lincoln, NE: University of Nebraska Press.

Robinson, Wm. Paul. 1998. "Groundwater Restoration Long Beyond Closure at the Homestake-Milan and United Nuclear-Church Rock Uranium Mill Tailings Piles, New Mexico, USA: Full-Scale Programs Requiring More than 20 Years of Active Treatment." In *Proceedings of Conference on Uranium Mining and Hydrogeology – II.* Claudia Helling, et al. editors, Technical University -Freiberg, Saxony, Germany.

Schrader-Freschette, Kristin. 1996. "Environmental Justice and Native Americans: The Mescalero Apache and Monitored Retrieval Storage." *Natural Resources Journal.* Volume 36, Number 4: 703.

Steiner, Stan. 1983. "Mother Earth and Father Energy." *Across the Board.* July/August: 30-36.

Takaki, Ronald P. 1979. *Iron Cages: Race and Culture in 19th Century America.* New York, NY: Alfred A. Knopf.

U.S. Bureau of Indian Affairs. 1976. Status of Mineral Resource Information for The Bad River, Lac Courte Oreilles, Lac Du Flambeau, Mole Lake Community, Potawatomi, Red Cliff, Public Domain and St. Croix, and Stockbridge — Munsee Indian Reservations of Wisconsin, Administrative Report BIA-20. Washington, D.C.

U.S. Congress. Radiation Exposure Compensation Act. Public Law 101-426 101st Congress. October 15, 1990. 42U.S.C. 2210.

U. S. Senate. Committee on Energy and Natural Resources. 1997. Hearings on S.839 — To Authorize the Secretary of Energy to Enter into Incentive Agreements with Certain States and Affected Indian Tribes Concerning the Storage and Disposal of High-Level Radioactive Waste and Spent Nuclear Fuel. Washington, DC: U.S. Government Printing Office.

Wones, R., Ruddack, K., Martin, V., Mandell, K., Pinney, S. and Buncher R. 1995. "Do Persons Living Near a Uranium Site Have Evidence of Increased Somatic Cell Gene Mutations? A First Study." *Mutations Research.* 335: 171-184.

6

The Circle of Life: Preserving American Indian Traditions and Facing the Nuclear Challenge

Cecilia Martinez and John Poupart[1]

Introduction

This chapter reviews the historical legal, political and cultural relationships between Indian tribes and the U.S. government in the context of nuclear policy. More importantly, it tells the nuclear story from an Indian perspective. We include a summary description of American Indian cultural worldviews as well as an evaluation of the Indian policy events that led to the establishment of a national military and civilian nuclear apparatus. Together with the chapter by Byrne and Hoffman in this volume, these papers highlight the complexities associated with the environmental justice field, and the deep cultural divisions that characterize this society's history. The two chapters also reflect how one value system and its truths may bring dire consequences to another culture and its people.

There are approximately 515 politically recognized Indian nations in the U.S. today[2] and while mainstream scholars and policy analysts tend to assume a homogenous pan-Indian culture, each tribe is unique with its own customs, history, traditions, and ceremonies. For non-Indians to develop authentic knowledge about Indian culture requires suspending application of European concepts and values, an extraordinarily difficult, though not impossible task. In truth, knowing the world from the "soul of the Indian" is a life commitment and must be learned primarily through oral history. As one tribal member states (Interview with Anishinabe tribal member from Lac du Flambeau):

> Imagine yourself in a far off country where a different language is spoken, a different value system is present (both material and social), a different appreciation of spirituality is expressed and people believe opposite of you as to how they came to be on this earth. And then, imagine that everything you believed in was expendable and replaceable by the other's understanding of the world. In other words, it would no longer be acceptable to believe in the ways that you had spent your entire life, up to that point learning.

In 1945, the first testing of the atomic bomb occurred near Alamagordo, New Mexico. This was the initial realization, albeit by an elite scientific few, of the magnitude of devastation made possible by nuclear energy. In the 1990s, after years of nuclear generated electrical power, the storage of radioactive waste that accompanies this energy source became a major national policy issue. A scant few miles from the place of the first nuclear test in New Mexico, lay the Mescalero Apache Indian reservation, one of several Indian reservations proposed for the storage of nuclear waste. In some ways this ironic cycle of events is consonant with American Indian's natural philosophical view that all things are part of the "circle of life." This belief rests on an understanding that everything is inextricably interwoven, and it is the nature of life for events to come full circle. But mainstream America has demonstrated that it is unable to relate to this Indian "sacred history," let alone understand it, and within education and scholarship there are few, if any, venues for learning about it.

In 1953, Felix Cohen observed that the relationship between Indians and European Americans was a marking point for U.S. democracy (Cohen, 1953):

> Like the miner's canary, the Indian marks the shift from fresh air to poison gas in our political atmosphere; and our treatment of Indians, even more than our treatment of other minorities, reflects the rise and fall in our democratic faith.

Sadly, U.S. American Indian conditions, both past and present, indicate a political system filled more with poisonous gas than fresh air. A premier example is illustrated in the political and legal relationship instituted between Indian tribes and the U.S. government for the development of a national nuclear power system. Since its inception the nuclear power enterprise has relied on uranium mined largely from Indian lands. Earlier in this volume, Byrne and Hoffman offered an historical evaluation of the inequality inherent in U.S. energy and nuclear policy and its impact on Indian nations. They also show how irresponsible corporate actions and the lack of effective environmental and health and safety governmental standards resulted in radioactive contamination of Indian people and their lands. However, uranium mining and processing is not the end of the story. The nuclear problem continues to plague Indian tribes. The latest attempt to use tribal lands for storage of radioactive waste from civilian nuclear power generation is still another example of the noxious elements that continue to plague the U.S. political system. In short, Indian tribal lands were, and are, foundational to the nuclear power enterprise, a fact that has escaped nearly every mainstream analysis of nuclear development.

The American Indian experience offers unique challenges to contemporary environmental justice models. Without addressing these challenges, environmental justice will not be effective in resolving the fundamental issues that are responsible for the negative conditions of indigenous peoples. If no resolution is found, as Cohen's analogy of the American Indian as the miner's canary indicates, the ultimate impact will come to rest not just on Indian peoples, but upon all life. And the consequence is the destruction of any possibility for a just, respectful, and democratic society. While we are unable to offer a truly authentic presentation of indigenous worldviews in this chapter (such an effort cannot be done in the English language, in written form, etc.), we present a basic review of some major characteristics of traditional Indian culture that are similar across tribes, and focus primarily on the Ojibwe (also known as Chippewa, but the original name being Anishinabe), with some references to other tribes as well. The literature cited here is intentionally limited to a number of classic works recognized as important contributions in Indian studies, and most importantly, to primary information derived from personal interviews with Indian elders.

The chapter is divided into four sections. The first section provides an introspective view of Indian culture and the importance of its preservation to Indians. It also allows for it to stand on its own merits. The second section presents a legal and political description of the foundational principle of Indian tribal sovereignty and its relevance to nuclear power development. The third section offers an overview of the relationship of man and the environment from an American Indian cultural perspective. It is important to note that this overview is a brief synopsis of American Indian values and beliefs and is intended to highlight the significance of Indian sovereignty and self-determination. The last section offers a review of the violation of Indian sovereignty and the contradiction between U.S. Indian policy and U.S. nuclear policy.

American Indian Worldviews: The Challenge for European American Frameworks of Environmental Justice

> A month or so ago, a delegation of White Men came to this village... They offered to buy the whole of our land for money and gifts... Since that meeting my dreams and my sleep has been troubled. I want to do what is right and just for both our people and the strangers. (Johnston, 1982: 169)

Two common assertions in mainstream society are that the North American continent was "discovered" by Europeans via their courageous explorations into unknown territories, and that indigenous peoples are descendents of Eurasian migrants that crossed over on a prehistoric land bridge. These beliefs have been sustained in part by the creation of a powerful social myth that European and European-American cultures are superior in intelligence. In contemporary society, this myth is rooted in three propositions that are used to explain the development and evolution of U.S. society. The first is the contention that a bold new experiment in democracy utilizing European derived liberalist political philosophy was successfully implanted in the "new world," and is politically and legally embodied in the U.S. Constitution. Second, that European American values are the source of modern civilization. Third, that European immigration spurred development of this nation's political, economic and technological systems, and thus serves as evidence of an advanced society.

These three propositions obscure the truth about the factual history of development on this continent. Native peoples, their culture and social organization, existed long before chronicles of democratic theory or ideas of exploration entered into European consciousness. But rather than formulate and accept a true understanding of native worldviews, the European mind has relied on centuries of self-conceived ignorance about Indian history and culture, and Indian-U.S. relations. Unfortunately, this is no less the case among scholars and policy analysts. Academic literature and the policy record abound with analyses that identified American Indians as heathen, uncivilized, ignorant savages. The European American worldview simply carried forward the European myth of superiority. In 1883, then Secretary of the Interior Henry Teller's views exemplify this U.S. posture toward Indian peoples and cultures (cited in Prucha, 1990: 160):

> If it is the purpose of the Government to civilize the Indians, they must be compelled to desist from the savage and barbarous practices that are calculated to continue them in savagery . . . Every man familiar with Indian life will bear witness to the pernicious influence of these savage rites and heathenish customs.

Clearly, the European American disposition toward Indian cultures provided the foundation for legislation and policies directed at destroying American Indian people and tribes. Despite these attempts however, native cultures and values survived and continue to exist into the present day.

After five hundred years of Indian-U.S. relations, European American and American Indian worldviews are as different today as they were at first contact. The relationship between man and nature is a focal point that highlights these fundamental differences in worldviews. Unlike European American distinctions between man and nature, native cultures are holistic and see everything in nature as having life. There is nothing that is inanimate or without soul in the native worldview. The soil of the earth, stones, lakes and rivers, and plants and animals all possess the power of knowledge, understanding, and communication. As one tribal member stated (quoted in Deloria, 1994: 90):

> Did you know that trees talk? Well they do. They talk to each other, and they'll talk to you if you listen. Trouble is white people don't listen . . . But I have learned a lot from trees; sometimes about the weather, sometimes about animals, sometimes about the Great Spirit.

Charles Eastman explains that native peoples know "that the spirit pervades all creation and that every creature possesses a soul in some degree . . . The tree, the waterfall the grizzly bear, each is an embodied Force, and as such an object of reverence" (1911: 14-15). In traditional Indian cultures the idea that life is in all things is not a metaphorical concept, it is reality. Every act, every interaction, every element is related, and in understanding the universe in this manner there is a moral obligation that all life should be treated with dignity, honor, and respect.

Human beings hold an important place in creation, but this is "tempered by the thought that they are dependent on everything in creation for their existence" (Deloria, 1994: 82). American Indians regard respect and harmony as core values, and traditions and customs help to inform and direct Indian people to act respectfully to all their relations. Historically, Indian tribes saw their well being directly tied to the well-being of other life. As Lakota spiritual leader, Black Elk explained, "once we were happy in our own country and we were seldom hungry, for then the two-leggeds and the four-leggeds lived together like relatives, and there was plenty for them and for us" (documented in Niehardt, 1979: 9).

Deloria notes that, "American Indians hold their lands—places—as having the highest possible meaning" (1994: 62). In native culture, the concept of lands is all encompassing, and includes every plant, animal, and earth life. Alternatively, western European American immigrants view land as an economic resource, and the constructed political concept of private property is used to assign rights of distribution. In contrast to the centrality of land, tradition and spirituality in American Indian life, European American society values mobility and innovation. Essentially, contemporary European Americans view "the movement of their ancestors across the continent as a steady progression of basically good events and experiences, thereby placing history-time in the best possible light" (1994: 62). Indian-U.S. relations are a collision of these worldviews.

In contrast to the native worldview, mainstream culture is rooted in a curious combination of Christianity and science. Judaeo-Christian religious origins offer an understanding of human-environmental relations in which "man" was the ultimate of God's creations and vested with higher reasoning and moral authority to rule over nature. "Be fruitful and increase in number; fill the earth and subdue it. Rule over the fish of the sea and the birds of the air and over every living creature that moves on the ground" (Genesis 1: 28).

For the Ojibwe the creation story is different (Johnston, 1982: 163-4):

Last the Great Mystery created man. To all the creatures had been given some of the mystery . . . When Geezhigoquae had descended, she asked for a morsel of soil—and the muskrat, the least of the animals, at last brought up a pawful of soil from the depths. Geezhigoquae took the lump of earth and, with her finger, traced it around the rim of the turtle's shell. Then, she breathed upon it; and the soil spread, covering the turtle's back, growing into an island which our forefathers called Mishee Mackinakong (Place of the Great Turtle).

Ironically, the emergence of science, generally regarded as a triumph of reason over religion, offers a hierarchical view of human relations with the natural world, similar to that in Genesis. Philosopher Renee Descartes, credited as being at the forefront of advancing the age of reason, envisioned that by "knowing the nature and behavior of fire, water, air, stars, the heavens, and all the other bodies which surrounds us…(we) make ourselves masters and possessors of nature" (1956: 40).

Whether rooted in religion or science, the European and European American mind has established a cultural paradigm in which intrinsic value is reserved only for human life. Plants, animals and the earth are contingent upon human assignment. Whether a species lives or dies, and if it lives what its purpose in the web of life will be, is seen as within the power and discretion of human society. The Indian, on the other hand, is taught to view not only the earth, but also the universe, and everything in it with co-equal standing. The European American mind seems to believe that human political and economic structures are the legitimate and final arbiters for these decisions.

The native worldview does not conceive of nature as a set of animate and inanimate objects or resources, nor does it contend that humanity has preeminent standing over others. Quite the contrary, as Deloria explains, the "physical world is so filled with life and personality that humans appear as one minor species without much significance and badly in need of assistance from other forms of life" (1994: 153). Native cultures regard the destiny of American Indians as physically and spiritually joined to the natural world, and subject to the will and wisdom of animals, plants or earth forces. In oral tradition (in European terms, substitute history for oral tradition), there are numerous examples in which Indian peoples have been assisted by other life forms. Records of these events are preserved in oral histories and are reminders that humans are fragile, and reverence to all life is the most fundamental moral obligation (Deloria, 1994: 40):

> American Indians look at events to determine the spiritual activity supporting or undergirding them . . . Indians know that human beings must participate in events, not isolate themselves from occurrences in the physical world. Indians thus obtain information from birds, animals, rivers, and mountains, which is inaccessible to modern science.

Recognition of birds, animals, rivers, and mountains as life with moral reasoning obligates people to act with reverence. Because of this understanding, it is natural that American Indian relations with the natural world are spiritual as well as physical. The holistic character of the traditional native worldview means that the physical, spiritual, and intellectual are interconnected and cannot be divided into separate domains. Fragmenting life into distinct spheres only serves to detach humans from their relatives in the natural world. Individualism is incomprehensible, as is the notion that humans would build citadels for worship detached from creation. Eastman explained that, "(t)here are no temples or shrines . . . save those of nature" (1911: 5). Like many of his contemporaries, Chief Seattle attempted to explain to European Christians and others to those who did not understand or respect this way of life (cited in Armstrong, 1971: 92):

> Every part of this soil is sacred in the estimation of my people. Every hillside, every valley, every plain and grove, has been hallowed by some sad or happy event in the days long vanished. Even the rocks which seem to be dumb and dead as they swelter

in the sun along the silent shore, thrill with the memories of stirring events connected with my people. The very dust upon which you now stand responds more lovingly to their footsteps than to yours, because it is rich with the blood of our ancestors and our bare feet are conscious of the sympathetic touch.

While Chief Seattle's statement can be read as one of despair of the treatment of Indian tribes, it is also intended as a warning to European immigrants that the web of life is fragile and if human beings disconnect themselves from it, they risk their own destruction. In this sense, American Indian spirituality is entirely different from the Judaeo-Christian concept of religion. According to the Anishinabe, creation is known as the Great Mystery, the Great Spirit, or Kitchee Manitou, and encompasses the natural spiritual connectedness of all things, even that which non-Indians see as inert and lifeless. Eastman explained that the soul of the American Indian knows that the "Spirit of God is not breathed into man alone, but that the whole created universe is a sharer in the immortal perfection of its Maker" (Eastman, 1911: 121). Similarly, Black Elk tells about the importance of the spiritual interconnection in his recounting of the story of the Lakota people. In a common way of beginning oral histories, he states (quoted in Niehardt, 1979: 1):

It is the story of all life that is holy and is good to tell, and of us two-leggeds sharing in it with the four-leggeds and the wings of the air and all green things; for these are children of one mother and their father is one Spirit. . . .

Oral tradition is the sacred stories, songs, and ceremonies of Indian people, and is the way information and knowledge is shared. One Ojibwe tribal member explains (Interview with Eugene Begay, Lac Courtes Oreilles, 2000):

My people are descendents of spiritual people. A lot of things we do today go back to spiritual values. How my people understand and relate to the environment is derived from the creation story of the Ojibwe people. It is a sacred story and when it is told through story and song, the ritual takes 14 days. It's a part of me . . . It is me . . . it's all part of the spirit world.

The discipline and reverence required to become a keeper of the oral tradition is considerable. Knowledge is shared through stories and song that take a lifetime to learn, in ceremonies that can take days, and sometimes years to complete. As interpreters of this knowledge, elders are the prominent and respected "leaders" in traditional Indian culture. They might be able to communicate with the spirit world and often demonstrate a life commitment of service to the community. Often mistaken as myths or fables, American Indian oral traditions are either dismissed as fictional entertainment or romanticized by mainstream culture. In fact, oral tradition is an essential part of preserving and sharing knowledge. Deloria states that the oral tradition disseminates "information about ancient events and precise knowledge of birds, animals, plants, geological features and religious experiences of a particular group of people" (1994: 36).

Other life in the natural world can and does offer lessons to humankind. Most Indian cultures acknowledge the intrinsic knowledge held by the natural world and this is exhibited in a variety of ways. For example, many tribes are organized around clan systems that replicate the relationships of the natural world. For the Ojibwe, these clans include the wolf, fish, bear, eagle, and marten, among others. Leadership roles and community obligations are based on clan structures. One Ojibwe tribal member summarizes the intricate relationships that traditionally existed in that tribal culture (Eugene Begay, 1998: 4):

> Ogitchedahs or clan leaders helped guide the band; each clan leader performed specific tasks and participated equally in solving the problems facing the band. While Ogitchedahs would discuss issues concerning the people, each clan retained specific leadership responsibilities. For example, the Ogitchedahs from the bird clan focused more on internal matters, the wolf clan negotiated with other bands to avoid conflict. The wolf clan is the warrior clan. But as warriors we do not only talk about war strategies. We do whatever is necessary to prevent war and bloodshed among people Traditionally a warrior could not be doctored with Indian medicine after battle until the blood of his enemy was removed through song. The warrior needed to be healed and one of the four songs for healing was dedicated to the fallen enemy.

In Indian cultures, spirituality, generosity, and commitment to the tribal community were considered the most important elements of leadership. Most mainstream historical analyses mistakenly view Indian leadership according to a hierarchical, Eurocentric paradigm, individualizing and almost exclusively identifying such skills with resistance leaders, such as Sitting Bull, Black Hawk, Geronimo and others. In fact, from a native worldview, leadership is consensual, communal, and spiritual. Firethunder notes that "Sitting Bull was also a spiritual man and because of this strengthened his people" (Firethunder, 1998: 8).

Misconceptions about Indian leadership and decision-making have existed since the first interactions between Europeans and Indians. American Indian norms emphasize deliberation and consensus, and Johnston explains "there were many practical reasons for 'taking time,' but dominating them all was a reverence for the 'word.' To be asked to make a decision was to be asked to give 'word,' an awesome request" (Johnston, 1982: 80). Mainstream norms that emphasize hierarchy, predominantly linear thinking, and individualism directly conflict with traditional Indian practice, a problem that continues to influence Indian-U.S. relations. The dichotomy established then, continues today.

In Ojibwe, the values of leadership are expressed as *namaji*, which means dignity, honor, and respect. The following description illustrates how traditional Ojibwe deliberations occurred according to the principles of *namaji*: "Ogitchedahs or clan leaders came together . . . Each could speak as long as they thought was necessary and nobody interrupted or challenged them. This could last hours or days. There were no disruptive or aggressive arguments . . . they would select one solution to try first . . . if it failed, they would try another" (Begay, 1998: 4). There are numerous accounts of U.S. governmental agents unfamiliar with these norms becoming exasperated by the length of Indian deliberations during treaty negotiations. Their frustration led to efforts to change and restructure Indian governance and decision-making to better accommodate European immigrant models.

Mainstream European American culture tends to operate as if its own norms, traditions and values are self-evident truths with universal acceptance and application. Derived from a mixture of Judaeo-Christian religious and liberalist political philosophy, it has perpetuated erroneous conclusions about Indian culture and behavior. These conclusions served as ammunition for an assault on the true identity of American Indians. Terms such as "savage," "heathen," and "uncivilized" were commonly used to describe American Indians, and this view was institutionalized into an egregious U.S. national Indian policy agenda. In 1889, then Commissioner of Indian Affairs Thomas J. Morgan stated that U.S. policy "should seek the disintegration of the tribes," and his successor in 1901 declared, "(b)orn a savage and raised in an atmosphere of superstition and ignorance, he [the Indian] lacks at the outset those advantages that are inherited by his white brother and enjoyed from the cradle" (cited in Prucha, 1990: 201). Over the years a comprehensive federal system of assimilation was devised and implemented to, as the designer of Indian boarding schools Richard Henry Pratt proposed, "kill the Indian and save the man" (cited in Iverson, 1998: 21). Secretary of the Interior Henry M. Teller proclaimed the characteristic understanding of the U.S. governmental intention toward American Indians in 1883; "If it is the purpose of the

Government to civilize the Indians, they must be compelled to desist from the savage and barbarous practices that are calculated to continue them in savagery . . ." (cited in Prucha, 1990: 160). Robert Williams describes the history of the U.S. policy framework of destruction as part of a European American genocidal need (cited in Getches et al, 1993: 328):

> European-derived legal thought has sought to erase the difference presented by the Indian in order to sustain its own discursive context; European norms and value structures. Animated by a central orienting myth of its own universalized, hierarchical position among all other discourses, the white man's archaic, European-derived law respecting the Indian is ultimately genocidal in both its practice and intent.

American Indian Sovereignty and the U.S. Trust Responsibility

Sovereignty as constructed by European and American legal philosophy is fundamental to the basic rights of a people to self-determination and self-governance and is the internationally recognized power of a nation to govern itself. It forms the legal and political basis for a people to establish custom, law, and traditions and is not conditional upon the consent of an external tribunal. Thus American Indians have as much right to their sovereign status as Europeans. To require external consensual authority defies the very principle of self-determination. Treaties between the U.S. government and Indian tribes are negotiated agreements between nations that granted special peace, alliance, trade and land rights to European immigrants, while confirming existing aboriginal rights of Indian tribes. Among those aboriginal rights are, the sovereign right to self-government, fishing and hunting, and jurisdiction over tribal lands (Kickingbird et al, 1980). Mainstream political analysis tends to inaccurately suggest that these rights were granted to American Indian tribes via treaty making, or that tribes are subject to "equal protection" under the Constitution. In fact, aboriginal rights pre-existed treaties, and treaties simply specified which rights, along with what land, Indian tribes agreed to cede to European and U.S. governments. This is the keystone of the nation-to-nation relationship between Indian tribes and the U.S. government.

Most accounts of the purpose and process of treaty making are described from a European American lens, and adopt a deterministic orientation. On the one had, there is an admission that cultural genocide was the guiding ethic of European and European-American political and legal strategies toward Indian tribes. Political arbitration was merely a more expedient and less costly avenue to acquiring land and resources to which other nations believed Indians held title (Getches, Wilkinson, and Williams, Jr., 1993: 2):

> Originally, Indians governed themselves free of outside interference or control. As the New World was colonized something had to be done about the continent's aboriginal inhabitants. Very early it was apparent that the tribes could be contained or decimated by force. But the costs in lives, materiel, time and conscience were far too great. Indians were in the way. . . Thus the United States' policy of negotiating land cessions in treaties and agreements, with certain promises and rights in return, was born of necessity and convenience.

Yet, pursuing the path of negotiation and political diplomacy meant that the rules of law, not the rules of war governed Indian relations, and required, by European-based standards, sovereign standing to Indian nations. As Getches et al state, "(o)ne of the ingredients of the process . . . was treatment of tribes as sovereign entities to the extent necessary to procure their consent to cession of their right to occupy the land" (1993: 2). While, the "motive was more to facilitate expedient colonization by the Europeans than it was to deal humanely with natives," unless the U.S. government openly advocated violation of its own system of law, Indian tribes could not be stripped of their sovereign standing. In 1789, the Secretary of War in condemning white violations of Indian rights stated, "Indians . . . possess the right of the soil. It cannot be taken from them unless by their free consent or by the right of conquest in case of a just war. To dispossess them on any other principle, would be a gross violation of the fundamental laws of nature, and of that distributive justice which is the glory of a nation" (cited in Prucha, 1990: 12-13).

Indian sovereignty has not gone unchallenged. Numerous attempts were made by states and by the U.S. Congress to undermine or dilute the sovereign status of Indian nations. One of the earliest of these attempts resulted in three landmark Supreme Court cases that continue to stand as the constitutional benchmarks for U.S.-Indian relations. Johnson v. McIntosh (1823), Cherokee Nation v. Georgia (1831), and Worcester v. Georgia (1832) are known as the "Marshall Trilogy" in reference to Chief Justice John C. Marshall who wrote the majority opinion. These cases echo the contradictions that characterized treaty making.

Relying on the Section 8, Article 3 of the U.S. Constitution, which empowers Congress to "regulate commerce with foreign nations, and among the several states, and with the Indian tribes" Marshall established that Indian nations occupy a unique legal standing incomparable to foreign nations and the several states (Cherokee Nation v. Georgia, 1831, cited in Getches et al, 1993: 132). Blending prevailing racist attitudes about the savage, childlike, and uncivilized Indian with tenets of U.S. law, Marshall created a unique legal creature, which he called "domestic dependent nation." Owing to the claim that the "condition of the Indians in relation to the United States is perhaps unlike any other two people in existence," Marshall advanced the concept that "the relations of the Indians to the United States is marked by peculiar and cardinal distinctions which exist no where else" (Cherokee Nation v. Georgia, cited in Getches et al, 1993: 132). In an odd bit of logic in which the point at issue seems to be fear that Indian nations could conceivably develop relations with foreign governments and enter treaties with such foreign states, Marshall wrote, "they (Indian tribes) . . . are considered by foreign nations, as well as by ourselves as being so completely under the sovereignty and dominion of the United States, that any attempt to acquire their lands, or to form a political connexion with them, would be considered by all as an invasion of our territory, and an act of hostility" (cited in Getches et al, 1993: 132). In order to prevent this possibility from becoming a reality, Marshall developed a legal argument based on these perceived "cardinal distinctions" and their effect on the legal standing of Indian sovereignty (Cherokee Nation v. Georgia, cited in Getches et al, 1993: 132):

> Though the Indians are acknowledged to have an unquestionable, and, heretofore, unquestioned right to the lands they occupy, until that right shall be extinguished by a voluntary cession to our government; yet it may well be doubted whether those tribes which reside within the acknowledged boundaries of the United States can, with strict accuracy, be denominated foreign nations. They may, more correctly, perhaps, be denominated domestic dependent nations. They occupy a territory to which we assert a title independent of their will, which must take effect in point of possession when their right of possession ceases. Meanwhile they are in a state of pupilage. Their relation to the United States resembles that of a ward to his guardian.

The construction of a "domestic dependent nation" has served to provide the U.S. government with a tool of legal ambiguity, which on the one hand, stipulates Indian tribes as sovereign nations, and on the other, establishes requirements that such authority is contingent upon assimilation into "civilized" European-based society. Legally, the upshot of these landmark cases is that only Congress has the constitutional authority to deal with, and pass legislation relative to, Indian tribes. Politically, however, Marshall's opinion gave support to racist ideologies of the time.

Historically, U.S. Indian policy has been dominated by the civilizing ethos. Regardless of the motive or intention, the underlying presumption of Indian tribes as savage or childlike is common. This belief has been forwarded by missionaries seeking to "Christianize" heathens, to liberal groups eager to save the Indian from unscrupulous whites, and to political and economic interests seeking to appropriate land and resources for profit. In fact, the opinion forwarded by Marshall in the trilogy was utilized to garner support and legitimize the next century of assimilation and appropriation policy. In report after report, U.S. Indian Commissioners reiterated the U.S. position. In 1848, Commissioner Medill stated, "apathy, barbarism and heathenism must give way to energy, civilization and Christianity; and so the Indian of this continent has been displaced by the European" (Indian Commissioner William Medill, 1848, cited in Prucha, 1990: 77). In 1872, Commissioner Walker stated (cited in Prucha, 1990: 141):

> Can any principle of national morality be clearer than that, when the expansion and development of a civilized race involve the rapid destruction of the only means of subsistence possessed by the members of a less fortunate race, the higher is bound as of simple right to provide for the lower some substitute for the means of subsistence which it has destroyed? This substitute is . . . helping them over the first rough places on 'the white man's road . . .'

The second fundamental principle undergirding U.S.-Indian relations is the principle of "trust responsibility." The term "trust responsibility" derives its name from the expectation that the U.S. government was "entrusted" to act in good faith and to fulfill obligations and commitments stipulated in treaties, among which included the provision of education, health, and welfare (Pevar, 1992: 26). Within the U.S. governmental structure, a succession of political and administrative instruments has developed over time to deal with Indian tribes. As early as 1786, the Continental Congress passed an ordinance that established a system of superintendents and agents adapted from British practice to govern non-Indians in U.S. territories trading with Indian nations. Despite clear and convincing language in the Articles of Confederation regarding the nation-to-nation relationship of the U.S. and Indian tribes, state governments pursued various efforts to undermine the legitimacy of Indian sovereignty. By 1787 the actions of state governments and an "avaricious disposition" of European immigrants were identified as "crucial problems" in Indian affairs (Committee Report on the Southern Department 1787, cited in Prucha, 1990: 11).

Later, responsibility for Indian affairs was included in the enabling legislation that created the War Department in 1789. In 1818, Congress formalized the offices of Indian agents and authorized monies for their compensation. In 1824 the Bureau of Indian Affairs (BIA) was created within the War Department, and in 1849 it was transferred to the Department of the Interior. Although there were numerous attempts to return the BIA to the War Department in later years, these proved to be unsuccessful. Between 1849 and 1975, the BIA and the Department of the Interior were the U.S. governmental units responsible for Indian programs. Although the BIA and the Department of the Interior continue to be the primary governmental agencies in Indian affairs, passage of the Indian Self-Determination and Education Assistance Act in 1975 authorized individual tribes, not the Secretary of Interior, to decide participation in any federal program. The American Indian Review Policy Commission, established by Joint Resolution in 1975 to study the historical and legal status of Indian tribes, specifically articulates the U.S. Department of Interior's responsibility inherent in the federal trust obligation to Indian tribes (1976: 1):

> The birth of the trust responsibility lies in the nature of treaties. In exchange for land concessions to the federal government, Indians were to receive protection from foreign nations, hostile Indian tribes, and individuals . . . protecting Indian tribes came to be regarded as a trust; that is, the fiduciary responsibility to protect.

The Commission further stated that in its opinion, the trust responsibility "extends beyond real or personal property" and includes the "obligation to provide services, and to take other appropriate actions necessary to protect tribal self-government" (1977).

As with all of the U.S. government's handling of Indian affairs, implementation of policy and law relating to tribal sovereignty and trust responsibility has been erratic, complex, and contradictory. In applying its own legal standards, the U.S. government has instituted a quagmire of rules and regulations, policies, and legislation that have been described as among the most complex of any bureaucracy in U.S. history. Was it the purpose of Indian policy to destroy all vestiges of Indian culture, eradicate native worldviews, and assimilate American Indian people into mainstream culture?

American Indian Nations and the Nuclear Encounter

The complex contemporary situation of American Indian tribes in the U.S. is based on two sets of historical facts. The first is the existence of a native worldview (the sacred history) that continues to be the cultural foundation of American Indian tribes despite comprehensive and systematic policies directed toward its annihilation. The second is the existence and evolution of a political and legal system that has never fully resolved its inherent contradictions. Substantial research exists documenting the exploitation of Indian tribal resources, the fraud that accompanied such exploitation, and the environmental consequences to Indian lands that followed. Flooding of Indian ancestral lands, ancient villages, and burial grounds as a result of dam construction, and pollution as a result of mining and other industrial activity has been all but too commonplace. Throughout the history of the U.S., Indian lands have been developed as national parks and forests, and exploited for a host of resources, including farmland, timber, water, oil, gas, coal, iron ores, copper, and gold. In short, U.S. development could neither have occurred, nor could it have been sustained for any length of time without access to Indian lands.

In one regard, the emergence of modern day environmental justice presents a model for explaining the experiences of indigenous tribes. Analysis of the inequitable impact of pollution can certainly be applied to Indian lands, as can the inequitable compensation paid for use of tribal natural resources. Establishment of a special tribunal in 1946, the Indian Claims Commission, to handle Indian claims against the U.S. is testimony to this fact. But the dilemmas posed by the American Indian experience challenge the boundaries of the environmental justice movement as well. Borne out of the necessity to confront mainstream environmental advocates to include the distributive impact of health and environmental degradation, the movement has brought the issues of the poor and the non-white to the national environmental platform.

Evidence of the disproportionate citing of hazardous industrial and waste facilities in low-income and racial communities raised awareness about the sophisticated mechanisms that continue to perpetuate and sustain a system of institutional racism. Given the conspicuous lack of policy attention to the condition of racial and ethnic communities, the environmental justice movement forced the policy agenda to specifically include considerations of social equity in the environmental arena. Consequently, proposed solutions to the problem of environmental racism include equal enforcement of environmental regulations and re-evaluation of fairness in methodologies used to assess environmental risk and impact, including long-term ramifications. These solutions are positive steps toward solving the issues and conditions identified in the initial environmental justice agendas. However, the American Indian experience offers a unique perspective from which to address the values and scope of contemporary environmental justice models. A poignant example of is illustrated in the case of American Indians and the U.S. nuclear enterprise.

The nuclear power system is among the most dangerous, complex, and wide-ranging systems in the world. It provides energy for both military and civilian purposes, operates out of a unique cooperative effort between private and public sectors, requires extensive research and development support from national laboratories and universities, and has been the most critical component of U.S. national security in the modern era (Martinez and Byrne, 1996). A host of historical accounts and analyses of the nuclear enterprise detail the extensive and intricate pattern of corporate and governmental actions that were necessary to construct the elaborate system of nuclear energy (see for example, Hewlett and Anderson, 1991; Rhodes, 1995). Others describe the impacts that continue to beset American Indian people and lands from uranium mining and processing during the early development stages of nuclear power in this country (see,   e.g., Churchill and LaDuke, 1992).

But the case of nuclear power and American Indian tribes extends beyond the disproportionate citing of mining and waste facilities on Indian lands on two counts. First, it begs the questions of how, and under what process and criteria, the U.S. was held accountable to its legal obligation to act in the best interests or to protect American Indian tribes. That is, how does one sovereign govern its relations with another "domestic dependent sovereign" when there is a direct conflict of interest? The second, and perhaps most important issue highlighted by the nuclear program, is one of cultural standing. American Indian cultures are not dead. They have been preserved by generations of Indians, often at great cost, and continue to guide and inform native peoples. Yet, the "rules of the game" are rooted in a European-based framework, which gives standing to European values and norms, and for all intents and purposes relegates American Indian cultures to mere quaint ideas or historical reminiscences.

How did the U.S. government implement and administer a national program of leasing Indian lands for the purpose of mining uranium deposits that was "in the best interests of the tribe," when by its own admission U.S. national security was at stake? This fundamental question remains to be answered. The federal government, through the BIA and the Department of the Interior, was responsible for the protection of Indian tribal lands and Indian people, at the same time it was embarking on a mission to implement a wholesale civilian and military nuclear program that necessitated access to fissionable uranium. More recently, the issue of nuclear waste accumulating from decades of civilian nuclear power operation has also become a national problem, and an even greater problem for Indian tribes. Once again, Indian lands are figured into the solution. The Office of the Waste Negotiator, established specifically for the purpose of finding a resolution to the problem, actively recruited Indian tribes to become hosts for "interim waste storage." 'Interim' refers to the fact that the U.S. Department of Energy is required, under the 1982 Nuclear Waste Policy Act to take permanent responsibility for nuclear waste. However, the federal government's designated depository at Yucca Mountain has undergone numerous delays, and as the waste is accumulating beyond what private facilities can hold, electric utilities are seeking storage sites until Yucca Mountain is operational. Uranium mining and nuclear waste storage signify two fundamental challenges to contemporary environmental justice paradigms. Both these issues are relevant to any comprehensive examination of environmental, nuclear, and Indian policies.

The U.S. as Guardian: For Whom, and For What Purpose?

As trustees of Indian lands, the Department of Interior has a "duty of protection," that is, an obligation to "protect the safety and well-being of tribal members" (Pevar, 1992: 26). Pevar explains that the trust responsibility to protect Indian lands can be traced to both federal statutes created in 1790 that required the U.S. to fulfill its treaty obligations, and to the majority opinion expressed by the Supreme Court in the Marshall Trilogy. One result of these interpretations was the institution of a "trust land" system, in which the BIA and the Department of Interior were assigned responsibility for managing Indian lands "in the best interests of the tribe." While the role of the Department of the Interior in trust management has evolved in recent years as tribal governments have assumed greater functional responsibility over tribal matters, ultimately the Secretary of the Interior must still approve decisions over trust land matters.

The stipulation of treaties as the sole method of separating Indian lands was made explicit in legislation enacted in the late 1700s. The Act of May 19, 1796 stated that no lease or other conveyance of lands from Indian nations or tribes were valid unless made "by treaty, or convention, entered into pursuant to the constitution" (cited in Cohen, 1988). However, in 1871 Congress unilaterally terminated U.S. treaty-making with Indian tribes, thus formally ending any legal method for granting or leasing Indian lands. Following this, a series of laws were passed authorizing leasing of lands of tribes, such as the Seneca, Blackfeet, Shoshone, Osage, Pueblos and Five Civilized Tribes, but leasing authority was limited to those tribes specified in the acts themselves. The first general legislation establishing authority for overall leasing of tribal lands was passed in 1891. Under this statute, tribal lands could be leased for mining and/or grazing for a period of up to ten years, "by authority of the council speaking for such Indians . . . and upon such terms and conditions as the agent in charge of such reservation may recommend and subject to the approval of the Secretary of the Interior" (Cohen, 1988: 327).

During the next 30 years several laws were passed to deal with various other issues associated with leasing tribal lands, including allotted lands, lands that had been reserved for school or agency purposes, and reservations that had been established by executive order. This period saw the development and enactment of laws that effectively established a set of European American values, codes, and procedures to govern Indian lands. By instituting such legislation, the U.S. Congress instituted a European derived worldview as the legitimate framework for understanding and governing human relationships toward Indian lands.

Two problems arise out of this early legislation. First is the disposition of Indian tribes in the decision-making process of both the legislation, and the administration of leases. Judicial review was reaffirming Indian tribes as nations, albeit with a dependent status. Preferring to rely on Supreme Court Chief Justice John Marshall's description of Indian-U.S. relations as that of "a ward to its guardian," the federal government's Indian lands leasing policy precluded Indian tribal participation. Cohen notes that this series of legislation, "as was characteristic of acts relating to tribal property enacted at that time, made no provision for Indian consent to such leases" (Cohen, 1988: 327). Secondly, the prevailing European American worldview of the value of land exclusively as an economic resource, inanimate, and an object to be owned was instated over Indian people and lands. The result was that policies governing the disposition of tI Indian lands were developed based on a European framework, as if it alone conceived of the truth about land and the natural world. American Indian truths were discarded as primitive, immoral, and wrong.

U.S. concerns of this early period primarily focused, not on any reconciliation of American Indian worldviews, but upon narrow legal distinctions between public lands and Indian lands and on the efficacy of legislation to "to give Indians the greatest return for their property" (Charles West, Acting Secretary of the Interior, 1937, cited in Cohen, 1988: 328). There was confusion about whether Indian lands could be managed in the same fashion as any other public lands, or whether Indian lands were legally distinct from public lands and therefore required a different management process. In a letter to Congress in 1937, the Acting Secretary of the Interior cited instances in which leasing procedures for public lands that gave lessees greater latitude in mining and exploration could not be similarly applied to Indian lands. The Act of May 11, 1938 was intended to resolve this situation and to reconcile mining legislation with the Indian Reorganization Act of 1934, which according to West, provided Indian tribes with the power to prevent leasing of tribal land. The 1938 Act was a comprehensive piece of legislation that supplanted the numerous piecemeal laws that had been passed since 1891.

According to the Act, the BIA was authorized to lease reservation land and mineral rights to private companies, through a bidding process approved by tribal resolution. Again ultimate approval of leasing rested with the Secretary of the Interior. Getches, Wilkinson, and Williamson, Jr. note that while, in principle, the 1938 Act gave tribes control over mineral leases, "in fact, they were often relegated to granting or withholding consent and playing a passive role as recipients of royalties under a lease negotiated between the Bureau of Indian Affairs and the mineral developers" (1993: 638). It was this act that governed the leasing of Indian lands for exploration and mining of uranium.

To this day, it is difficult to measure the numbers of exploration and mining permits that occurred on Indian lands during this period. It is also difficult to determine the exact amount of uranium extracted from Indian lands over the course of the years. While the majority of uranium mining occurred on Navajo lands, other reservations such as Pine Ridge in South Dakota, were also affected, in addition to several pueblos in New Mexico and reservations in Washington and Wisconsin. By 1970, over 1,185,000 acres of Indian land had been under lease for uranium exploration and development (Garrity, 1980). As noted by Byrne and Hoffman (this volume), the consequences to Indian lands and to Indian people of uranium mining and milling enterprises has been sub-

stantial. Mining and milling companies operated with virtually no regulation or oversight, and tribes are still in the process of attempting to
locate the abandoned mine shafts and waste sites for cleanup.

Indian lands were critical to the development of both military and civilian nuclear power. The nuclear enterprise required access to uranium,
and Indian lands were the geological sites of large uranium ore deposits.
After World War II, the Atomic Energy Act of 1946 established the Atomic
Energy Commission as the governing body for the nuclear program. The
subject of much national debate and several revisions, the Act finally put
in place a "peacetime" administrative structure for the atomic industry.
The legislation granted the AEC sole ownership and control over the production and use of fissionable materials; authorized it to sponsor basic
and applied research as well as the development of militarily necessary
nuclear projects; and vested it with responsibility for the promotion and
commercialization of nuclear-generated electrical power. In short, with
establishment of the AEC the government had designated the research
and commercialization of atomic energy a state monopoly.

Congress recognized that with regard to the nuclear program a
new structure of government would be essential. Thus, the Atomic
Energy Act also established an innovative legislative device to specifically deal with nuclear development. The Joint Committee on
Atomic Energy (JCAE) was created and given "full jurisdiction" over
all matters relating to the AEC and to the nuclear program. Only
select Congressional members of the JCAE, on behalf of Congress,
were privy to the details of AEC policy; and even they had access to
only partial information. National security became the paramount
issue in the organization of the postwar nuclear program. Revision
of the Atomic Energy Act occurred in 1954, and provided for private ownership of nuclear reactors and the licensing of nuclear materials. The intent of these provisions was to strengthen the role of
corporate industry in the nuclear program. The effort was extremely successful and by 1963 AEC contracts and subcontracts for materials, supplies and equipment totaled approximately $3.4 billion. The national
nuclear program became a large-scale governmental sponsored enterprise for both military and civilian purposes and Indian lands, the geological sites for large reserves of uranium ores, were critical to the viability of the program.

On the one hand the federal government, under the AEC, was responsible for maintaining a military nuclear capacity as well as the develop-

ment of civilian nuclear generation for electricity. On the other hand, the federal government, under the BIA and the Department of Interior, was responsible for protecting Indian lands as part of its trust responsibility. Given the extensive exploration, mining and processing that occurred on Indian lands, and the degradation to Indian lands and life that occurred as a result of the nation's nuclear program, it is clear that "national security" won out over the "best interest of the tribe." Fifty years later, as tribes struggle to address the consequences of uranium mining, they were revisited by a new nuclear problem—high-level radioactive waste storage.

In 1982 Congress passed the Nuclear Waste Policy Act. This act required the Department of Energy to begin taking spent fuel from civilian nuclear utilities by January 1998, and also directed the Department of Energy to address the problem of a permanent repository. Almost immediately, electric utilities and DOE entered into agreements which stipulated that DOE would take responsibility for the spent fuel and utilities would pay 1/10 of a cent per kilowatt hour of nuclear generated electricity into a federal fund in payment for the development and implementation of the repository. In 1986, DOE submitted a proposal for a Monitored Retrieval Storage (MRS) system to be located at a federally owned facility near Oak Ridge, Tennessee. It was suggested that this site minimized the transportation distance for spent fuel, since most reactors were located in the eastern U.S. According to the Congressional Research Service, the "total amount of spent fuel stored at the site, in sealed concrete casks, was to be limited to 15,000 metric tons, or about 20% of the amount planned for the permanent repository" (2000).

Strong public opposition eventually resulted in the cancellation of this proposal. In 1987, amendments to the 1982 Act directed DOE to concentrate on Yucca Mountain, Nevada as the permanent repository for the nation's high level waste from civilian electricity generation. In light of the fact that a permanent repository would not be available by 1998, the legislation also established the Office of the Nuclear Waste Negotiator for the purpose of seeking interim storage sites until Yucca Mountain was operational. Under the Act, "DOE was authorized to site, construct, and operate an MRS facility, but not until substantial progress was achieved on the permanent underground repository" (Congressional Research Service, 2000). In addition, the amendments revoked the selection of the Tennessee site and put a ceiling of no more than 10,000 to 15,000 metric tons of spent fuel allowed in any MRS facility.

The position of Waste Negotiator was filled by David Leroy, a former Lieutenant Governor and Attorney General of Idaho. Although the office was directed to seek voluntary agreements with states and/or Indian tribes for resolving the interim problem, Leroy's primary focus was to immediately recruit Indian tribes. Among the inducements that Leroy was authorized to offer were "guarantees of local oversight, highway and airport improvements, higher education programs, economic development activities, health care programs, direct federal payments, and the siting of desirable federal facilities" (Congressional Research Service, 2000).

Among Leroy's first actions was to address the National Congress of American Indian Tribes and encourage native leaders to draw from their "Native American culture and perspective" and "timeless wisdom" and take on the responsibility of acting as stewards of the nations high level radioactive waste (Hanson, 1995). Leroy quoted Chief Seattle's statement that "every part of this soil is sacred," and suggested that "no matter where the waste ended up it would still be on sacred ground" (Hanson, 1995). Leroy's perverse logic implied that because of American Indian's unique understanding and knowledge about the natural world, they should, on behalf of the rest of society, be the guardians for the most deadly and destructive material in existence today.

Expectably, by 1992, twenty grants of $100,000 had been authorized to 20 tribes for investigation as possible sites. Not a single state government had applied for such grants. Nine tribes applied for the $200,000 grants authorized for the second phase of the process. Three tribes, including the Mescalero Apache tribe in New Mexico, were to be awarded Phase IIb grants of up to $2.8 million, when Congress stopped authorization of the grants because of strong opposition by New Mexico congressional delegates. Ultimately, the federal problem of securing a tribal host for high-level nuclear waste rested on the concern about the political popularity of overriding state and congressional opposition to such agreements, not on any concern for Indian tribal people and lands. The authority for the Waste Negotiator was terminated in 1995, but by that time the office had achieved its goal. As the federal government retrenched from active involvement in the development of an interim storage facility, a consortium of utilities was formed to essentially accomplish the same task through a private contract with Indian tribes. The consortium includes such utilities as Northern States Power (now Xcel), Genoa FuelTech, American Electric Power, Southern California Edison, Southern Nuclear Company, GPU Nuclear, Consolidated Edison, and Florida Power and Light. Under the new project name of Private Fuel Storage (PFS), these utilities have whittled down the tribal contenders to one—the approximately 87-member Goshute Tribe in Skull Valley, Utah. The proposal before the Nuclear Regulatory Commission is to lease 820 of the 18,000 acre reservation for a PFS. The facility will be able to store up to 4,000 above-ground storage casks, with each cask having the capacity to contain 10 metric tons of spent fuel, an amount four times (40,000 tons) larger than first proposed in the federal MRS facility in Tennessee.

American Indians, Environmental Justice and the Future

According to Chambers and Price, the Secretary of the Interior adopts a view of Indian trust land "as a resource to be used singularly for the production of income in the form of lease revenues" (in Getches et al, 1993: 630). This purely economic understanding of land and its value to the circle of life is a distinctly European view and violates traditional American Indian principles. Ultimately, federal decisions that approved uranium and other mining on Indian lands, and then authorized efforts to secure tribal sites for nuclear waste storage, violate the most basic of Indian values. Chambers and Price elaborate (italics added, cited in Getches et al, 1993: 628):

> If reservation land is simply a source for income production, then it should be devoted to its "highest and best use" in order to maximize lease revenues. That is a conventional goal of trust management. If, on the other hand, reservation land has multiple purposes and should be utilized as a part of an overall resource development plan that has as its goal the economic and cultural viability of an Indian tribe, there would be trade-offs of various kinds which should be considered by the Secretary in exercising his approval power: between income and jobs, income and services, income and economic growth, income and *conservation of an Indian culture on the land*.

Environmental justice cannot and should not be divorced from a more comprehensive analysis of justice that addresses the ethical foundations of the relations of one society with another. The BIA, a creature of the U.S. government, perceives things in the best interests of Indians in a far different manner than Indians do for themselves. When adopting a native frame of reference, everything changes. If native cultures had demanded of European immigrants allegiance to the native worldview, a wholly different set of relations with Indian lands would have occurred. But, what if this had been the case? What if U.S. negotiators were required to adopt the native form of decision-making? They would have had to return, gather their leaders, and consensually reach a decision, contingent upon approval of women leaders. What if fur traders, railroad and timber companies, were required to communicate with the earth and the trees before they proceeded to extract their bounty? They would have had to learn how to communicate with the trees, the soil and the animals. What if the U.S. government was obligated to honor the sacredness of the land, above any concept of national interest? Quite possibly the contaminated places we have today would be places where the honor and dignity of life would be honored and celebrated.

To some, requiring these actions might sound like ignorance or quaint primitivism, but this would be valid only if there is a presumption of superior knowledge or if truth is contingent upon cultural coercion. Paradoxically, native tribes did tend to view such requirements on European immigrants as foolish, not because of any reservations about their own beliefs, but because of American Indian norms of noninterference. Just as the traditional native worldview accepted and revered the rights of other life forms, there was also an underlying respect for the rights of other cultures to believe and act for themselves. Goodtracks notes that "if the Indian told the Anglo that he was being intrusive, the Indian would himself be interfering with the Anglo's freedom to act as he sees fit" (1973: 497).

Over the years a tendency developed to romanticize about Indian people among non-Indians critical of unchecked economic and technological growth. In some ways, growth of the environmental movement and an environmental ethic has influenced this perspective. Some research has focused on the traditional practices of American Indian tribes as an alternative for the mainstream economistic framework of nature-society relations. Traditional Indian cultures have even been cited by some as the "first ecologists" or as the first "stewards of the land." Such references, while more tolerant of American Indian cultures and values, are still rooted in a European framework. Stewardship implies that humans have empowered themselves with an authority to oversee, to protect, and have guardianship over the natural world. Yet, this conception is alien to the native cultures. In the American Indian worldview the concept of justice includes all life, and recognizes that human beings are but a minor actor in the web of creation. Whether humans demonstrate wisdom and reverence to the natural world is a matter of choice, but ultimately all life, even human life, cannot escape accountability.

American Indians may well serve as the miner's canary, but in the end the effects will be borne by all of society. Chief Seattle is quoted as saying (cited in Armstrong, 1971: 92):

> But why should I mourn at the untimely fate of my people? Tribe follows tribe, and nation follows nation, like the waves of the sea. Your time of decay may be distant, but it will surely come, for even the White Man whose God walked with him and talked with him as friend with friend, cannot be exempt from the common destiny. We may be brothers after all, we will see . . .

Chief Seattle's admonition is as poignant for us today as it was for his contemporaries. In reflecting upon the condition of Mother Earth, it is clear that life's elements are, indeed interdependent. Global warming, acid rain, toxic waste, changing climatic conditions and other environmental threats continue to signal the risks of our current development path. From a native perspective, the experiences of American Indians and nature are related. They are both interconnected consequences of the continuation of the ethnocentric philosophy of Manifest Destiny. Chief Seattle, in a manner characteristic of native non-interference, is warning of the consequences of treating the circle of life with disrespect. He advises that the American Indian experience is an early warning of what is to come for all peoples. No one can escape this destiny.

Notes

1. The authors would like to acknowledge Dawn Scharnberg and Adam Nyan for their extensive research and editorial assistance for this chapter.
2. This number refers to federally recognized Indian nations. Due to policies implemented unilaterally by the United States government, many tribes were stripped of their federally recognized status. Most of these tribes continue to demand federal recognition.

References

American Indian Policy Review Commission. 1977. *Final Report*. Washington, D.C.: GPO.

American Indian Research and Policy Institute. 1998. *Reflections on Traditional American Indian Ways*. St. Paul, MN: American Indian Research and Policy Institute.

Begay, Eugene. December, 2000. *Personal Interview*. Saint Paul, MN.

_____. 1998. "Traditional American Indian Leadership," In *American Indian Leadership: Traditional to Contemporary*. 1998 Annual Forum Proceedings. St. Paul, MN: American Indian Research and Policy Institute. pp. 2-4.

Churchill, Ward and Winona LaDuke. 1992. "Native North America: The Political Economy of Radioactive Colonialism." In M. Annette Jaimes (ed). *The State of Native America: Genocide, Colonization, and Resistance*. Boston, MA: South End Press.

Cohen, Felix. 1988. *Handbook of Federal Indian Law*. Buffalo, NY: William S. Hein Co.

_____. 1953. "The Erosion of Indian Rights, 1950-1953." 62 *Yale Law Journal* 348, 390. (p. 30). In David Getches, Charles F. Wilkinson, and Robert A Williams, Jr. (1993). *Federal Indian Law. Cases and Materials.* Third Edition. St. Paul: West Publishing Co.

Committee for the National Institute for the Environment. 2000. *Civilian Nuclear Spent Fuel Temporary Storage Options: Need for Additional Storage Capacity.* Congressional Research Service Report for Congress 96-212 ENR. In Committee for the National Institute for the Environment [online]. Washington, DC, 2000 [cited 4 February 2001]. Available online at: *<http://www.cnie.org/nle/waste-20c.html#Appendix:%20History%20 of%20U.S.% 20Nuclear%20Waste%20Policy*

Deloria, Jr. Vine. 1997. *Red Earth, White Lies. Native Americans and the Myth of Scientific Fact.* Golden, CO: Fulcrum Publishing.

_____. 1994. *God is Red.* Golden, CO: Fulcrum Publishing.

Eastman, Charles. 1980. *The Soul of the Indian: An Interpretation by Charles Alexander Eastman (Ohiyesa).* Lincoln, NE: University of Nebraska Press.

Firethunder, Cecilia. 1998. "Heroic Leadership." In 1998 Annual Forum Proceedings. *American Indian Leadership: Traditional to Contemporary.* St. Paul, MN: American Indian Research and Policy Institute.

Garrity, Michael. 1980. "The U.S. Colonial Empire is as Close as the Nearest Reservation: the Pending Energy Wars." In Holly Sklar (ed). *Trilateralism: the Trilateral Commission and Elite Planning for World Management.* Boston, MA: South End Press.

Getches, David, Charles F. Wilkinson, and Robert A. Williams, Jr. 1993. *Federal Indian Law. Cases and Materials. Third Edition.* St. Paul: West Publishing Co.

Good Tracks, Jimm, G. 1973. "Native American Noninterference." In Francis J. Turner (ed). *Differential Diagnosis and Treatment in Social Work.* New York, NY: The Free Press. pp. 496-502.

Hanson, Randel. 1995. "Indian Burial Grounds for Nuclear Waste." Reproduced from *Multinational Monitor, Voume XVI, No. 9, September 1995.* [cited 4 February 2001]. Available online at: *<ftp://ftp.halcyon.com/ pub/FWDP/ Americas/nukewast.txt>*

Hewlett, Richard G. and Oscar E. Anderson, Jr. 1991. *The New World: A History of the United States Atomic Energy Commission, 1939-1946, Volume 1.* [Orig. 1962] Berkeley, CA: University of California Press.

Iverson, Peter. 1998. *We Are Still Here.* American Indians in the Twentieth Century. Wheeling, IL: Harlan Davidson, Inc.

Lac du Flambeau tribal member. December 2000. Personal Interview. Saint Paul, MN.

LaDuke, Winona. 1979. "The History of Uranium Mining." *Black Hills/Paha Sapa Report,* Volume 1, Number 1.

Johnston, Basil. 1982. *Ojibway Ceremonies.* Lincoln, NE: University of Nebraska Press.

Martinez, Cecilia and John Byrne. 1996. "Science, Society and the State: The Nuclear Project and the Transformation of the American Political Economy." In John Byrne and Steven M. Hoffman (eds.). *Governing the Atom: The Politics of Risk.* New Brunswick, NJ and London: Transaction Publishers. pp. 67-102.

Neihardt, John G. 1979. *Black Elk Speaks: Being the Life Story of a Holy Man of the Ogalala Sioux.* Lincoln, NE: University of Nebraska Press.

Pevar, Stephen. 1992. *The Rights of Indians and Tribes: An American Civil Liberties Handbook.* 2nd Edition. Carbondale, Illinois: Southern Illinois Press.

Prucha, Francis Paul (ed). 1990. *Documents of United States Indian Policy. Second Edition, Expanded.* Lincoln, NE: University of Nebraska Press.

Rhodes, Richard. 1995. *The Making of the Atomic Bomb.* New York, NY: Touchstone Books.

Task Force Seven: Reservation and Resource Development and Protection. 1976. *Final Report to the American Indian Policy Review Commission.* Washington, D.C.: Government Printing Office.

United States, Department of Energy. 1979. *Statistical Data of the Uranium Industry.* GJO-100 (79). Grand Junction, CO.

United States Federal Trade Commission, Bureau of Competition. 1975. *Report to the Federal Trade Commission on Mineral Leasing on Indian Lands.* Washington, D.C.: Government Printing Office.

Utter, Jack. 1993. *American Indians: Answers to Today's Questions.* Lake Ann, MI: National Woodlands Publishing Company.

7

Powering Injustice: Hydroelectric Development in Northern Manitoba

Steven M. Hoffman[1]

Introduction: Hydropower's Green Myth

In a world in search of "green" energy, hydropower is often proposed as an environmentally positive option. According to the industry's supporters, dams do not produce emissions that might exacerbate the greenhouse problem, acid rain or urban smog—ineluctable consequences of using fossil fuels. Nor do they generate volumes of waste that create a range of harms for future generations. And, unlike natural gas, the future of hydropower is secure. According to the National Hydropower Association, the trade association representing U.S. hydropower interests (www.hydro.org):

> Hydropower is an emissions-free, renewable and reliable energy source that serves our national environmental and energy policy objectives. With zero air-emissions, hydropower helps in the fight for cleaner air. Hydropower's fuel—water—is essentially infinite and is not depleted in the production of energy. This helps to preserve our nation's independence from supply disruptions overseas. And, as a source of energy, hydropower excels at preserving the stability and reliability of the electrical grid due to its unique operating characteristics.

Like all things promoted as virtually risk free, however, the reality of hydro turns out to be more complicated than promised. A survey of the world's proposed and operational dams reveals a litany of environmental and social ills on scales that are comparable to those of thermal and nuclear generation of electricity (International Rivers Network at *www.irn.org*):

- In Africa, the government of Namibia is currently planning a huge hydroelectric scheme on the Kunene, which is one of just five peren-

147

nial rivers in Namibia. The dam's reservoir would evaporate twice as much water as the entire country uses each year—a major issue in a country that continually suffers from drought and water shortages.

- Namibia, along with Angola, is also proposing to dam the Okavango River, which rises in the Angolan highlands, and flows over 1000 miles, passing through Namibia before entering Botswana and forming the Okavango Delta, a 9,000-square-mile rich and varied habitat for thousands of mammals, birds, fish and other animals. A Namibian government proposal to extract water from Okavango River to supply the rapidly growing population in Windhoek also threatens the future of the Delta. In addition, the Angolan government has proposed more than ten dams and other developments for the headwaters of the Okavango. If completed, the dams would flood over 70 square kilometers of the river valley, inundating the river and destroying the richly diverse forest and its wildlife.

- In Latin America, the Biobío River is threatened by a number of hydroelectric projects. The river springs from the Icalma and Galletue lakes in the Andes, flows through steep and narrow gorges and forests of araucaria pine, passes through agricultural lands and cities, until it reaches the Pacific Ocean, 380 kilometers from its source. The river's watershed has a surface area of 24,260 square kilometers and is 380 kilometers long. Over one million people use the resources of the Biobío for drinking and irrigation water, recreation, and fisheries. ENDESA, the largest private company in Chile, plans to construct six hydroelectric dams on the Biobío. The first of these, Pangue, was completed in 1996 while construction of the second has been temporarily halted due to a variety of indigenous land claims.

- In South America, the Porto Primavera Dam, begun in 1979, will flood 2,250 sq. km (869 square miles), creating the third largest reservoir in Brazil. The dam will force the last members of the Ofaiê Xavante Indian tribe to abandon their lands and homes. Thousands of other fishermen, ceramic workers and small farmers will lose their livelihood as a result of the dam. The reservoir will drown the ecologically valuable varjão, or wetlands, of the Paraná River, which provide habitat to a rich diversity of species including the endangered marsh deer, maned wolf, giant anteater, broad-snouted caiman, giant river otter, and black and spotted jaguars. Three protected areas will be inundated, without the legislative authorization required under the Brazilian constitution. Porto Primavera is acknowledged to be an economic boondoggle. Originally budgeted at $2.2 billion, it is now estimated that the final cost of the 1,800 megawatt dam will exceed $9 billion. Around two-thirds of the dam's cost is likely to be borne by Brazilian taxpayers since the cost of energy generated by the dam will be 15 US cents per kilowatt-hour, nearly four times that currently charged to customers.

- In Asia, the Mekong basin has been targeted for large-scale dam building with more than 100 large dams having been proposed for the region over the last ten years. Some of these dams are already under construction and others are in advanced stages of planning. Together, these dams will have widespread impacts on the livelihoods of Mekong communities and on the natural ecology of the river system.

But perhaps the most spectacular example of new dam building is the Three Gorges Dam presently under construction in China. Located in Sandouping, Hubei Province, China, the dam will measure some 2,000 meters in length, have a total storage capacity of 39.3 billion cubic meters of water, and generate some 17,680 megawatts (MW) of electricity. When completed at an estimated cost of $27 billion, the project will inundate a stretch of land 632 kilometers long. Nineteen cities and 326 towns will be flooded, forcing the relocation of at least 2 million people. The project faces increasingly sharp criticism for its enormous and largely unaccounted social costs, a cavalier attitude toward construction risks, and operational issues related to sedimentation buildup and reduced water flows (Adams and Reinner, 1999; Sklar and Sklar, 1997; and Sullivan, 1999). According to one critic, the "project represents an energy dinosaur" especially given present trends away from large-scale power (see comments by John Byrne, 1999, www.cnn.com/SPECIALS/1999/china.50/asian.superpower/three.gorges/).

It is not surprising that most of the world's newest or proposed mega-hydro projects are located in the third world since the bulk of hydrological resources in North America and Europe were fully exploited by the end of the 20th century (Reisner, 1986; Wooster, 1985). Today's projects are, however, linked to those of the past by a consistent "ideology of progress" that transcends any specific cultural context. As argued by Byrne and Hoffman (1996), development guided by this way of thinking is based upon the premise that the environmental and social harms which generally accompany large, technically complex projects are considered acceptable, indeed even necessary, to a modern way of life.

One example of the logic and power of this ideology, and the manner it which it allows for the rationalization of damage to both ecology and society, is the hydroelectric project engineered and constructed by Manitoba Hydro, starting in the 1960s. Unlike other mega-hydro projects around the globe such as the Three Gorges Dam or Hydro Quebec's Great Whale project (see Niezen, 1993), the re-engineering of one of North America's major hydrological systems by Manitoba Hydro has received little international scrutiny. The conditions faced by Aboriginal communities located within the geographic scope of the projects have also largely been ignored by the residents of Manitoba, North American electricity consumers, and, to a great extent, the world's human rights community. Yet, the pattern of ecological destruction and the dislocation of Aboriginal peoples in northern Canada caused by the Manitoba Hydro project make it an important case of environmental injustice deserving of greater attention.

Canada's Hydro Economy

Canada is uniquely dependent upon its hydroelectric resources. As shown in Table 1, while many countries display greater reliance upon hydro as a percent of total domestic capacity, Canada stands alone among those countries with a generating capacity greater than 100 gigawatts (GW). For instance, Norway, Austria, and New Zealand all have a greater percentage share of domestic hydro capacity (99, 66, and 62%, respectively), but their combined total hydro capacity of 44 GW is dwarfed by Canada's 117 GW. Indeed, only the United States' 839 GW and Japan's 239 GW exceed Canada's hydro capacity (International Energy Agency, 2000).

Table 1
Total Generating and Hydroelectricity Capacities, Selected Nations and Regions

Country	Total (GW)	Hydro Capacity (GW)	Hydro Capacity (%)
United States	839	100	12
Japan	239	45	19
Canada	117	66	56
France	115	25	22
Italy	75	21	28
Norway	28	27	99
Austria	18	12	66
New Zealand	8	5	62
North America	956	166	17
Pacific	289	58	20

Source: International Energy Agency. 2000. Statistical Abstract, Annex 1.

Table 2 further demonstrates the importance of hydropower to Canada's electrical economy. While both Japan and the United States consume greater volumes of electricity (1003 and 3652 terrawatthours (TWh), respectively) neither demonstrate comparable degrees of "hydro-dependency." In fact, Canada's use of hydro as a share of fuel used in electric generation is almost 3.5 times larger than that of the average IEA country (International Energy Agency, 2000).

The use of hydropower is even greater in some of the nation's provinces. For instance, of Quebec's nearly 37 GW of total capacity, 94% is hydroelectric (www.hydroquebec.com). BC Hydro, while somewhat more diversified, nonetheless generated some 80% of its 1999 total of 46 TWh from its hydroelectric system (www.BCHydro.com).

Canada's dependence upon hydroelectricity has resulted in a particular kind of energy economy, one that depends upon the acquisition and control of vast amounts of land and the reengineering of entire hydrological ecosystems. The history of Manitoba Hydro and the projects it has undertaken in the last quarter century is a powerful illustration of this developmental logic.

Table 2
Share of Fuel in Electricity Generation

Country	Total Output (TWh)	Share in Hydro (%)
United States	3,652	10
Japan	1,003	8
Canada	571	62
France	508	13
Italy	239	17
Norway	104	99
IEA Total	8,119	16
North America	4,223	17
IEA Europe	2,680	17
Pacific	1,216	10

Source: International Energy Agency. 2000. Statistical Abstract, Annex 1.

Manitoba: The Hydro Province

Manitoba Hydro is a Crown corporation, owned by the Province of Manitoba. The utility serves the entire province except for the inner portion of the City of Winnipeg, which is served by the city-owned Winnipeg Hydro. The two utilities are interconnected, operating as a single integrated system, with Manitoba Hydro responsible for providing the vast majority of the province's power requirements. The utility is also responsible for determining the province's future electricity requirements and for designing, constructing, maintaining, and operating all the facilities needed to meet those requirements.

Manitoba Hydro's history is consistent with many of Canada's state-owned utilities: a continual guarantee of cheap power for its provincial customers based upon the development of ever-larger and more powerful generation technologies; a historical series of consolidations, mergers, and acquisitions designed to assure provincial monopolization of the electric supply system; long-term efforts to encourage the consumption of electric energy; the integration of the supply system into larger regional ones; and, consistent with its other hydro-dependent neighbors, an aggressive use of Manitoba's hydrological resources, culminating with the Churchill River Diversion (CRD) and Lake Winnipeg Regulation (LWR) projects of the 1960s and 1970s.

Electric power was first brought to Manitoba on March 12, 1879 when an electric light was used by the "Honourable Robert A. Davis, proprietor of Davis House . . . to illuminate the front of his building" (Manitoba Hydro, no date: 2). Seven years later, the province's first electric light company, the Manitoba Electric and Gas Light Company, was formed through an Act of the Manitoba legislature, which granted MH wide powers to "supply light and heat in Manitoba by gas, electricity or other means" (Manitoba Hydro, no date: 2). For the best part of the next thirty years, a variety of companies served the province and, most importantly, the city of Winnipeg, ultimately resulting in the formation of the Winnipeg Electric Railway Company (WERCo).

To counter the privately held monopoly power of WERCo, the City of Winnipeg Hydroelectric System was formed in 1906. The tension between public and private power was ultimately resolved in 1961 when Manitoba Hydro (MH) was formed through the consolidation of the Manitoba Hydro Electric Board and the Manitoba Power Commission (MPC).

The "march northward," i.e., the continuous expansion of MH to more remote parts of the province, was, by the middle of the century, accompanied by a parallel effort to expand it's operations east- and westward across Canada and southward to the United States. The first export of power to the United States from Manitoba occurred in 1936 when the Dominion Government issued a license to export a limited amount of power to Interstate Power Company, which served parts of North Dakota and Minnesota. The connection to the south was more firmly established in 1964, when Manitoba Hydro and the Mid-Continent Area Power Planners (MAPP) of the U.S. signed a memorandum of understanding for possible interconnection of transmission lines to carry out large-scale exchanges of power to and from U.S. utilities (Manitoba Hydro, no date: 17, 34).

The potential for large-scale power exchanges was realized less than a decade later, when Canada's National Energy Board gave MH a permit to build a 232-kilometer, 230 kV transmission line from Winnipeg to Grand Forks, North Dakota. The line allowed Northern States Power Company of Minnesota and several smaller Minnesota-based companies and cooperatives to exchange power with MH during respective peak seasons and periods of maximum power production (Manitoba Hydro, no date: 34). The company currently sends more than 40% of its total power output to the United States at some of the lowest rates available to any U.S. utility.

The ability to serve its' domestic and international loads hinged upon the exploitation of Manitoba's hydrological resources. While initially modest in terms of size and capacity, as the century progressed the idea of modernization was explicitly linked to projects that became successively larger in scale and geographic scope.

The exploitation of the region's hydrological resources began in 1900 with the construction of the Minnedosa River Plant. This was followed by the Pinawa Generating Station on the Winnipeg River in 1906 which was the first plant in the region to operate on an annual basis. Following the pattern of power plant construction typical of the era, other stations followed in rapid order, all being larger and operating with relatively higher dam heads. Ultimately, however, the Winnipeg River was inadequate to meet the region's growing electricity demands and MH began to look north to the Nelson and Churchill Rivers.

By any measure, the Nelson and Churchill River drainage area is a massive hydrological and ecological system. Together, the basins cover over one million miles, from the Rockies in the west to the Mississippi and the Lake Superior drainage basins in the south and east and throughout the bulk of the Canadian provinces of Alberta, Saskatchewan, Manitoba and Ontario (Manitoba Hydro, *The Hydro Province, Fact Sheet*). While a tentative step in placing hydroelectric resources on the Nelson River had been taken in 1960 with the construction of the Kelsey Generating Station, a systematic inquiry into the full hydroelectric potential of this watershed had to wait until 1963, when the province of Manitoba entered into a cost-sharing agreement with the Government of Canada to investigate the feasibility of large-scale hydroelectric development on the Nelson. Also in 1963, MH commissioned a study to investigate the economic feasibility of developing hydroelectric generating stations on the lower Nelson River which emptied directly into Hudson Bay (Manitoba Hydro, no date: 31-34).

The 1960s, therefore, marked a new era in MH's history, one that was to see the re-engineering of entire hydrological systems and even the redesign of the human communities located within the geographic scope of this development. Though potentially daunting, these plans were understood as a prerequisite for "provincial continental modernization." According to Alex Netherton (1993), this policy was based upon a mix of old and new assumptions, including long-held beliefs that power must be cheap and that the province's hydro policy must be based upon the most efficient use of financial resources. Added to these traditional assumptions were at least two new and critically important beliefs: first, that electricity generated in the far north would have to find extra-provincial markets in order for the projects to be economically viable; and second, that MH possessed the only legitimate claim to northern land and water resources. Institutional changes were also needed, including the creation of a large, integrated provincial utility not bound by previous interutility agreements and the establishment of mechanisms to remove Aboriginal communities from lands and resources used for hydro (Netherton, 1993: 294-5).

The Churchill River Diversion and the Lake Winnipeg Regulation projects (CRD/LWR) are extraordinary efforts at ecological re-engineering. In essence, the CRD project reversed the directional flow of the Churchill River to increase the volume of water moving through the Nelson River, while the LWR project manipulated seasonal discharges from Lake Winnipeg into the Nelson.

The first phase of the project required diverting the Churchill's flow into the Nelson River. According to Larry Krotz (1991: 38):

By 1976, the engineers had achieved their dream. A control dam at Missi Falls 400 kilometers from the mouth of the Churchill River, cut the flow from an average of 1,050 cubic meters per second to an average of 150, and turned all that water back through 180-kilometer long Southern Indian Lake, then through a man-made channel and several smaller rivers into the Nelson.

Simultaneously with the CRD, MH began constructing the first of a series of dams located on the Nelson River. In addition to the Kettle Generating Station, which was brought on line in 1974, MH built three other facilities on the river, representing almost 3,600 MW of generating capacity.

The second part of the project involved the regulation of Lake Winnipeg, primarily to coordinate the outflow of the lake with seasonal electric demand. Unfortunately for MH, the natural water flows out of the lake are lowest in the winter, when the demands for export power are the highest. In order to optimize hydroelectric production, MH needed to control the Lake's natural water flows, a feat accomplished with the construction of the Jenpeg control structure and generating station, located 10 miles from the Aboriginal community of Cross Lake. As described by MH (www.hydro.mb.ca):

> [The] station on the upper arm of the Nelson River is one of the key elements in the successful development of the hydroelectric potential of northern Manitoba. In addition to generating [128 MW of] electricity, Jenpeg's powerhouse and spillway structures are used to control and regulate the outflow waters of Lake Winnipeg, which in turn is used as a reservoir to store water to ensure enough water is available to run the northern generating stations.

A number of channels were also constructed, including the 2-Mile Channel, the 8-Mile Channel, and the Ominawin Channel (Manitoba Hydro, *Information Sheet, Kettle Generating Station).*

The CRD/LWR projects allowed Manitoba Hydro to develop the Nelson River as a "power corridor" and to turn Lake Winnipeg into a gigantic "storage battery." The projects irreversibly altered the hydrological and ecological characteristics of some 50,000 square miles of northern boreal rivers and forest. In achieving these results, MH was able to ignore two key considerations: first, the environmental consequences created by the projects; and second, the interests of and impacts upon the Aboriginal communities located within the geographic scope of the projects, i.e., York Factory, Nelson House, Split Lake, Norway House, and Cross Lake.

Canadian-Aboriginal Relations[2]

MH's actions were hardly surprising given the historical realities of Canadian-Aboriginal relations. As in the United States, these relations have been marked by a historical process of conquest and assimilationist ideology (see Byrne, Hoffman and Martinez, 1992 and the references therein).

The Royal Proclamation of 1763 served to define the initial relations between the indigenous societies of Canada and the new European settlers. The Proclamation addressed the difficult issue of Aboriginal status under the Crown by reserving for Aboriginals virtually complete sovereignty. Designed by the British, the Proclamation established a relationship in which Aboriginal peoples were autonomous nations under the protection of the Crown, allowed to maintain traditional forms of self-government as "assemblies of Indians" who controlled their respective territories independent of British intervention. Under the terms of the Proclamation, Aboriginal peoples were to be recognized legally as second parties in any land transfers (Fleras and Elliot, 1992).

In the 1800's the rough equality established by the Proclamation began to erode as settlers grew in numbers and power. Commercial relations that sustained the attitudes upholding the Proclamation faded as the fur economy declined due to the cumulative effect of over-hunting. The erosion of commercial arrangements was accompanied by the erosion of political relations and the displacement of the cooperative nature of the white-Aboriginal relationship at the core of the 1763 Proclamation (Fleras and Elliot, 1992).

With the rise of the Canadian confederation, Aboriginal interests soon conflicted with the new nation and the framework of the Proclamation could no longer be sustained. On the eve of the 1867 unification of Nova Scotia, New Brunswick, Quebec and inland Ontario, Canadian Prime Minister John A. Macdonald began an intense campaign of colonialist expansion based upon the British North American Act which designated all Aboriginal lands as subject to government regulation and under control of the Dominion (Royal Commission on Aboriginal Peoples, 1999).

McDonald first exercised the state's new authority when he laid claim to one of Canada's largest territories, colloquially known as Rupurt's Land. This sale included the vast region surrounding Hudson Bay, which encompassed areas in present-day Ontario, Manitoba, central Saskatchewan and portions of the North West Territories. The Rupurt's Land claim was viewed as a transaction between the Crown and the Hudson Bay Company, entirely excluding the Aboriginal peoples who lived there. No Aboriginal assembly was notified of the deal or included in the land transfer negotiations.

Canada next created two more provinces, Manitoba in central Canada and British Columbia on the west coast of the country. These new provinces coincided with the development of an Aboriginal policy that acted as the national mechanism for increased land acquisition and further Aboriginal submission, namely the Indian Act of 1876 and the Amendments of 1884. Together, they consolidated previous Aboriginal legislation in hopes of solving the 'Indian problem' through forced assimilation and the nullification of previously honored arrangements of Aboriginal sovereignty and the subsequent dispossession of traditional Aboriginal territories (Flores and Elliot, 1992).

The 1876 Indian Act dealt with three main areas of aboriginal sovereignty, i.e., land, Aboriginal status and local government, while the later amendments created additional measures that outlawed major social, economic and political institutions of indigenous societies. Cultural staples, such as the Potlatch ceremony of the west coast tribes and the Sundance of the prairie tribes became illegal. Traditional tribal order was outlawed with the forced election of band councils that were overseen by the Federal Department of Indian Affairs. Self-determination and Aboriginal governance of traditional lands was greatly restricted by the Department of Indian Affairs, which controlled both land and cultural practices of traditional society.

Land reserves restructured Aboriginal-state relations mandated by the Indian Act through the consolidation of Aboriginal populations. Such consolidation simplified the administration of services in locations where Aboriginal peoples could be supervised by the state. The reserve system led to a systematic deculturation mainly through the use of residential school systems that were intended to, in essence, educate the Indian out of Aboriginal children. Traditional ways were discouraged, as Aboriginals were mainstreamed into Canadian society.

The disintegration of traditional society under these assimilationist pressures also caused the passive absorption of their territories into the administrative state of Canada. By the mid-1900's, after the devolution of virtually all power, Aboriginal peoples found themselves almost totally dependent upon a federal system that served the state's economic interests. Aboriginal governance had been dissolved in fact, if not in statute.

This history has caused some in the white community of Canada to rethink relations with Aboriginal communities. 1982 amendments to the Canadian Constitution, for instance, represent structural accommodations that could restore some Aboriginal sovereignty. Under this schema, a kind of "citizen-plus" status was granted that potentially affords Aboriginal peoples a political identity along the lines that were once guaranteed by the Royal Proclamation of 1763. The amendments also acknowledge the special problems of assimilation and dispossession. The collective expression of identity of Aboriginal peoples as distinct societies is validated and protected as a constitutional right (Fleras and Elliot, 1992).

While Canadian-Aboriginal *relations* have arguably improved in the last 20 years, the *actual conditions* experienced by Aboriginal communities across Canada are still dismal. For instance, the rate of infant mortality is almost twice as high as the Canadian national average; the rate of sudden unexplained death for Aboriginal infants is three times as high as the overall Canadian rate; the rates of infectious diseases such as tuberculosis and hepatitis are up to forty-three times higher than among non-Aboriginals born in Canada; the rate of suicide is at least five to six times higher than that among non-Aboriginal youth and three times higher for all age groups in Canada; and there are significantly higher levels of overcrowding and unemployment among Aboriginal populations relative to Canadian averages (Grand Council of the Crees, 1999: 46-53).

The Royal Commission on Aboriginal Peoples has recently found that "Aboriginal peoples have had great difficulty maintaining their lands and livelihoods in the face of massive encroachment" and that "this encroachment is not ancient history" 1996, Volume 2: 425). Hydroelectric development was perhaps the single most important vehicle for the perpetuation of this history in the last decades of the 20th century.

Hydro Development and Aboriginal Relations

The Canadian federal government, the Provincial government of Manitoba and MH all sought to portray the CRD/LWR projects as technically straightforward and environmentally and socially beneficial. In fact, the "parties faced ill-defined alternatives, the consequences of which were not well-understood" (Netherton, 1993: 380).

From the outset, none of the state parties, i.e., the federal government, the provincial government and MH, considered in any meaningful way the environmental effects that might arise from the projects. According to Lorraine Land, while the "threshold of expectation with respect to environmental assessment (particularly assessment of impacts of industrial development on indigenous communities) has risen since 1977 . . .

the decision not to conduct an environmental review of this project was not even in keeping with the principles for decision-making on mega-projects at the time" (1999: 8). Where environmental consequences were considered, it was oftentimes to deny the potential for harm. For instance, MH insisted that the projects would not damage the native fisheries, going so far as to state that "fishermen would benefit from [the] improved transportation" infrastructure associated with the projects (Neizen, 1999: 2).

By failing to conduct a comprehensive environmental review or undertake baseline studies, MH was also able to successfully ignore the social consequences of altering the land base upon which Aboriginal communities (especially the Cree) depended. Thus, when the Project "was announced the social and spiritual effects it might have were not at all thoroughly considered . . . The social consequences of flooding, community relocation, and displacement from the land were nowhere seriously discussed by those most responsible for them" (Niezen, 1999: 2-3; see also Land, 1999: 8).

With the passage of time, the state parties were forced to acknowledge that the projects were creating both environmental and social damages. According to MH, however, the impacts were fairly modest and largely indirect. At Cross Lake, for instance, the little flooding that was to occur was to be upstream of the Jenpeg structure and was portrayed as having "no impact on any Cross Lake Reserve Lands and only affected a small area within the Cross Lake Resource Area" (MH, Background Paper #3: 7). But subsequent analysis has shown this claim of little or no impact to be incorrect (MH, Background Paper #3: 7):

> [T]he most drastic change was in the seasonality of water level changes and the monthly fluctuations. Traditionally, the Cross Lake water elevations followed a seasonal pattern with highs occurring in late summer (August) and lows in Spring (April) annually. Following LWR, average highs occurred in January and average lows in June. The effect during the open water season was that the total volume of water in Cross Lake decreased by an average of 53%.

Of course, the shifted high flows to January accords well with the need to provide electricity for export in the winter. In this regard, the LWR project starkly exhibits the conflict between environmental and social interest and economic advantage.

Similar impacts have been reported with regard to domestic fisheries, trapping, and recreational activities (see MH, Background Paper #3 generally). Krotz (1991), for instance, argues that the experience at South

Indian Lake, the site for early hydro developments, is an instructive example of what has happened throughout the Nelson River watershed. Prior to construction, MH's engineers estimated that it would take five years for the South Indian Lake shoreline to re-establish itself subsequent to the changes in the water regime and the fluctuations caused by the normal operations of the control structures and the dams. However, these estimates were not based upon any experience in areas dominated by permafrost, a soil type particularly sensitive to changes in water levels and flows. Instead of a fairly rapid period of restabilization, fifteen years after the projects began operations Krotz observes that (Krotz, 1991: 41):

> [T]he only places where the shores of [South Indian Lake] have stabilized are where some solid backshore has been reached. Along most of the lake, however, it has been a continuous cycle of erosion and slumping. Water thaws permafrost, the shoreline slumps; then water extends further, causing yet more erosion.

Studies done by Robert Newbury of Winnipeg's Freshwater Institute indicate that it will take "80 years before a 90-percent recovery of the shoreline is achieved, and complete stability may be 300 years away" (quoted in Krotz, 1991: 42).

Despite disagreements over the extent and severity of the impacts, the parties were successful in establishing a mechanism for dealing with the adverse effects generated by the CRD/LWR. Finalized in 1977, the Northern Flood Agreement (NFA) was entered into by the governments of Canada and Manitoba, Manitoba Hydro and the Northern Flood Committee, a group represented by the chiefs of Nelson House, Norway House, Cross Lake, Split Lake, and York Landing (Wiebe, 1999). The NFA was seen by Manitoba Hydro as a means for negotiating damage claims brought forward by individual landowners and communities in return for exercising the pre-existing right to flood lands legally owned by the Canadian government. MH never assumed that the Aboriginal communities had any right to intervene in a way that would prevent or even delay construction, despite the fact that the projects were being built almost entirely on Aboriginal lands. Any idea that the construction of the dams could be halted was simply not considered. The best that the Northern Flood Committee could hope for was to negotiate a price for the damages and suffering of Aboriginal people who had no choice but to accept that their land would be lost.

Even after the NFA went into effect, however, MH was anxious to avoid admitting any *direct* responsibility for environmental damage and associated social harms caused by the projects. For example, it has argued that while "the Projects would create foreseeable changes . . . such changes would occur against the background of unforeseeable natural events" (Manitoba Hydro, Background Paper #1, 1999: 1-3). Any extraordinary damage cited by the communities could be a consequence of natural disruptions, since "one cannot provide firm forecasts of future events in nature," much less their effect (Manitoba Hydro, Background Paper #1, 1999: 1-3).

MH has also consistently pointed to the poor economic status of the affected communities prior to the projects as a way of avoiding direct responsibility, a position the corporation has never relinquished. For instance, in recent testimony at an Inter-Church inquiry, MH argued that "the five Reserves were experiencing serious problems of poverty and unemployment long before construction of the Project . . . [and to] . . . assess the specific effects of the Project" or "to quantify the costs and damages of the Project on the NFA communities" is extremely problematic (Manitoba Hydro, Background Papers #1 and #4, 1999: 1-3 and 4-9).

This pattern of denial and self-exemption from responsibility has been commented upon by numerous independent investigators. In 1996, the Royal Commission on Aboriginal Peoples (RCAP) found that the "history of the NFA has been marked by little or no action in implementation of [its] obligations and a long, drawn-out (and continuing) process of arbitration to force governments to implement their obligations" (1996, Volume 2: 517). The RCAP concluded that Canada, Manitoba, and MH (1996: 120):

> [D]id not intend, and have never intended, to cooperate energetically in measures designed and determined to be effective in confronting the adverse impacts of the project. They have instead used every legal device to limit their individual liabilities under the Agreement. The sixteen-year history of the Northern Flood Agreement is largely a record of the deployment of those devices . . . To the communities [the history of the Northern Flood Agreement] is a manifestation of bad faith by both levels of government. It has done little to address the impacts which continue to confront the communities.

A similar finding was issued by the Report of the Aboriginal Justice Inquiry of Manitoba in 1991. First, the Inquiry endorsed the Northern Flood Agreement as a modern-day treaty, stating that (cited at www.mcc.org):

> [T]he Northern Flood Agreement is a 'land claims agreement' within section 35(3) of the Constitution Act, 1982 and that the rights within the Northern Flood Agreement

are treaty rights within section 35(3). As a treaty, the Northern Flood Agreement must be interpreted liberally from the Indian perspective so that its true spirit and intent are honoured.

The report then concludes that the governments failed to adhere to the terms of the treaty and formally recommended that "the governments of Manitoba and Canada recognize the Northern Flood Agreement as a treaty and honour and properly implement the Northern Flood Agreement's terms" (www.mcc.org).

A report of the Auditor General of Canada, issued in 1992, reached a similar conclusion. The report acknowledged the direct impacts of the Hydro Project on the communities, including significant flooding of the Reserve lands of each of the five involved Aboriginal communities; damage to recreational and commercial areas; decreases in the quantity and quality of fish, including an increase in mercury toxins; contamination of drinking water; increased scarcity of wildlife for hunting and trapping; travel hazards due to water fluctuations and un-natural melting and freezing honored (cited at www.mcc.org). Despite the obvious nature of these damages, the report noted that "parties to the Northern Flood Agreement have taken an adversarial approach in implementing the Agreement" (www.mcc.org). In coming to this conclusion, the Auditor cites an internal government document which noted that in "many respects, it is not too harsh a judgement to conclude that the Department entered into this Agreement in 1977 and then promptly forgot the five involved communities" (March 1982 letter from Department of Indian Affairs and Northern Development Director of Economic Planning E.E. Hobbs to the Assistant Deputy Minister, cited at www.mcc.org).

The Department of Indian Affairs and Northern Development (DIAND) has also been characterized as negligent in implementing the terms of the agreement. The Nielson Report (The Task Force on Program Review, 1986), a comprehensive review of government programs commissioned by Prime Minister Brian Mulroney and headed by Deputy Prime Minister Erik Nielsen, provided evidence that DIAND supported the agreement primarily because it would save the Department money. According to the report, Federal negotiators interpreted the NFA as requiring a minimum of contractual obligations on the part of Canada and encompassing several desirable, but discretionary, activities that would actually reduce government expenditures. The Nielsen Report documents that DIAND did, in fact, achieve a cost-cutting goal that was consistent with a pattern of approving 'enriching' agreements between First Nations and governments that ended up having the opposite effect expenditures (www.mcc.org).

By 1990, frustration over the failure of governmental parties to fully and faithfully implement the NFA prompted the five communities to initiate a negotiation process that ultimately resulted in Master Implementation Agreements (MIA). According to MH, the four communities that have accepted the MIAs have done so because the agreements provide an "enhanced land package, firm operational agreements, resource management structures, locally operated claims processes and the flexibility afforded by secure financial arrangements created by means of a trust structure" (Manitoba Hydro, 1999, Background Paper #2: 2-4). Only the Pimicikamak Cree of Cross Lake have declined to become a party to a Master Implementation Agreement.

While the MIAs do in fact represent an alternative to the failed promises and obligations of the NFA, they also impose a significant cost, namely the extinguishment of all Aboriginal land claims and their transfer to the government of Canada, which, in turn can make them available to private parties for development. In other agreements such as the James Bay Northern Quebec Agreement (1975), Gwich'in Agreement (1992), and the Sahtu Dene and Metis Agreement (1993), extinguishment requires "Aboriginal people to 'cede, release and surrender' inherent Aboriginal rights and title to lands for the 'benefits' of land claims agreements" (Grand Council of the Crees, 1998: 35-36). In the present case, the Cree people's government has concluded that (Grand Council of the Crees, 1998: 33):

> [R]ather than fulfill their obligations under the NFA Treaty, the treaty parties . . . embarked upon an initiative of escaping their continuing duties under the Treaty once and for all by inducing the Cree communities to accept a one-time cash buy-out in exchange for full and final extinguishment of their Treaty rights.

In this respect, the MIAs complete an historical process that began more than a century ago with the Rupert's Land claim. White society's economic ambitions and the aims of Manitoba and MH to modernize the landscape of the province's north country have been fulfilled. Victims of the result, as discussed below, have been whole ecosystems and Aboriginal communities.

Environmental Justice and Manitoba Hydro

Ronald Niezen has extensively studied the effects of mega-hydro developments on Cree populations in both Quebec and Manitoba. In his recent work, he notes the link between mega-hydro projects and community health (1999:3):

> In the academic literature one of the few discussions of displacement resulting from hydroelectric mega-project development can be found in the book *World Mental Health* . . . [which concludes] that 'the common consequences of dislocation include impoverishment, malnutrition, increased morbidity, dependency, and the breakdown of community norms and mutual support systems. Dams and resettlement projects mean not only a loss of home and the identity that comes from a sense of place; they can obliterate generations of practical culture and knowledge'. Further, if compensation for this trauma is 'delayed withheld, inadequate or poorly distributed . . . [it] leaves painful memories, exacerbates loss and feelings of impotence, fuels distress and discontent, and can haunt a project with a rankling sense of grievance.'

Although *World Mental Health* (Dejarlais et al, 1995) dealt primarily with the resettlement effects of mega-hydro projects such as the Aswan Dam and the Three Gorges project, Niezen argues that its findings are directly applicable to the Cree communities affected by the CRD/LWR projects. In Niezen's view, the point of reference is that of a "culture based upon mobile forest subsistence" (1999: 4). Quoting from a report prepared for the Province of Manitoba, Neizen argues that Aboriginal residents "identify with a concept of home which reaches [into the] lands and waters traditionally used for hunting, fishing, trapping and recreation" (Nelson River Group, 1986: 20). In this context, the loss of use of traditional lands, i.e., those lands inundated or rendered inaccessible because of shoreline erosion, silting, etc., can likewise be expected to result in the health effects associated with displacement. As he notes (1999: 4):

> To find situations of displacement, therefore, we do not need to look just for people living in settled communities that have been relocated from one site to another. To the extent that their activities on the land have been disrupted, the Crees have been displaced; and we should be alert to traumas occurring in Canada's north of the kind associated with forced relocation elsewhere in the world.

The CRD/LWR projects raises at least two questions central to the discourse on environmental justice: (1) can the physical impacts and the resulting social conditions occasioned by the projects be reversed or mitigated; and (2) can the affected communities participate meaningfully in decision making processes to redress the violations to their lives, their culture and their lands?[3]

Restoring the ecological integrity of the Nelson River watershed is, of course, a theoretical possibility. The dams, channels, and control structures could be removed and the natural flows of the Nelson and Churchill

Rivers and Lake Winnipeg could be allowed to return their pre-construction states. As a practical matter, however, none of the parties are suggesting such a course of action.

Large-scale environmental restoration is also considered by most experts to be impossible. Indeed, even minor restoration efforts are problematic given the scope of the damage. For instance, the cleanup of the Jenpeg forebay and the construction of a weir[4] built upriver from Cross Lake, have been heralded by MH as a major step towards environmental mitigation (Background Paper #3, 1999). However, the forebay constitutes a tiny fraction of the total impacted area and the weir has done little to deal with the water quality problems experienced at Cross Lake. Even with the wier, the summer months generally bring a proliferation of marsh grass and aquatic weeds, sometimes reaching across the expanse of the Nelson River (Stewart, 2000). In addition, the hundreds of miles of eroded shoreline and the constant fluctuations in water levels required for the continuing operations of the dams, particularly given the sensitive nature of boreal forest shoreline and soil systems, makes restoration or even stabilization of the vast majority of the affected area virtually inconceivable (Krotz, 1991).

The irreversibility of the hydro projects greatly undermines the viability of returning to a land-based way of life. The resource areas available for traditional hunting, trapping and fishing have been severely compromised and land exchanges envisioned under the NFA and the MIAs, while significant, are all problematic for the communities (personal interviews, November, 1999). In addition, the communities have lost much of the traditional knowledge base required for long-term cultural restoration (Niezen, 1999).

Perhaps the most realistic remedy is the development of mechanisms for meaningful self-determination. Yet there is much debate within the northern communities about the appropriate means to incorporate even a semblance of self-determination.

Some communities, led by Split Lake, are opting for a kind of "revenue-sharing" based upon the development of additional hydro capacity along the Nelson. Even the Split Lake community, however, acknowledges the devastating impacts of hydro development to the region (2000: 2-3):

> The 1970s was a decade of . . . major social and environmental change, as the entire Project made up of Lake Winnipeg and Nelson River regulation and Churchill River diversion began to operate . . . The adverse effects caused by this development were

beyond the worst fears of our people. The Nelson River pattern of higher flows in the spring and summer, with declining and low flows in the fall and through winter, dictated by Mother Nature, was reversed and flooding of our lands occurred. Our local environment was fundamentally, and permanently, disrupted. Wildlife patterns and habits we knew and depended upon changed. Hydro development was the final step in removing forever our opportunity to support ourselves in our traditional ways development.

Given its inability to maintain a traditional way of life, Split Lake argues that they must "embark upon an appropriate and determined effort in the area of economic development" (2000: 14). Thus, the community is (2000, 15):

[E]xploring an opportunity to form a business relationship with Manitoba Hydro for the possible joint development of a 560-megawatt generating station at Gull Rapids within the Split Lake Resource Area. All of the problems and opportunities of being a co-owner are being carefully investigated. We have clearly defined objectives, including environmental stewardship, shared financial benefits and job opportunities. At the beginning of the Gull planning discussions, Chief Norman Flett said 'Only Split Lake will decide if a generating station at Gull Rapids is built and whether we want to participate in the construction, operations and ownership.'

A radically different approach is being pursued by the Cross Lake community. Having withdrawn from the MIA process, and believing that the NFA must be implemented, the community has chosen to pursue an intensive public relations campaign centered in Minnesota and the upper Midwest. The immediate goals are to prevent expansion of MH's generation and transmission capacity and to educate American consumers about the consequences that their energy demands impose upon the northern communities.

The differences among Cross Lake, the other Northern Communities, and the government parties, regarding the meaning of the NFA are fundamental. According to MH, the NFA "was intended to provide a way to deal with the adverse effects of the LWR/CRD hydro Project on the participating communities" by providing a mechanism for determining the economic value of all land claims or damages resulting from the project and making one-time cash payments that would provide relief to the governmental parties, including MH, from all future claims (Background Paper #3, 1999: 3-4). The Cross Lake community, on the other hand, sees the "NFA is a treaty that promised to ensure the viability of a growing Cross Lake First Nation resident at Cross Lake and to eradicate mass poverty and mass unemployment for the Cross Lake Residents." In response, MH argues that "regardless as to the treaty status of the NFA (which is not agreed to by the Government parties or Manitoba Hydro) the view of Canada, Manitoba and Manitoba Hydro is that the NFA was not intended to be a funding arrangement to meet all of the needs of these five First Nations forever" (Background Paper #3, 1999: 3-4).[5]

The criticisms directed at the various parties reflect these differences. Opponents to Split Lake's position, for instance, view the MIAs, as well as any future agreements, as part of an explicit government strategy to divide the communities and ultimately destroy their ability to resolve any Aboriginal land claims (Grand Council of the Crees, 1998 and 1999). From this perspective, an expectation that future agreements will be honored, including those concerning future Nelson River hydro developments, is to disregard the historical record of Canadian/Aboriginal relations.

Critics of the Cross Lake position argue that the community cannot expect Manitoba Hydro or the governments of Manitoba and Canada to restore a now-extinct way of life. Further, these critics argue that reliance upon traditional treaty rights will only exacerbate already desperate conditions and deepen welfare dependency upon the Canadian state (personal interviews with Split Lake and other Northern Community representatives, April, 2000).

Conclusion

The impacts of hydroelectric resources in northern Manitoba extend far beyond the traditional lands of the Crees and, indeed, far beyond the boundaries of Manitoba. As pointed out above, at least forty percent of MH current generation flows to U.S. markets and future plans call for the construction of additional capacity meant almost exclusively for export to the U.S. Canadian export power is at the center of a number of political controversies, including the construction and/or expansion of transmission lines in both Minnesota and Wisconsin. The resolution of these controversies will have major consequences for the development of additional wind and solar resources in Minnesota and the upper Midwest generally.

It is also important to recognize that the electricity being generated at such enormous cost to both Aboriginal communities and Canadian ecosystems is destined for a consumer culture prodigious in its ability to waste a huge share of its electrical resources. To date, however, none of these costs have been acknowledged either by American utilities or by the consuming public. Indeed, officials from Xcel Energy Company,

Manitoba Hydro's single largest wholesale customer, have publicly stated that the issue is an internal matter and that any effort by U.S. interests to intercede in the matter would be inappropriate. Nor is there evidence that American consumers have any knowledge of where and under what conditions their electricity is delivered to them.

The development of Manitoba's northern resources offers a case of transnational environmental injustice breathtaking in its scope. Yet, the development of northern Manitoba as a source of cheap energy required to satisfy the demands of a rapacious consumer culture did not begin the process of Aboriginal de-culturation. It is, however, a powerful force for its continuation and has served as a vehicle for the final acts of dispossession required for the full exploitation of Canada's northern resources. Efforts by Manitoba Hydro to distance itself from the consequences of its actions can only be understood as an effort to deny its role in this historical process.

Notes

1.   The author wishes to thank John Byrne and Ann Stewart for their assistance in the development of this chapter. All errors and omissions are, of course, the responsibility of the author.
2.   This section was written with the assistance of Jermaine Toney, Aron Khoury, and Kristin Lukes of the University of St. Thomas.
3.   These questions are derived from a general reading of the environmental justice literature. See generally Bullard, 1990; Fritz, 1999; Gupta, 1997; Hofrichter, 1993; *Social Science Quarterly*, 1997; and Taylor, 1999.
4.   The forebay is an area of water or reservoir created to provide for times when the river's water level is low. The dam also creates a head of water, or waterfall, to ensure the water has enough force to spin the turbines. A wier is a dam-like structure which has the effect of preventing excessive low water in periods of drought and facilitating the passage of water more quickly in flood years. The weir, along with a number of excavations, was built at the outlet of Cross Lake (MH, Background Paper #3: 8).
5.   Interviews were conducted in Winnipeg and Cross Lake with officials from Manitoba Hydro and with the leadership of the Cross Lake community in November, 1999. Other discussions were conducted at an April, 2000 conference held at the University of St. Thomas on April 15, 2000. The conference was entitled *Energy Policy and Environmental Justice in the Upper Midwest*. The fundamental differences spoken to by the Company was evident during all of these interviews.

References

Adams, Patricia and Gráinne Ryder. December, 1999. *The Three Gorges Dam: A Great Leap Backward For China's Electricity Consumers and Economy.* Probe International. Published online at www.irn.org.

Bullard, Robert D. 1990. *Dumping in Dixie: Race, Class and Environmental Quality.* Boulder, CO: Westview Press.

Byrne, John and Steven M. Hoffman. 1996. "The Ideology of Progress and the Globalization of Nuclear Power." In John Byrne and Steven M. Hoffman (eds). *Governing the Atom: The Politics of Risk.* New Brunswick, NJ and London: Transaction Publishers. pp. 10-46.

Byrne, John, Steven M. Hoffman, and Cecilia R. Martinez. 1992. "The Industrialization of Native American Lands." *Proceedings of the 7th Annual Meetings of the National Association for Science, Technology and Society.* pp. 170-181.

Desjarlais, Robert et al. 1995. *World Mental Health: Problems and Priorities in Low-Income Countries.* New York, NY: Oxford University Press.

Fleras, Augie and Jean Leonard Elliot. 1992. *The Nations Within: Aboriginal-State Relations in Canada, the United States, and New Zealand.* Toronto, CA: Oxford University Press.

Foreman, Christopher. 1998. *The Promise and Peril of Environmental Justice.* Washington, D.C.: Brookings Institution.

Gupta, Francis. 1997. "Coming to the Nuisance or Going to the Barrios? A Longitudinal Analysis of Environmental Claims." *Ecology Law Quarterly.* Volume 24, Number 1 (February): 1-56.

Grand Council of the Crees. 1999. "To the Edge of Cultural and Political Extinction. A Response Concerning the Covenant Rights of Aboriginal Peoples in Canada to the Government of Canada's Fourth Periodic Report on the Implementation of the International Covenant on Civil and Political Rights." *Submission of the Grand Council of the Crees to the United Nations Human Rights Committee.* Nemaska, James Bay, Quebec: Author.

_____. 1998. "Reciting the Symptoms, Ignoring the Cause: The Systematic Dispossession of Aboriginal Peoples in Canada. A Response to the Government of Canada's Third Periodic Report on the Implementation of the International Covenant on Economic, Social and Cultural Rights." *Submission of the Grand Council of the Crees to the United Nations Human Rights Committee.* Nemaska, James Bay, Quebec: Author.

Hofrichter, Richard (ed). 1993. *Toxic Struggles: The Theory and Practice of Environmental Justice.* Philadelphia, PA: New Society Press.

IEA (International Energy Agency). 2000. Statistical Abstract, Annex 1.

Krotz, Larry. 1991. "Dammed and Diverted." *Canadian Geographic.* Volume 111, Number 1 (February/March): 36-44.

Land, Lorraine Y. 1999. "Playing Environmental Roulette with Aboriginal Cultures?" *Submission to the Inter-Church Inquiry into Northern Hydro Development and the Churchill-Nelson Hydro-Electric Project.* Presented in Winnipeg, Manitoba. June 21-22, 1999.

Manitoba Hydro. No date. *A History of Electric Power in Manitoba.* Winnipeg, Manitoba: Author.

_____. 1999. "Background Paper #1: Overview of NFA Origins and Provisions." *Background Information from Manitoba Hydro to the Inter-Church Inquiry into Northern Hydro Development.* Winnipeg, Manitoba: Author.

_____. 1999. "Background Paper #2: Recent Implementation Agreements with Four First Nations." *Background Information from Manitoba Hydro to the Inter-Church Inquiry into Northern Hydro Development.* Winnipeg, Manitoba: Author.

_____. 1999. "Background Paper #3: Hydro Impacts and Implementation to date at Cross Lake." *Background Information from Manitoba Hydro to the Inter-Church Inquiry into Northern Hydro Development.* Winnipeg, Manitoba: Author.

_____. 1999. "Background Paper #4: Manitoba Hydro Impacts within Manitoba's Economy." *Background Information from Manitoba Hydro to the Inter-Church Inquiry into Northern Hydro Development.* Winnipeg, Manitoba: Author.

Niezen, Ronald. 1999. "The Social Consequences of the Hydroelectric Development for the Pimicikamak Cree Nation." *Speaking Notes for an Inter-Church Inquiry into Northern Hydro Development: Winnipeg and Cross Lake.* June 21-25.

_____. 1993. *Power and Dignity: the Social Consequences of Hydroelectric Development for the James Bay Cree.* Toronto, CA: University of Toronto Press.

Netherton, Alex. 1993. *From Rentiership to Continental Modernization: Shifting Policy Paradigms of State Intervention in Hydro in Manitoba: 1922-1977.* Ph.D. Dissertation. Carlton University.

Reisner, Marc. 1986. *Cadillac Desert: the American West and Its Disappearing Water.* New York, NY: Viking.

The Royal Commission on Aboriginal Peoples. 1996. *Report of the Royal Commission on Aboriginal Peoples. Volume 2, Part 1.* Ottawa: Ministry of Supply and Services Canada.

Sklar, Leonard S. and Amy L. Sklar. 1997. *Report on a Site Visit to the Three Gorges Dam, Yangtze River, Hubei Province, China, October 17-18, 1997.* Available online at www.irn.com.

Social Science Quarterly. 1997. Special Issue devoted to Environmental Justice. Volume 78, Number 4 (December).

Split Lake Cree First Nation. 2000. *Our People, Our Land, Our Water, Our Future, Our Voice.* Position Paper regarding developments in the Split Lake Resource Area. Split Lake, Manitoba: Author.

Stewart, Ann. 2000. Public Information Officer. Pimicikamak Cree Nation. Cross Lake, Manitoba. Personal Interview.

Sullivan, Lawrence R. 1999. "The Three Gorges Dam and the Issue of Sustainable Development in China." In Norman J. Vig and Regina S. Axelrod (eds). *The Global Environment: Institutions, Law, and Policy.* Washington, D.C.: Congressional Quarterly Press. Pp. 300-316.

Taylor, Dorceta (ed). 1999. "Special Issue: Advances in Environmental Justice: Research, Theory, and Methodology." *American Behavioral Scientist.* Volume 43, Number 4.

United Church of Christ. 1987. *Toxic Waste and Race in the United States: A National Report on the Racial and Socio-economic Characteristics of Communities with Hazardous Waste Sites.* New York, NY: Author.

Wiebe, Menno. 1999. "The Northern Flood Agreement: In Whose Interest." A paper presented at the *Current Status of the Northern Flood Agreement*, a conference sponsored by the Society for Applied Anthropology of Manitoba. University of Winnipeg.

Wooster, Donald. 1985. *Rivers of Empire: Water, Aridity, and the Growth of the American West.* New York, NY: Pantheon Books.

8

The Global Commons and Environmental Justice—Climate Change

Anil Agarwal, Sunita Narain, and Anju Sharma

Introduction

To date, the international response to the global crisis of climate change has reproduced the patterns of advantage and disadvantage that plague the global community of nations. Within the international negotiations to address climate change, the interests of the world's poorer nations and of the environment itself have taken second place to the dominant economic interests of the richer nations and corporations.

Global economic dependency on carbon-based fuels for economic growth is resulting in an increasing accumulation of carbon dioxide and other greenhouse gases (GHGs) in the atmosphere, the effect of which is which is heating up the planet. Many harmful social and environmental effects will result from a warmer global climate. Weather patterns will change with higher temperatures, more extreme weather events, loss of glacial and polar ice and an irreversible rise in global sea level, inundating low-lying islands and coastal lands. As the level of concentrations of GHG (mostly carbon dioxide but also methane, nitrous oxide and chloroflurocarbons), continue to build up in the earth's atmosphere the severity of these impacts increases.

Sufficient reduction of GHG emissions will slow, and eventually reverse, their accumulation in the atmosphere—although the long atmospheric 'residency' of GHGs means that a long-term effort at emissions abatement is necessary. Preventing the alarming prophecies associated with climate change from coming true, according to scientists, requires reducing global emissions by 50-70% below their 1990 levels (IPCC, 1990). Realizing such a goal means reducing, or altogether abandoning, the use of carbon-based fuels.

Such a simple remedy belies the immensity and complexity of the task involved, for the use of carbon-based fuels, and hence carbon emissions, are closely linked to economic growth and lifestyle. Every human being contributes to the carbon dioxide concentrations in the atmosphere in some way, but the size of that contribution depends on the person's lifestyle. There is a close association between a nation's GHG emissions and its economy. Historically, the more prosperous a country becomes, the higher its per capita income and fossil fuel consumption, and accordingly, the higher its GHG emissions. Part of the challenge for climate change policy is to break this historical association and to forge new ways to meet energy service needs.

The prosperity of industrialized nations is due to years of historical emissions, which have accumulated in the atmosphere since the start of the Industrial Revolution, and also to a high level of current emissions. However, the world's developing countries have only recently set out on the path to industrialization, and their per capita emissions are still comparatively low. The GHG emissions of one U.S. citizen, for instance, are equal to 19 Indians, 30 Pakistanis, 17 Maldivians, 19 Sri Lankans, 107 Bangladeshis, 134 Bhutanese or 269 Nepalese in 1996 (Marland et al, 1999). Under these circumstances, any limit on carbon emissions from developing countries amounts to a limit on their potential for economic growth, turning climate change mitigation into an intensely political issue.

International efforts to curtail global GHG emissions center on the United Nations Framework Convention on Climate Change (FCCC), which seeks to stabilize atmospheric GHG levels so as to "prevent dangerous interference with the climate system." Developed nations, called Annex 1 nations under the FCCC, have a current interim GHG reduction target that amount to 5.2% below 1990 levels, to be achieved in the period 2008-2012. This target was set under an agreement known as the Kyoto Protocol. Yet how that target will be met has many implications for developing nations and for the future climate itself. International negotiations under the FCCC have turned into a tug of war with rich countries unwilling to compromise their lifestyles, and poor countries unwilling to accept a premature cap on their right to basic development.

The atmosphere is a 'global commons' (i.e., a common property resource), to which every human being has an equal right. Yet some people have used up more than an equitable share of this global resource, and others, less. Through their own industrialization history and current lifestyles that involve very high levels of GHG emissions, the industrialized counties have more than used up their share of the absorptive capacity of the atmosphere. In this regard, the global warming problem is their creation, so it is only right that they should take the initial responsibility of reducing emissions while allowing developing countries to achieve at least a basic level of development.

Throughout the history of international negotiations over the FCCC, many in the developed world have sought commitments for emissions reduction from the developing world. In response, developing countries have refused to reduce emissions at their current stage of development and demanded 'space to grow.' Since asking developing countries to reduce carbon emissions amounts to asking them to freeze their standards of living at their current stage of development, the implications are that existing global inequalities between nations would remain permanent.

As a result of these political complexities, negotiations under the FCCC have turned into a game between unequal partners, with the G77 (the negotiating block of developing countries) on one side and the industrialized nations on the other. Though the European Union (EU) and the U.S. often come to the negotiating table with divergent viewpoints, with the EU pressing for tighter commitments and the U.S. unwilling to give in, the two have almost formed a habit of resolving issues among themselves. The EU ends up giving in to the lax U.S. position, and the two expect the developing world to accept their conclusions. To date, the G77 has frequently been outmaneuvered by the allied two main industrialized country groups, the U.S. and the EU.

Climate change is a complex scientific issue with the implications of research into emissions, climate processes, and potential climate change impacts having a great bearing on the global response to the issue. Predicting the adverse effects with some degree of reliability and pinpointing responsibility requires investment and scientific expertise that is available mostly to industrialized countries. As a result, developing countries, which have made little effort to expand their scientific capacity, are dependent on Northern scientists and institutions to tell them the extent and fallouts of global warming. This has enabled the developed nations to lead the negotiations in what is an intensely science-driven Framework Convention. Science has been used several times in the past to implicate developing countries, either by showing their future GHG contributions as increasing and counterproductive to developed country action, or by making no distinction between 'survival emissions' of the South and the 'luxury emissions' of the North.

As developed nations have produced the majority of climate change research, their interests have largely shaped the research agenda. This North-driven scientific process often makes developing country concerns a low priority. Very little research has been conducted on the possible impacts of climate change on different countries and regions, so that nearly all the inhabitants of developing nations are totally unprepared to handle the adverse effects of climate change. Some scientists allege this outcome reflects a 'conspiracy of silence,' since it avoids any findings that may show that the most damage will occur in developing countries. If this is true, there is a danger that the incentives for industrialized countries to take action to take action against global warming will be comparatively low.

Creating a Fair and Effective Policy Response

Within the fractious and competitive world of international climate change negotiations there are three main 'camps' of nations. The first comprises those nations that want to take extensive action on global warming. This camp includes the Association of Small Island States, who are in desperate position—many are faced with partial or complete inundation with the next century. It also includes some European nations who have strong pro-environment positions and Green parties in their Parliaments. For this group, the Kyoto Protocol must lead to ecologically effective action through effective and rapid reductions in global GHG emissions.

The second group is made up of most of the developed nations who consider that extensive emissions reductions will be expensive and are searching for as low cost solutions as possible. For this group, led by the U.S. (which has the highest level of national emissions), the Kyoto Protocol must lead to economically effective action. The third group consists of poor nations who want appropriate 'environmental space' for their future economic growth, given the fact that development within a carbon energy economy is closely related to carbon emissions. This group, led by India, China, and other developing nations, want the Kyoto Protocol to undertake equitous and socially just actions.

Creating Economic Solutions

To a great extent, the sheer scale of emissions reductions required of the developed world forms the basis of the climate change dilemma and the issue of how these nations' economies can be transformed without economic harm. A key feature of the Kyoto Protocol is that it allows developed nations some flexibility in meeting their national emission reduction targets (often known simply as 'flexmex') by including a number of market-based mechanisms as alternatives to domestic emissions reductions. All are essentially international trading or exchange mechanisms to facilitate the developed nations to develop market-based mechanisms around the commodity of emissions reduction. Three types of flexmex exist: the Clean Development Mechanism (CDM), joint implementation (JI), and emissions trading. Flexmex as envisaged in the Kyoto Protocol obviously provides an extremely effective means for cheap emissions reduction by OECD countries. Therefore, emissions reductions by Annex I nations will have to come from three sources: 1) domestic action; and/or 2) emissions trading with other Annex 1 nations and from credits obtained through CDM projects between Annex 1 countries; and/or 3) through CDM projects with developing countries.

Arguably, many Annex I nations have delayed taking significant reductions until these instruments begin operation. Carbon dioxide emissions grew in most industrialized countries between 1990 and 1996 and there are grounds for believing this growth trend will continue in the absence of effective policy responses. The International Energy Agency (IEA) forecast that carbon dioxide emissions from OECD countries will grow from 2,798 megatonnes of carbon (mtC) in 1990 to 3,269 mtC by the year 2010 under a business-as-usual scenario (IEA, 1998: 53-54). To meet the Kyoto Protocol targets, they will have to reduce emissions by another 192 mtC. This adds up to a total reduction of 1022 mtC under a business-as-usual scenario.

One factor that will greatly influence the extent of Annex I emissions reduction is the way in which the international emissions reduction system deals with emissions from former Warsaw Pact nations. As a consequence of their economic decline, these nations now produce less GHG emissions than in 1990. Accordingly, these nations have a GHG 'credit' which those Annex I nations with increasing emissions are seeking to purchase in order to avoid more costly domestic GHG abatement (this form of emissions trading is the so-called 'hot air trading'). The impact of hot air trading could be very significant. Emissions from transition economies are expected to be 166 mtC below their 1990 levels by 2010, even allowing for some GHG increases as their economies improve over the forecast period (IEA, 1998: 53-54). If trade in these hot air emissions is allowed, then industrialized countries will only need a reduction of 867 mtC (IEA, 1998: 53-54).

The Royal Institute of International Affairs, London, estimates that the total emissions of OECD are projected to exceed their targets by 580-1160 mtC in 2010 (Vrolijk, 1999). If all reductions come only from domestic action, the cost could be as high as US$120 billion a year, according to a study conducted as the Massachusetts Institute of Technology (MIT), though experts like Vrolijk criticize the study for taking very high emission growth rate figures, and disregarding 'no regret options.' As the Kyoto Protocol expects Annex 1 countries to meet the stipulated targets as an average of a five year period from 2008 to 2012, the total cost, according to the old-fashioned MIT study could be as much as US$600 billion. However, with trading between Annex B countries, this figure could drop by as much as 87%. If there is also large use of CDM at low costs, reductions cost drop by about 95%.

A Dutch study has even questioned the wisdom of the EU proposal of putting restrictions on emissions trading, including 'hot air' trading, and predicts that it will increase emissions reduction costs (Bollen et al, 1999). According to the study, the EU will have to pay higher costs while the U.S. will actually gain economically from such restrictions. The restrictions, surprisingly do not prevent the 'hot air' from the Former Soviet Union (FSU) from being used up, and even tend to increase global emissions. It concluded (Bollen et al, 1999):

> . . . although quotas have been agreed in Kyoto, the burden sharing is still highly dependent upon the rules and guidelines that still have to be agreed upon. Unequal burdens will affect competitiveness and international trade patterns, which are becoming important issues in the debate.

Less developed countries are concerned, meanwhile, that CDM will bypass them, and go mainly to the more industrially advanced among them, such as China and India.

Despite its appeal to those favoring economic policy tools, there are strong reasons to question the ability of the CDM to actually deliver GHG emission reductions when operating: CDM appears likely to act as an obstacle to a non-carbon based energy future. The net results of flexmex may ultimately be substantially higher emissions reduction costs. The U.S. Government's Council of Economic Advisors suggestion that the U.S. will seek to rely heavily on flexmex to satisfy its Kyoto Commitment, exemplifies this problem, for it allows no preparation for the much deeper cuts ultimately required to prevent climate change. Any strategy seeking to obtain least-cost carbon emission reduction options will inevitably focus on improving energy efficiency in the carbon energy sector.

Ecologically Effective Actions

There are two aspects to the task of responding to climate change with GHG emissions reduction; firstly to ensure that total GHG emissions do not surpass an unacceptable level and secondly, to ensure their substantial decline. Determining acceptable absolute levels and necessary rates of decline is highly complex, but some scientific guidance is available. According to IPCC studies, if atmospheric GHG concentrations stabilize at 450 parts per million by volume (ppmv) by the end of the 21st century, global average temperature will increase by 0.7°C, accompanied by a sea level rise of 10-65 centimeters (cm). Though this temperature rise exceeds natural variability, it would allow many—though not all—ecosystems to adapt. Therefore, 450 ppmv GHG concentration can be tentatively taken as an upper limit that will produce on the tolerable rate of climate change. Because we are dealing with a carbon cycle, it takes considerable time for emissions reductions to produce lower atmospheric concentrations.

To stabilize at 450 ppmv, cumulative GHG emissions have to be limited to about 600-800 gigatonnes of carbon (gtC) between now and the end of the 21st century, by which time annual emissions should diminish to less than 3 gtC per year. Reaching such an ecologically-oriented target involves reversing the global trend of increasing emissions. For example, under a business-as-usual scenario, cumulative emissions between now and 2100 will be about twice a high, at 1500 gtC, with annual emissions reaching 20 gtC per year and accelerating upward (Kartha, 1998). As a climatic consequence, we could expect a warming of 1.4 to 2.9°C and a sea level rise of 19 to 86 cm by 2100 which will adversely affect natural habitats, agricultural system and human health, and have severe implications for coastal and inland ecosystems and their human communities.

The 450 ppmv stabilization trajectory, despite being a dramatic deviation from business-as-usual, is itself not without considerable risks. It commits the world to accelerated global warming, and takes the climate system into a realm where our predictive capacity is weak. Scientific models of climate change impacts, alarming as they are, may be unduly optimistic. Evidence from prehistoric climate records is increasingly supporting the view that the climate system can change rapidly with dramatic ecological impacts. Relatively small human-induced changes could thus be amplified by positive feedback that operates within larger systems that cannot be controlled by human beings (Katha et al, 1998).

Despite the urgency and importance of reducing GHG emissions, much of the talk of stabilization is idealistic and theoretical—such is the gap between current global emissions and the stabilization targets discussed above. Our current global concentration of carbon dioxide alone (ignoring other GHGs) is around 360 ppmv. Stabilization at this current concentration is considered virtually impossible within two hundred years because of the residency period of this gas in the atmosphere and the sheer difficulty of weaning the global economy from its thirst for fossil fuel energy forms. International negotiations have not considered the prospects of stabilization at 750 ppmv, even though business-as-usual scenarios show concentrations rising well above 750 ppmv.

Translating the targets of global emissions reductions into a personal responsibility (i.e. per capita targets) reveals something of the immensity of this ecological challenge. Such an analysis reveals that the nations of both the North and South will have to reduce per capita emissions substantially. The North must reduce its current carbon emissions of about 3 tonnes per capita from fossil fuel sources to about one-tenth of this amount. The South must eventually reduce its own per capita carbon emissions of about 0.5 tonnes per capita by half even as its population and economies motorize and industrialize in the years to come (Katha, 1998).

Such is the character of this global ecological problem that the Northern nations are to protect their long-term interests they can neither adopt strategies to avoid effective emissions reduction themselves, or to shift that responsibility onto the South. For even if the North reasoned that it could withstand the effects of future climate change, it could not be similarly assured that the resulting upheavals resulting from the impacts on the developing world—such as migratory, economic, and geopolitical disturbances—would leave it unaffected. Having developing nations assume disproportionate responsibility for emissions reductions would lead to similar outcomes as the first strategy. However, such reasoning has yet to penetrate into the international negotiations, as the North continues pursuing a strategy that offers to neither satisfactorily address the threat of climate change, meet the needs of developing nations, nor be reasonably considered to display any pursuit of justice.

Forging Renewable Energy Systems

Climate change cannot be satisfactorily addressed without bringing the dominance of fossil fuel energy sources to an end and using renewable energy sources to meet energy service needs. That international negotiations have virtually ignored the necessity of this transformation is indicative of the extent to which most developed nations wish to perpetuate the status quo, despite the known social and environmental costs. Global negotiations have thrown up energy efficiency as the most economically effective strategy for emissions reduction, and equal per capita entitlements and convergence as the key components for equity and global solidarity. But there has been very little discussion on what constitutes ecologically effective action.

An effective response to global warming means nations must leave the path of carbon-intensive ways to meet energy needs through improving energy efficiency, but also move quickly towards the ultimate goal of a zero-carbon energy-based economy. These goals are not mutually exclusive but complementary-however, an exclusive focus on energy efficiency measures could jeopardize the transition to a zero-carbon energy transition. A narrow focus on energy efficiency could 'lock in' fossil fuels for a much longer time than desired and 'lock out' renewable energy sources. Many studies show that governments must take a proactive role in promoting the transition here and now. Though a zero-emissions future looks more promising today than ever before, the transition will not take place by itself.

Certainly it is misguided or excessively optimistic to think that the problem will solve itself simply through the diminution of the reserves of fossil fuels. If the world waits for a large part of its oil and gas resources to be exhausted before the shift to a zero-carbon energy system occurs, which will not be before the 22nd century, then more rapid and greater global warming than is already occurring becomes inevitable.

Despite the urgency of the need to transform the world's carbon-based energy system, the current international approach of using market-based policies in responding to climate change works against the prospects of changing the energy system in the desired manner. Rather than producing policies that will assist in the transition to renewable energy, there are elements within the Kyoto Protocol that will inhibit the transition by reinforcing the role of carbon-based energy forms. Comparing forecast emissions shows an indication of the limits to energy efficiency savings for energy efficiency improvements alone and when used in combination with increased application of renewable energy. Using only energy-efficient fossil fuel scenario, global emissions will rise from 6.23 gtC in 1990 to almost 22 gtC by 2050 (Anderson, 1996). A combination of renewable energy and energy efficiency could return global carbon emissions to just slightly above their 1990 global carbon emissions.

The study's author, Dennis Anderson, a senior advisor in the World Bank's industry and energy department, concluded that ". . . it will not be possible to prevent the accumulation of carbon in the atmosphere unless non-carbon (or not-net carbon-emitting) alternatives become available." (1996:10-13). As long as GHG emission trends remain identical with growth in global energy demand, energy efficiency alone will have little overall effect. Anderson reasoned that a continuation of global trends could conceivably produce 10 billions tonnes of carbon emissions in 20 years time and ". . . this would be in an energy efficient world." (Anderson, 1996:10-13).

A University of Hawaii study has forecast the potential impact of solar energy penetration on future carbon emissions against a baseline scenario in which global carbon emissions grow for nearly 180 years and reach a peak of 49 gtC in 2175, causing average global temperatures rise to a maximum of 6°C (relative to 1860) (Chakravarty, no date). Under the most optimistic solar energy penetration scenario, under which the prices of solar energy systems fall by 50% per decade, global carbon emissions will peak at only about 13 gtC in 2035. Global average temperature will rise by 1.5°C and begin to decline after 2055, making global warming a problem that can be dealt with within the first half of the next century (Chakravarty, no date).

Solar energy would have to become competitive enough to replace fossil fuels in every economic sector by 2065.

Even a relatively pessimistic scenario in which solar energy costs decline by 30% per decade makes a salutary difference. If this 30% decline is accompanied by a carbon tax on fossil fuels of about US$100 per tonne (raising coal prices by about US$70/tonne or 300%, and oil prices by about US$8 per barrel), the effects are the same as the earlier scenario, with a 50% solar decrease in solar energy prices every decade.

Cleaning up existing fossil fuels has similarly limited impacts, such as moving towards clean coal technology. The model assumes that a new coal combustion technology will become available by 2020 which removes 50% of the carbon dioxide emitted by coal (Chakravarty, no date). In this case, peak temperatures rises by about 4°C but prior to 2045 clean coal technology does help to control temperatures and delay global warming even more than the most optimistic solar energy penetration scenario of 50% rate of solar cost reduction per decade. But once oil and natural gas run out, the global energy economy will become totally dependent on clean coal and temperatures begin to rise rapidly. In other words, clean coal has a good short term, but bad long term, implications.

Analysis by the International Institute for Applied Systems Analysis (IIASA) and the World Energy Conference (WEC), entitled *Global Energy Perspectives* reveals the importance of renewables (Nakicenovic et al, 1998). With appropriate "technology push and pull," renewables could contribute as much as 37-39% of the global primary energy supply by 2050 and as a result net carbon emissions could be below 1990 emissions by as much as 15%, argue the authors.

The IIASA/WEC study shows that gross global carbon emissions from fossil fuel combustion rising from 6.23 gtC in 1990 to anywhere between 5.93 gtC to 16.00 gtC in 2050 and per capita emissions increasing from 1.18 tC in 1990 to anywhere between 0.59 tC to 1.59tC. Gross carbon emissions of OECD countries could rise from 3.03 in 1990 to anywhere between 0.79 gtC to 4.42 gtC in 2050. Those of developing countries could rise from 1.85 gtC in 1990 to anywhere between 4.2 gtC to 9.02 gtC in 2050 (Nakicenovic, 1998).

Both in the case of OECD and developing countries, gross carbon emissions remain at the lower end of 2050 projections only where governments take a proactive position to push for non-polluting renewable energy sources and for energy efficiency. In such a scenario, OECD countries will be able to cut their 1990 carbon emissions by about 75% and developing countries will be able to stay within 2.5 times their 1990 carbon emissions. If this were to occur, the world as a whole will be able to return to the gross carbon emissions of 1990. However, without any effort to transform the world's fossil fuel energy system, by 2050, the world will not be able to reduce its gross carbon emissions below the 1990 levels, which in itself are 2-3 times higher than those which are considered to be environmentally sustainable.

The difficulty in transforming the energy system lies in the enormous scale of the changes required; for example, the capital turnover rates (the time it takes to recover investment) of energy supply technologies, and particularly of infrastructures, are five decades or longer (Nakicenovic, 1998). Research investments made in the next few decades that will shape the technology options available to the world even after 2020. The more the world gets locked into fossil fuel based systems, especially efficient and low-cost systems, the longer it will take to get out of them. Already, despite major technological innovations and cost reductions, renewable energy technologies are failing to penetrate the U.S. market significantly. Renewable energy technologies not only have to compete with the costs of fossil fuel systems but also with the falling costs of increasingly efficient fossil fuel systems in the future.

It is clear that the existing mechanisms of the Kyoto Protocol promote the operation of the existing energy system and will cause the continual build up of greenhouse gases, especially when we take into account that huge energy investments will be made by developing countries in the next 3-4 decades. If these investments lock developing countries into a carbon energy economy like industrialized countries, it will be very difficult for them to get out of it fast. According to a recent analysis, the amount of zero-carbon energy needed by 2050 to stabilize at 450 ppmv will be twice the current total global primary energy requirement. This amount can be reduced, however, if energy efficiency were to increase rapidly than in the past.

Transforming the energy system in order to reduce the extent of harmful climate change is a task that cannot be left to market forces or corporate interests. Governments of the world have to play a key role in 'reinventing the energy system' in the 21st century, just as they have played a key role in determining the modern energy supply structure ever since the 19th century. The 20th century has actually seen a major transition away from renewable sources of renewable energy, towards a fossil fuel-based global economy. Between 1900 and 1997, world energy use grew over 10 times—but even though the actual contribution of renewables increased by nearly 5 times, its share dropped from 42% to only 19%. The challenge for the 21st century is to return once again to a much bigger share for renewables. This will mean a switch from traditional uses of renewables to modern uses of renewables, including biomass energy (Brown and Flavin, 1999).

Public and political awareness of the status and potential of renewable energy continues to lag behind its actual condition, leaving many in the community unaware of its progress and achievements in recent years. Renewable energy is a fast-growing source, faster than any other method of electric generation (Priddle, 1999). For example, between 1990 and 1997, wind power capacity grew by 25.7% every year (Brown and Flavin, 1999: 16) and the global installed capacity of wind turbines doubled between 1990 and 1995 (Priddle, 1999). The recent slowing of the world economy has proved advantageous for wind energy. Favorable market developments, including the recent decline in interest rates due to global economic problems have benefited wind power—because of its higher up-front capital costs compared to fossil fuel systems—making it the 1990s fastest-growing energy source (Gray, 1999).

Photovoltiac energy sources are also developing rapidly. Between 1990 and 1997, photovoltaics (PV) increased by 16.8% per year (Brown and Flavin, 1999: 16) and their annual production is doubling every five years (Priddle, 1999). Annual U.S. sales of solar energy technologies are already about US$1 billion and cumulative purchases of PV worldwide by 1997 were about 800 MW (Brown and Flavin, 1999: 28). Technological advances are also taking place in the use of hydrogen as a source of energy, which could have a major impact on the transport sector. By 2010, vehicles operated on fuel cells are expected to be on the road (*The Economist*, 1999a, b). The cost of fuel cells has been falling dramatically to only a few thousand dollars per kW, though it must fall further to about $50-100 per kW to compete with the internal combustion engine.

Modern biomass energy offers similarly immense potential. New biomass technologies can help produce ethanol from agricultural wastes, which can be used in cars (Clinton, 1999). On August 12, 1999, U.S. President Bill Clinton announced a program for biofuels with the goal of tripling U.S. use of bioenergy by 2010. These technological developments have led energy experts to be reasonably optimistic about the future of renewables. WEC has developed a scenario in which as much as 45% of the world's electricity is produced from renewables by 2020.

Encouraging as these developments are, the fact remains that renewables are still unable to penetrate the market without government support and the removal of unfavorable government policies. Where it receives government support, the market for renewable energy is expanding rapidly. However, renewables still require government assistance to overcome numerous existing institutional and economic barriers before it can become fully competitive with fossil fuel energy.

The biggest obstacles facing renewable energy technologies are: low fossil fuel prices; fossil fuel subsidies in many countries; declining public sector research and development; and plummeting private sector research and development as the deregulation of energy markets increasingly focuses attention on short-term returns (Katha et al, 1998). As a result, the rate of penetration of renewables-based electricity in the 1990s compared to the 1980s, despite major technological advances, and rapid increases in wind power capacity and PV sales in recent years (OECD, 1998). Even though fossil fuel prices will continue to fluctuate in the coming decades, they will are not change drastically, making the rapid expansion in the use of zero-carbon technologies possible only with a proactive official policy aimed at increasing research investment, and creating favorable economic conditions so that mass production can bring their costs down further.

Compounding the effects of these trends is that Government research and development investment of renewable energy in recent years has been extremely poor. In 1995, it was a mere US$878 million in all industrialized countries put together, less than 10% of the total reported government expenditure on energy research and development (IEA/OECD, 1997). During the 1980s the level of official investment actually fell dramatically, although there has been a slight increase in the 1990s (IEA/OECD, 1997). Yet opportunities for increasing research and development are not small. A carbon tax of US$5 per tonne of carbon will increase the price of oil by just US$0.65 per barrel but it will generate US$10-15 billion in the U.S. alone, which could be used to fund research in solar energy.

There are many successful examples around the world of governments promoting renewable energy; in fact a large part of the current world demand for PV is based on government programs. As part of Japan's rooftop program, more than 6,800 systems were installed in 1998. Shipments to Japan increased from 35 MW to 49 MW, reflecting strong indigenous support for grid-connected PV. Just as Japan is playing a major role in the current demand for PV, the Iceland government is playing a major role in promoting fuel cells. In 1999, Iceland pledged to become the world's first hydrogen powered economy. The country's capital, Reykjavik, suffers from severe automobile pollution even though the country gets most of its electricity from clean hydroelectric and geothermal sources. Iceland's commitment has immediately attracted Shell, Daimler-Chrysler, and Norsk Hydro, a Norwegian energy firm experienced in making hydrogen, who have set up a joint venture with local firms. In 1999, Daimler intends to introduce fuel-cell buses. The country hopes to replace all cars and the fishing fleet with fuel cell-powered transport.

Initiatives by the Californian government have forced car manufacturers to take fuel cells seriously in the U.S. and this has led to significant investments by the automobile conglomerates. The state has decreed that by 2004, one-tenth of all cars sold in the state must be zero-emission vehicles or else the companies could be barred from the market. As a result, by next year, carmakers and specialist fuel cell companies will have spent some US$1.5 billion on fuel cells (*The Economist*, 1999a, b).

Several studies show that renewable have not only reached a stage where they can take off with government support, but importantly that in the long run they could also lead to much lower energy investments compared to those made in fossil fuel technologies. Authors of the IIASA/WEC study *Global Energy Perspectives*, have shown that if energy investments are made carefully, then both annual and cumulative energy sector investments will be lowest in the case of renewables and energy efficiency scenarios (Nakicenovic et al, 1998). The combination of zero-energy sources and highly efficient technologies will be a critical element of adhering to a low-carbon trajectory so that failing to develop advanced energy producing and energy-using technologies would cause the ultimate costs of GHG mitigation to be dramatically higher than otherwise.

Disconcertingly, projections of the high costs of reducing GHG emissions could become a self-fulfilling prophesy if society, daunted by the exaggerated costs of addressing climate change, defers action and fails to adequately stimulate technological innovation and diffusion. According to SEI, if technological innovation and diffusion is postponed, processes of technological 'lock-in' and 'lock-out' can occur, preventing the market entry and associated development of nascent technologies that would ultimately be superior to the status quo, but require a period of continued technological innovation, learning-by-doing, and expanded consumer awareness before they can diffuse widely (Katha et al, 1998).

Through enlightened policy, the developing world can assume the lead role in transforming the world economy to one based on renewable energy. Developing countries can create a global market for zero-carbon energy technologies because they have two distinct advantages over their developed counterparts in this regard. Firstly, they enjoy relatively greater solar energy resources. Secondly, there are more than 2 billion people today without access to electricity. This group is a potential market comprising several hundreds of thousands of villages that are not yet touched by the carbon grid. It could be argued that providing these villages with access to renewable energy constitutes rural development, not 'emissions reduction.' Additionally, there are emissions benefits from reducing fossil fuel use in the developing world, as there is substantial use of fossil fuels by people who are outside the electric grid. For example, in Indian villages, diesel and electricity used for operating irrigation pumps constitutes a significant proportion of India's diesel and power consumption.

Development need not slavishly follow the pattern of Western industrialization, but can 'leapfrog' from existing conditions to adopt more advanced or environmentally benign technologies, thereby bypassing those intermediary technologies with their high social and environmental costs. An excellent example of how technological leapfrogging can help both developing countries' national objectives and the global warming problem comes from the Indian transport sector. In the U.S., there is one car for every 1.6 people. If India were to have the same ratio, the number of cars in the country would grow from 4 million, to more than 550 million. While such an outcome is unlikely, it is entirely possible that by 2020, Indians will be riding one hundred million motor scooters that burn gasoline and are far less friendly to the environment than cars. As with most Asian cities, motor scooters are very popular in India, accounting for 70% of the motor vehicles registered in India in 1995-1996. If investments in highway and traffic infrastructure and pollution control technology lag behind, one can imagine the widespread mayhem and pollution on the roads of the kind already seen in big cities from Bangkok to Delhi. Polluted cities could provide a huge and rapidly growing market for fuel-cell scooters (Agarwal, 1997).

The future for developing countries will not be the same as that process of industrialization that characterizes the developed nations. Experts at SEI point out that because of the fossil fuel-based historic industrialization of the North, the South today finds itself facing a 'severely compromised' climatic system if it follows the well-trodden path of the North. The South, therefore, has to bear the extra cost of taking a different path and has to 'get it right the first time.' Production of energy is based on long-lived capital, which, once built, commits a society to lifetime's worth of emissions. A power plant built today will still be emitting 30 years from now, by which time global carbon emissions would have to be reduced by 25% from the business as usual scenarios.

The South is undertaking rapid economic growth based on fossil fuel sources and its major energy investment decisions in the immediate decades will significantly contribute to global emissions. Such is the current momentum of this approach to development that there is very little that can be done to change the fossil fuel-based path for the next 20 years. But if efforts to make renewables begin to compete by 2020 are not made now, then the world will be committed to a carbon based energy economy well into the next century. A slower rate of reduction today will mean either faster rates of reduction later or a high risk of climate change and results in a very heavy burden being passed to future generations (Katha et al, 1998).

Addressing the Equity Issue

Developing a response to climate change that is economic and ecological cannot be justified unless the critical matter of the existing inequities in the global system of GHG emissions and their consequences is resolved. Equity cannot be considered separately or left to narrow international negotiation, but needs to be part of an effective approach to reduce global GHG emissions. For while per capita carbon dioxide emissions are closely related to a country's level of economic development and standard of living, it is obvious that as long as the world remains bound to a carbon based economy, it cannot delink its economy substantially from carbon dioxide emissions.

Because of the current nexus between a carbon-based energy economy and GHG emissions, equitable sharing of 'atmospheric space' becomes a critical issue, especially for poor developing countries who need the maximum space for their future economic growth. The enormous inequity in carbon dioxide emissions, as it currently stands, is best represented by the comparison between U.S. per capita emissions and those of South Asian nations, which are amongst the world's poorest nations. Though the gap is narrowing, this extraordinary inequity makes it very difficult for political leaders, especially in nations with an electoral democracy, to agree to a common action plan unless there is clear recognition of the need for equity in sharing available atmospheric space. Without sharing equitably, global solidarity will not be possible.

Although the importance of equity has been stressed in several governmental and non-governmental fora, including the European Parliament and the heads of nonaligned Nations, very few studies have been undertaken to conceptualize and operationalize the implications of equity. Now that there is a standoff between the U.S. demand and the developing countries' reluctance over the 'meaningful participation' of key developing countries, some efforts are being made to discuss what is meant by equity. As a result, it is now critical to examine equity more closely and to find a way to ensure its inclusion in a revised approach to creating effective global climate change policy. Indeed, it is also interesting to note that the emissions reduction commitments of member nations of the EU are highly equitable

The most fundamental means to ensuring equity is to allocate GHG emissions on a per capita basis. The concept of equal per capita emissions entitlements was incorporated in the Buenos Aires work plan at CoP-4 at the insistence of G77 and China. A few studies have tried to elaborate this concept and two basic approaches have been adopted—one includes historical emissions and the other builds a system of entitlements on current and future emissions. The concept of equal per capita emissions entitlements using current and future emissions entitlements has been elaborated by the New Delhi-based Centre for Science and Environment (CSE) using four approaches.

Sinks

Under this approach, the emissions absorbed annually by the global atmospheric sinks, especially global commons like the oceans, could be distributed equally among all the people of the world, providing each person with an equal entitlement. In order to avoid global warming, the world will have to produce no more emissions than the world's sinks are capable of absorbing. According to IPCC, 1990 emissions must come down by over 60% if atmospheric concentrations of GHGs are to be stabilized (IPCC, 1990). The average annual production of carbon dioxide between 1980 and 1989 has been estimated at 7.1 btC. The annual average absorption by all the sinks for these years was 3.8 btC.

There are mainly two types of sinks for carbon dioxide—oceanic and terrestrial. Terrestrial sinks are national property, but oceanic sinks, which absorb to the order of 2 btC per year, belong to humankind and are common global property (IPCC, 1996). As the 1990 world population was 5.3 billion, this gives a per capita sink availability of 0.38 tC, which can be considered each person's entitlement.

But this entitlement is so low that while some countries will reach their limits very fast, there are many developing countries that have already well above such an entitlement. India's carbon dioxide emissions in 1990 from burning fossil fuels, gas flaring and cement production, for instance, was 0.22 tC. India should then be entitles to increase emissions up to 0.38 tC and, in the meantime, trade unused emissions, or bank these for later use. Major developing countries which were emitting less than this level in 1990 included all the seven countries in South Asia, African countries like Tanzania, Ghana, Kenya, and Nigeria, Asian countries like the Philippines and Indonesia, and South American countries, such as Peru and Brazil. However, several developing countries like Egypt and China had already crossed this level.

Industrialized countries, way above this per capita level, will find it almost impossible to come down as long as they remain within a carbon based energy economy. Their emissions will keep contributing to the build-up of carbon dioxide levels in the atmosphere.

Budget

Recognizing that the build up of GHG emissions in the atmosphere is inevitable in the decades ahead, the budget approach first fixes the future atmospheric concentration limits for the major GHGs which cannot be exceeded by a certain date. These concentrations will have to be fixed at levels that do not threaten to seriously destabilize the climate and comprise a global emissions budget over a specified time period, to be distributed among all nations in the form of equal per capita entitlements. This approach demands that the targeted atmospheric concentration be subject to periodic scientific reviews, and changed appropriately. Therefore, per capita entitlements based on this approach, too, would be subject to review. If a country does not use its budget during a particular year, it would have the right to trade its unused budget.

IPCC has estimated the total amounts of carbon dioxide emissions that can be emitted in a 110-year period from 1991 to 2100 to reach specified atmospheric concentrations. If the world were to aim for a maximum atmospheric concentration of 450 ppm of carbon dioxide by 2100, then the world can emit an average of 5.73 to 5.91 btC every year, which would have provided in 1990 a per capita entitlement of 1.08-1.12 tC. For a 550 ppm atmospheric concentration, the 1990 per capita entitlement would be 1.49-1.53 tC (IPCC, 1995).

Moving entitlements

Under this approach, nations agree on a moving per capita emissions entitlement which could begin with, such as 2.0 tC or even 2.5 tC. This entitlement would be subject to periodic reviews, allowing reductions based on the latest scientific information on the seriousness of the threat of global warming.

The approach may appear ad hoc, but there is already a lot of 'pragmatic adhocism' in the climate negotiations. The amount that industrialized countries are going to emit by 2008-2010 as specified in the Kyoto Protocol, for instance, is pegged to their emissions in 1990. The choice of the base year 1990 is an ad hoc selection—but it has been accepted because industrialized countries have to show that they are reducing their emissions relative to some year. As long as they reduce emissions, it does not matter which year is chosen as the baseline.

Some countries in economic transition, in fact, have been given the option to choose their own baseline year. The choice of the amount by which each industrialized country is going to reduce its emissions relative to 1990 emissions was also voluntary and ad hoc. Once again, the targets have been chosen simply in the interest of moving ahead. An ad hoc enticement amount can similarly be chosen to get the principle of equity and convergence enshrined within the FCCC, and get North-South cooperation moving through emissions trading (Nakicenovic, 1998).

Convergence

This approach sets a common per capita allocation for the inhabitants of all nations, regardless of their development status of any nation, with the intention that global emissions would result in stabilization of GHG concentrations. Accordingly under this common goal, developed nations must reduce emissions significantly from their current levels and developing nations will be able to increase their emissions up to the limit set by their total populations, thereby both North and South 'converge' on a common allocation. Such an approach is the most equitable arrangement to setting per capita allocations.

Practical Implications of the Entitlements Approach

An entitlements-based scheme offers many advantages over the market-based approaches currently being promoted through the international negotiation process, but its success would depend on resolving a number of potential problems through careful design. One of the most contentious problems is that of hot air trading. Hot air can become an issue of concern with any form of entitlements, especially in the case of countries that are unlikely to use up their emission entitlements in the near future. If they trade their unused amounts, this would amount to trading in 'hot air.' This problem can be taken care of by placing certain restrictions on their right to trade unused emissions, and allowing these countries to trade only those emissions that they would have produced had they not undertaken measures to improve energy efficiency or use zero-carbon sources.

Another difficulty with the entitlements approach is the apparent contradiction with the Kyoto Protocol. At present, the Protocol bases the industrialized countries' emissions reduction targets on the basis of their current emissions. In the event that developing countries based their emission reduction targets on equitable entitlements, the North and South would be pursuing different emissions reduction approaches. However, there is no compelling reason why North and South must follow identical routes, so that this contradiction can be resolved easily by accepting both principles. No nation would like to unravel the Kyoto Protocol as long as all agree that they will ultimately reach a convergence point. In this way, industrialized countries can start reducing emissions on the basis of their 1990 baseline, whereas developing countries can agree not to go beyond their 'emission entitlements' and undertake measures to moderate their emissions growth path using financial resources generated from emissions trading.

A lot of economic activities will relocate from developed countries to developing countries to escape the limits imposed in industrialized countries, argue various interest groups in industrialized countries (particularly the oil and automobile lobby in the U.S.). Because only industrialized countries (being Annex I nations) take on emission reduction commitments, the effectiveness of the FCCC measures will be greatly eroded. These interests fear that this 'leakage' will lead to economic and job loss in industrialized countries. Clearly, an effective set of emission reduction mechanisms needs to consider these particular problems and their complex implications.

A good indication of the potential of this problem is shown in a study which found that if the EU reduced its emissions by 20%, global emissions will not come down by the expected 3%, but only 0.7%. The reason why the benefits of reduction would not be realized was that nearly 70% of the advantage of EU's reduction would be lost through leakage (Pezzey, 1992).

Another dimension to the problem of 'leakage' involves the matter of 'embodied emissions,' which is when the production process for a particular good destined for export involves the release of GHGs. For example, one study has calculated that in 1990 there was 1.2 million tonnes of methane embodied in agricultural goods like rice, meat, and milk products imported by Germany, Japan, France, Canada, U.S., and the UK from developing countries (Subak, 1995). This is a substantial amount of methane, being about 7% of the emissions from livestock in the six importing countries. Indeed, it amounts to more than the total anthropogenic methane emissions produced by 103 countries out of 140 countries surveyed (Subak, 1995). It is reasonable to speculate that as Western nations reduce their agricultural subsidies and import tariffs, the livestock and crop production from developing countries will become more competitive, with the result that trade in methane-embodied products could increase.

One solution to this problem is to ensure that Western nations' GHGs inventories include the GHG emissions embodied in imported commodities, thereby avoiding the possibility of 'leakage' to non-participants, while being counted towards the developing nation's national reduction target. An alternative solution, and one that appears simpler more equitable, is to extend GHG emission targets to all countries participating in the climate convention. There is some evidence supporting this approach; for example a group of MIT modelers have shown that if developing countries begin participating in emissions control and reductions only after they reach a per capita income trigger of US$4,500, there will be considerable leakage (Jacoby et al, 1998). However, if participation occurs when per capita income is only US$3,000, then emissions leakage is greatly reduced (Jacoby et al, 1998). On the basis of these findings, it appears that developing countries should start participating sooner, rather than later. One clear advantage of a system of emission entitlements which allows trading of unused emission entitlements is that countries would be wary of allowing the entry of high GHG-emitting activities, thereby providing a strong disincentive against leakage.

That the tradable equitable emissions approach immediately engages developing countries and provides an incentive to keep emissions low is a great appeal of the concept. Unlike CEE countries and Russia, which cannot use their assigned amounts built on 1990 emissions because of their economic problems, developing countries are growing at a very rapid rate. And although developing country entitlements will be used up rapidly, it is unlikely that they will use up their entitlements in the potential to trade their unused entitlements. The effect of this provision would immediately provide an incentive to move towards a low emissions developmental path so that the benefits from emission trading can stay with them a long time. The trading system would provide sufficient financial resources and an "enabling economic environment for technology transfer" to take place, as indicated in article 10 of the Kyoto Protocol (Agarwal and Narain, 1998).

Some critics of the entitlements approach have cited population growth as a factor that destroys the effectiveness of the proposed scheme by altering the size of each nation's entitlement over time, especially where population is growing rapidly. Nations with stable populations could be arguably disadvantaged by this approach because there is a theoretical incentive for other nations to add to their population totals. By increasing their populations, nations would be entitled to increase their emissions over the years under a per capita entitlement scheme.

Such an argument is hardly realistic, for who would have more babies simply because they want to increase their emissions quota? In any event, this problem can be easily resolved by taking the global distribution of population at a given base year—ideally that of the year of the agreement. As a result, each nation's emission entitlement is fixed and if its population grows, then its per capita emissions entitlement will decline.

Ecological and Economic Effectiveness with Equity

International policy development to date has highlighted the antagonisms between economic interests and those of community, sustainability, and environment—yet there are ways in which economic factors can be used to respond effectively to the problems of global GHG emissions that are ecologically and socially desirable. Negotiations at the international level have devised a climate change policy response that is 'economically efficient.' Emissions trading, both at the project level under JI and CDM, and at the national inventory level under emissions trading, provides extremely cheap options for emissions reduction. Yet such economic efficiency comes only through a continuation of ecological damage. Least cost emissions reduction options are entirely in the carbon energy sector, but if nations seek only these options through flexmex, they will further lock countries into the carbon energy system. Climate change and its impacts can be kept to a minimum within the 21st century only by moving as rapidly as possible towards zero-carbon energy. The longer we delay this transition and allow countries, especially developing countries, to get locked into carbon energy systems, the longer it will take to get out of it. Ecological and social prospects in the 21st century will be determined by what happens in its first few decades.

Developing countries offer considerable opportunities for promotion of zero-carbon technologies, and equity and global solidarity demand an agreement based on the twin principles of equal per capita entitlements and convergence. Energy efficiency measures on the demand side are also extremely valuable for developing and developed nations because they will help reduce future investments required in renewable energy systems. Furthermore, reduced total energy demand in developed nations is essential if renewable energy systems are to assume the role of providing energy services currently based on carbon-based energy.

What is required is the effective pursuit of three related objectives: economic and ecological effectiveness; equity; and global solidarity— and putting these together to develop an action plan to keep climate change at tolerable levels. Equal per capita emission entitlements offer the most just, effective and 'meaningful' way of getting developing countries to engage with the climate change problem. These entitlements have the added advantage of providing developing countries with an incentive to keep their emissions growth path as low as possible, so that they have unused emissions to trade for financial gain. A study conducted by experts at MIT clearly shows that China keeps its emissions low as compared with the U.S. when an emissions trading regime is in place (Jacoby et al, 1998).

There can be a role for emissions trading, but it should be only used for projects that promote the zero-carbon energy system, and should not be allowed for projects that promote the carbon energy system. If CDM is used to influence emissions in projects where added costs are only in the range of 2-20% of the projects' costs, then a CDM project worth US$10 billion can influence energy projects worth as much as US$100-500 billion (Vrolijk, 1999). As a result, further support of these types of these energy projects will further lock the developing world into the carbon energy sector. CDM applied to carbon-based energy projects becomes a economic subsidy that further disadvantages renewable energy and will in all probability lock out renewables for an inordinately long time to prevent serious climate change. It is indeed ridiculous to subsidize the carbon energy system in order to prevent climate change.

CDM can be used, however, as an effective way to promote renewable energy and assist in the transition to a greatly reduced level of global GHG emissions. Renewable energy is not going to be the cheapest policy option for reducing emissions in the short term. While the U.S. is looking for least-cost options in the range of US$17-23/tC, solar thermal power plants will only produce reductions at a cost of US$64-82/tC, as Janet Yellen suggests. However, future renewable energy costs will be lower.

A study carried out by SEI for the World Bank estimates the additional capital cost of switching over from a coal-based power plant to a solar thermal power plant in India to be about US$0.532 million per MW of installed capacity. In other words, a CDM market worth US$25 billion alone can help to set up some 55,500 MW of solar power plants. Data presented in the 1999 *Annual Energy Outlook* of the U.S. Energy Information Administration shows that the capital cost of a photovoltaic power station over a coal-based power station is about US$41.81 million (in 1997 dollars). An input of US$25 billion will help to set up 16,500 MW of photovoltaic power plants, compared to the current cumulative capacity of less than 1000 MW. This will play a critical role in bringing down the world prices of solar cells.

As industrialized countries are already locked into a carbon system, they should invest in energy efficiency measures. But since the resources available through the emissions trade are going to be limited, they should be used in a catalytic manner for the first commitment period to help the cost of renewables to drop to a level that enables them to compete with carbon based technologies on their own. Once this happens, the fossil fuel era and the climate change problem comes to an end. It is also important to note that developing countries will undertake more and more energy efficiency measures as their economies grow and energy markets are liberalized and competition grows. Worldwide statistics already show that developing countries are culling energy subsidies, and energy efficiency in developing countries is already improving rapidly (World Energy Council, 1999; Brown et al, 1999).

According to the IIASA/WEC study, between 1990 and 1996, the commercial energy intensity decreased by 0.9% per year in South Asia—the best record of the world—and well beyond the expectations of even the environment-friendly case C of the IIASA model. Normally, the model would have expected primary energy intensity to increase because of the shift from traditional non-commercial fuels in the region, outweighing any improvements made in actual engineering or structures. Yet South Asian energy experts considered this achievement as far too little given what can be achieved, and given the enormous scope for further improvements which will take place even faster with improved economic growth (Nakicenovic et al, 1998: 222).

In Centrally Planned Asia and China, commercial energy intensities have decreased substantially by 6% per year despite high economic growth rates (Nakicenovic et al, 1998: 209-211). In Central and Eastern Europe, too, where the economy collapsed between 1989 and 1993, primary energy intensities have been falling with the onset of economic recovery (Nakicenovic et al, 1998: 193). In contrast, Western European and North American energy experts felt more satisfied with energy intensity improvements in their regions (Nakicenovic et al, 1998: 222). In the North American region (U.S. and Canada) primary energy intensity decreased by only 0.4% per year, even more slowly than expected in the case of the IIASA model (Nakicenovic et al, 1998: 156).

Therefore, if financial resources from emissions trading are limited, they should be focused mainly on the promotion of renewables because all the factors leading to increased market competition will lock renewables out.

Conclusion

The prospects of climate change are forcing the world to reconsider the way its uses fossil-fuel energy to drive its economy and to serve as the basis for the conventional models for economic and social development. Addressing the needs of developing nations and the environment necessitates a revised approach to the crisis of climate change and the adoption of strategies that feature renewable energy systems. Once the renewables strategy is accepted, the purpose of per capita emission entitlements also gets redefined. Its key purpose then is not to create a framework which forces all countries to converge to a sustainable level of emissions but to create a framework for engaging poor nations such that the world can kick start a movement towards a zero-carbon energy transition. Once the world seriously starts moving towards such a transition, the entitlements framework becomes increasingly redundant.

Extending the dominance of the carbon energy economy prolongs and worsens the problems it creates. Poor nations will demand adequate 'environmental space' for their growth, whereas industrialized countries will find it extremely difficult to reach the low levels of per capita emissions that are needed to restrain climate change. Highly industrialized nations cannot reduce their per capita carbon dioxide emissions without a major move towards zero-carbon energy systems. However, it is clear that such a move will require farsighted political leadership, not one that falls prey to the dinosaur-age oil and automobile industries.

Developing countries should not accept a response to climate change built on the principle of emissions trading in order to provide a lucrative opportunity to reduce emissions cheaply. Emissions trading cannot simply be carried out to achieve economic efficiency, but must be undertaken in an environment that also promotes ecological efficiency and social justice and global solidarity. The purpose of equity and an equal per capita entitlement principle is not to force industrialized countries to drastically curtail their economy. It is to create a framework for global cooperation so that the world can move as fast as possible towards a world economy that can keep on growing by using renewable energy. A three-pronged combination of emissions trading, equitable entitlements, and promotion of renewables thus constitutes a truly 'meaningful' plan of action and has the potential to ensure that these responses to climate change provide justice to all the world's peoples regardless of their national address and to the environment itself.

References

Agarwal, Anil and Sunita Narain. 1998. "Sharing the Air." *Down To Earth.* August 15.

Agarwal, Anil. 1997. "The Way of the West is Poison." *Time.*

Anderson, Denis. 1996. *Energy and Environment: Technical and Economic Possibilities.* Washington, D.C.: Finance and Development, IMF.

Anon. 1999. *"Clinton on Biomass Industry."* U.S. Information Service, New Delhi. Press Release.

_____. 1998. *National Environmental Policy Plan 3.* VRCM, The Hague.

Boden, T. A. et al. 1995. *Emissions of Global, Regional, and National Co2 Emissions from Fossil Fuel-Fuel Burning, Hydraulic Cement Production, and Gas Flaring: 1950-1992.* Oak Ridge, TN: Carbon Dioxide Analysis Center, Oak Ridge National Laboratory. Electronic database.

Bollen, Johannes et al. 1999. "Clubs, Ceilings and CDM: Macroeconomics of Compliance with the Kyoto Protocol." *The Energy Journal.* Kyoto Special edition. Volume 1:177-207.

Brown, Lester R. and Christopher Flavin. 1999. "A New Economy for a New Century." In Lester R. Brown et al. *State of the World 1999.* New York and London: W. W. Norton. pp. 3-21.

Chakravarty, Ujjayant et al. No date. *Extraction of Multiple Energy Resources and Global Warming.* University of Hawaii. Mimeograph.

Clinton, Bill. 1999. "Remarks by the President at Bio-energy Climate Event." U.S. Information Service, New Delhi. Press Release.

Flavin, Christopher and Seth Dunn. 1999. "Reinventing the Energy System." In Lester R. Brown et al. *State of the World 1999.* New York and London: W. W. Norton. pp. 22-40.

Gray, Tom. 1999. "Wind is Getting Stronger and on Course for the Next Decade." *Renewable Energy World.* Volume 3: 2.

IEA (International Energy Agency). 1998. *World Energy Outlook.* Paris: IEA.

IEA/OECD (International Energy Agency / Organization for Economic Cooperation and Development). 1997. *IEA Energy R&D Statistics 1974-1995.* Paris: IEA/OECD.

IPCC (Intergovernmental Panel on Climate Change). 1995. *Climate Change 1994: Radiative Forcing of Climate Change and an Evaluation of the IPCC IS92 Emissions Scenarios.* Cambridge, MA: Cambridge University Press.

_____. 1990. *IPCC First Assessment Report: Overview.* Geneva: WMO/UNEP.

Jacoby, Henry D. et al. 1998. "Toward a Useful Architecture for Climate Change Negotiations." Presented at the OECD Experts Workshop on Climate Change and Economic Modelling: Background Analysis for the Kyoto Protocol, Paris, September 17-18. Mimeograph.

Kartha, Sivan et al. 1998. "'Meaningful Participation' for the North and South." Presented at the SEI/CSE Workshop on Towards Equity and Sustainability in the Kyoto Protocol, Buenos Aires, November 8. Mimeograph.

Marland, Gregg et al. 1999. "Global, Regional, and National Carbon Dioxide Emission Estimares from Fossil Fuel Burning, Cement Production and Gas Flaring: 1751-1996." ORNL/CDIAC-90, NDP-030. Oak Ridge National Laboratory, Oak Ridge, TN.

Nakicenovic, Nebojsa, Arnulf Grubler, and Alan McDonald (eds). 1998. *Global Energy Perspectives.* Cambridge: Cambridge University Press.

OECD (Organization for Economic Cooperation and Development). 1998. *Energy Statistics and Balances in Non-OECD Countries.* Paris: OECD.

Origkeit, Janina and Joseph Alcamo. 1998. *Stabilisation Targets and Convergence of Per Capita Emissions, Workshop Report: First Answers Towards Buenos Aires.* Presented at the Seventh International Workshop on using Global Models to Support Climate negotiations. September. Mimeograph.

Pezzy, John. 1992. "Analysis of Unilateral Carbon Dioxide Control in the European Community and the OECD." *The Energy Journal.* Volume 13, Number 3: 159-172.

Priddle, Robert. 1999. "Energy and Sustainable Development." *IEA Bulletin.* Volume 41.

Subak, Susan. 1995. "Methane Embodied in the International Trade of Commodities: Implications for Global Emissions." *Global Environmental Change.* Volume 5, Number 5: 438-446.

The Economist. 1999a. "Stepping on the Gas." July 24: 19-20.

_____. 1999b. "Fuel Cells Meet Big Business." July 24: 59-60.

Tse, Kinping and Ujjayant Chakravarty. No date. *Transition from Fossil Fuel to Renewable Energy: Evidence from a Dynamic Simulation Model with Endogenous Resource Substitution.* University of Hawaii. Mimeograph.

UNDP (United Nations Development Programme). 1998. *Human Development Report 1998.* New York, NY: Oxford University Press. pp. 140-142.

USEIA (United States Energy Information Administration).1999. *Annual Energy Outlook.* Washington,DC: USDOE.

Vrolijk, Christian. 1999. "The Potential Size of the CDM." *Global Greenhouse Emissions Trader.* Geneva: UNCTAD. Issue 6.

WEC (World Energy Council). 1999. *Energy Production and Supply: Statistics.* Available online at: http://www.wec.co.uk

Part III

Expanding the Discourse

9

Ecosocialization and Environmental Justice

Nicholas Low and Brendan Gleeson

Introduction

The ethics of international political economy shape and are shaped by a process of 'socialization' of the nexus of economic relationships of 'the global economy'—or, in the terminology of an earlier age, of 'capital.' We shall argue that environmental injustice occurs in the process of unequal exchange in which commodities are produced from nature. In this chapter we consider whether a new form of socialization can be constituted around the principle of ecologically sustainable development, and what part environmental justice may play in its ethical framework.

We picture ethical discourse as part of a wider social historical canvas. The picture we see painted today is not one in which ethics sits decoratively atop a structural edifice of human relations created by class and capital as Marx portrayed. Nor do we see ethics as the foundation of all political freedom and market relations as Hayek (1944: 20-22) argued. Rather, we see ethical discourse as participating centrally in a drama of social relations and historical struggle: ethics as dialectic (Bhaskar, 1993). The struggle has an ethical dimension in which people construct the assumptions which fire political action, and on which they base the governance of the institutions, which in turn rule their lives.

We position our own work (Low and Gleeson, 1998a and b; Gleeson and Low, 2001) in relation to two very different texts which also depict this wider canvas: those of Daly (1996) and van der Pijl (1998). These authors depict the global economy as today threatening to over-reach its physical and social limits (Daly, 1996) or 'exhausting' its natural and social substrata (van der Pijl, 1998). Though the point of departure of the two authors varies, these precepts form a common 'pre-analytic vision': that the system through which we produce, consume and exchange goods and services, the economy, is supported by a natural ecosystem which provides the economy's resource inputs and accommodates its waste outputs, and a human society which makes the economy politically possible, in that people obey certain rules. The economy, these authors argue, is an open subsystem of a social and ecological system of limited capacity. Socialization is the term used to explain the institutional adaptation of the economy to its social and ecological conditions. Socialization is the constantly shifting outcome of social struggle. It is not necessarily always a benign and protective outcome.

In the first section of the chapter we explain the concept of socialization, the role that ethics play within it, and how the recent discourses of 'sustainable development' and 'environmental justice' define a new turn in the struggle for socialization, with an outcome as yet unrealized, which we might call 'ecosocialization'. In the second part we re-examine the ethic of environmental justice in the light of ecosocialization. We follow the conceptual route laid out in earlier work (Low and Gleeson, 1998a: Chapter 7) in which justice is conceived as a dialectic.

Socialization and Sustainable Development

The idea of socialization (*Vergesellschaftung*) is reviewed at some length by van der Pijl (1998). Drawing on the work of Karl Marx, Max Weber, and Karl Polanyi, van der Pijl charts the continuing metamorphosis of capital as it encounters limits of commodification and checks on accumulation.

Van der Pijl conceives of socialization as "the planned or otherwise normatively unified interdependence of functionally divided social activity" (1998: 15). A market society works through myriad adjustments of individual households and firms to each other's acts of production and consumption. In this sense there is no direct steering of production and consumption on the part of an agency acting on behalf of the collective. Social activity is 'functionally divided'. Yet there also have to be some rules for this game, otherwise the adjustment process by which individuals accommodate to one another's behavior could not take place efficiently and productively.

Standards, rules, or guidelines (forms of 'normative unification') are needed to co-ordinate production, consumption, and exchange. An example given by van der Pijl of socialization at one level is the series of steps taken by a British machine tool manufacturer to prepare for the conversion of its product line to the metric system following the 1965 decision of the British Government to adhere to the international measurement standard. In this example, the major goal is to coordinate British production with world markets for British machine tools (van der Pijl, 1998: 15). This may seem a rather pedestrian example, but the adoption, dissemination, and enforcement of production standards is just one small part of an extensive normative structure which includes policies, targets, accounting measures, and ultimately, ethical precepts.

Being prepared to abide by rules for the coordination of an industry is one kind of normative unification: the assumption that everyone benefits from a rule which applies to all. In a more traditional sense, shared ideas of justice-of rights, deserts, and needs-bind people together in society. "Justice," Adam Smith observes in *The Theory of Moral Sentiments*, "is the greatest pillar that holds up the whole edifice. If it is removed, the great, the immense fabric of society ... must in a moment crumble into atoms" (1759: 86). Bellah et al (1985: 253) remind us that the founders of the American republic believed that 'republican government ... could only survive if animated by a spirit of virtue and concern for the public good." These authors argue that it is the spirit of community within American society, less celebrated than rugged individualism, that holds American society together. "Generosity of spirit is thus the ability to acknowledge an interconnectedness-one's 'debts to society'- that binds one to others whether one wants to accept it or not" (Bellah et al, 1985: 253). In the 1950s, this sense of mutual concern was institutionalized in welfare systems based upon need: a governance system sometimes termed 'corporate liberalism' (van der Pijl, 1998: 63). Polanyi (1957: 76) argued that a framework of social protection accompanied the spread of capitalism: "a network of measures and policies was integrated into powerful institutions designed to check the action of the market relative to labor, land, and money."

The transformation of global capitalism in the 1980s and 90s by 'neoliberalism,' however, is no less a process of socialization accompanied by normative precepts. Here are a few: every value is a preference; no person's preference is to count more than anyone else's; preferences are generated within the individual; preferences are made effective by money in markets; the greatest satisfaction of preferences in aggregate is the aim of public policy; in a market no-one distributes wealth, wealth accrues as a result of the many choices made by individuals; individuals are responsible for and must accept the consequences of the choices they make; individuals are entitled to the property they legitimately acquire; taxation is theft— in short, the ethic of property rights and micro-economic rationality.

The onset of economic stagnation accompanied by inflation in the late 1960s, the flight of capital from the industrial heartland into new territories of cheap labor, the consequent breakdown of the Bretton Woods accord, and the unraveling of the 'welfare state' paved the way for the assertion of the new 'truth' of neo-liberalism. The limited 'social protection' of the New Deal and the Marshall Plan which had functioned well for two decades to stimulate economic growth was seen to have weakened the discipline of capital over labor. That discipline had to be restored if non-inflationary economic growth was to continue: "The core of the new concept of control which expressed the restored discipline of capital, neo-liberalism, resides in raising micro-economic rationality to the validating criterion for all aspects of social life." (van der Pijl, 1998: 129).

If the threats to the social substratum, prevalent from the early 19th century and erupting in Depression and War in the 20th, provoked an impulse of *social* protection, we might expect the threat to the natural substratum to provoke an impulse of *environmental* protection culminating in the idea of ecologically sustainable development (ESD). For about thirty years, following an accumulation of evidence of threats to the environment from economic growth, there has indeed been a movement in that direction. But that impulse appears to have been checked by neo-liberalism and by the mobilization of reactionary pressures in support of interests vested in traditional industrial production technologies (in particular the fossil fuel industry and its dependent industries).

Prades (1999), looking to Durkheim, argues that the critique of the 'spirit of capitalism' will give birth to an ethic of sustainable development governing the economy, which will in turn change society's 'totemic principle.' The latter is the term Durkheim used for the 'sacred' at the heart of ethics (Durkheim, 1976 [1912]). Renewal of the totemic principle involves a change at the core of modern life, that is to say a change in what is 'sacred', a move away form 'particularistic individualism.' The result is a change in functional solidarity, or 'the compulsory functional interdependence which links and integrates the forces and resources of every human society' (Prades, 1993: 7-18).

Certainly renewal of religious experience on the revelation of the Earth's fragile ecology is sometimes discussed in sober journals (see, for example Levine, 1994; Booth, 1999). But society and economy are *already* functionally integrated, and by a discipline and ideology far from ecologically sustainable (Falk, 2001). A number of scholars from both Left and Right depict a gloomy scenario for the impact of current tendencies in world capitalism on the human and natural environment (see Martin and Schumman, 1997; Athanasiou, 1998; and Gray, 1998). Our own work suggests that the adoption of the agenda of the 1992 earth summit (United Nations Conference of Environment and Development) 'Agenda 21' around the world has been quite limited and patchy (Low et al, 2000; Low, 1999).

Luke (2000) for example, argues that environmentalism as an international force has suffered in the U.S.A. from the national mood of resistance to globalization. Lake (2000) points out that in the U.S.A. very few municipalities have adopted Local Agenda 21 plans and of those few, the underlying motives have little to do with sustainable development. In the developing world, sustainable development is little more than a rhetorical smokescreen for business as usual, and in some relatively advanced peripheral countries like Australia, the rhetorical is all that remains of sustainable development as a policy driver (Christoff and Low, 2000). Market environmentalism, imposing micro-economic rationality as the 'validating criterion' for environmental protection, seems today to be rapidly supplanting every other logic in the project of sustainable development (see Low and Gleeson, 1998a: 160-68).

According to van der Pijl's interpretation of the process of socialization, the gradual transformation of the world economy takes place both as a result of struggles from below and initiatives from above. The two are not necessarily concatenated. Pressures generated by groups outside the state form either within nations or at a global level ('globalization from below' in Falk's (1996) terms). They may reinforce or counteract planning by global elites. Examples are the environmental justice movement in the United States, the 1995 mass movement in France against a program of 'disciplinary neo-liberalism', the popular revolt against genetic modification of food in Britain, movements against agribusiness in India, against ecological destruction by Shell in Nigeria and by the Australian multinational Broken Hill Proprietary (BHP) in Papua New Guinea (van der Pijl, 1998: 49; Low and Gleeson, 1998b; and Shiva, 1999).

Van der Pijl shows how the 'cadre' stratum, consisting of global planners, consultants and functionaries, plays a central role in coordinating socialization. Thus he writes: "The cadres have all along tended to adopt positions which look beyond the straight class antagonism ... the cadres are the class that historically performs the role of shaping the structures for a classless society in the context of a class society (van der Pijl, 1998:165). He recounts the role of international economic planning groups in forging a ruling class consensus on the management of the global economy. For example, the Bilderberg Conferences were instrumental from 1952 in setting in motion long term planning for 'corporate liberalism': they "assembled in the spirit of corporate liberalism, representatives of Right and Left, capital and organized labor" (van der Pijl, 1998: 121). Subsequently, the Mont Pèlerin Society and its offshoots did for neo-liberalism what Bilderberg had done for corporate liberalism (see Cockett, 1995: 129-43). For van der Pijl, planning must look beyond short-term class interest, even though the instruments used (markets, prices, and state regulation) are compatible with existing class society. Indeed, "humanity will only survive if ... a classless society, a planetary community of fate, *replaces* the capitalist one" (van der Pijl, 1998: 165, our emphasis).

In summary, we conclude that there are certain necessary conditions for the evolution of socialization away from neo-liberalism. These conditions are:

- The growing certainty of the threat of human damage to the earth's ecology (the natural substratum),

- The continuation of struggles outside the state directed both at changing the discourse of growth and development—the limits of market environmentalism have to be exposed—and at winning contests where growth projects are pitted against local opposition seeking to protect local environments,

- The existence both of material technologies, institutional structures, and organizational techniques geared to the principle of sustainable development; the latter, in particular, grounded in a changed and renewed ethical system, and

- Planning initiatives on the part of international elites at the core of government of the global economy.

The scientific study of the human impact upon the environment has made rapid advances. Despite attempts to present anthropogenic climate change as controversial 'theory' rather than consensual 'fact'

(Gelbspan, 1997), the weight of evidence of evidence continues to suggest the reverse: that the facts, on which the majority of climate scientists are agreed, are opposed by a very few 'theorists.' We will not comment here on the popular struggles which continually erupt over environmental issues, or on the mobilization of organizations in global civil society (see Wapner, 1996). At the global level there is no ruling class economic planning organization for sustainable development comparable with Bilderberg or even the Mont Pèlerin Society. The Club of Rome which might have fulfilled that function appears to have been marginalized, and the World Business Council for Sustainable Development (WBCSD) does not seem to be thinking of a major shift away from neo-liberal orthodoxy. The members of the WBCSD are transnational corporations whose profits stem from large scale, unsustainable exploitation of the environment. Athanasiou (1998: 241) comments: "A small group of upper executives, many of them heads of major corporations with criminal environmental and social records, have signed on to a public relations manifesto that is notable only for its recognition of the need for reformed business practices more sensitive to the demands of efficiency and waste reduction."

At the level of the state, the work of institutes concerned to develop policy on the basis of ecological sustainability is laying some of the foundations for eco-socialization. The work of the Rocky Mountain Institute in the U.S.A. and the Wuppertal Institute in Germany engages directly with economic growth and interests of business. Their aim is to develop both the production technologies and the normative structures necessary to shape an economy around the concept of ecologically sustainable development. Their message is upbeat and optimistic: "We can accomplish everything we do today as well as now, or better, with one-quarter of the energy and materials we presently use" (von Weizacker et al, 1997: xxi). The SuE model developed by the Wuppertal Institute is a decision support tool for measuring flows of materials and resources, a 'tool for examining the overall impact of specific policies upon an economy" (Spangenberg et al, 1998: 25), and targets for resource productivity. Of sustainability, Spangenberg (2001: 39) writes, "It is a new, integrated, ethically based normative system of rules". Methods of resource efficiency accounting are being developed using the concept of 'material intensity per unit of service': MIPS (Orbach and Liedtke, 1998). The United Nations Development Program (1999: 7) calls for a reinvention of global governance, including "a global code of conduct for multinational corporations and a global forum for their monitoring" (UNEP, 1999: 100). Even the OECD is now examining the debate on the environmental effects of free trade (Scheicher, 1997; Adams, 1997). The environmental question is beginning to find its way into some orthodox economics spheres (Krugman, 1999: 167-172; OECD, 1997). In 1997, 2500 economists, including Nobel laureates Robert Solow and Kenneth Arrow, signed a 'Statement on Climate Change' calling for serious measures to limit the emission of greenhouse gases. Krugman argues for a 'green tax shift' in which the burden of taxation is placed on polluting activities without the overall scale of taxation increasing.

If we are able to detect the beginnings of eco-socialization, what part will environmental justice play in its further development? For the Wuppertal Institute, social justice is one of the pillars of sustainable development. But it has yet to be shown that social justice is *necessarily*, and not contingently, related to ecological sustainability. Rather, as Falk (2001: 222) observes, it is not difficult to conceive of a world whose economy is geared to ecological sustainability without it being in the least 'humane': "One could easily believe in the prospects for the emergence of an authoritarian control system imposed on the world so as to preserve unequal access to resources in the face of intensified scarcities and environmental decay" (Falk, 2001.). How, then, might we conceive of the relationship between ecologically sustainable development as a mode of socialization and environmental justice?

Sustainable Development and Environmental Justice

If socialization entails 'normatively unified interdependence' then 'eco-socialization', following Daly's thinking, entails a transformation of the economy to deliver a just distribution of environmental values among inhabitants of the earth now living (geographical justice), and a just distribution of those values to population over time into the future (intergenerational justice).

The three central perceptions of Daly's 'economics of sustainable development,' however, are not normative but factual. The first is that the environment is not outside the economy but rather passes through, and is transformed by, the economy. The second is that the physical capacity of the environment is limited and thus 'scarce.' Moreover, it is scarce in a particularly rigorous sense, in that no more of it can be created. We cannot create or add to the environment, we can only change it. Usually that means degrading it, simplifying it, and subjecting it to entropy. The third is that the rate of growth of today's global economy is rapidly approaching the limits of the capacity of the environment to supply inputs without depletion, and absorb waste outputs. Together, these perceptions form Daly's 'pre-analytic vision.'

The economy, in Daly's vision, is a process of transformation of nature, and as he reminds us (following Georgescu-Roegen, 1971), it is a physical process subject to the laws of thermodynamics. Ultimately there is only one renewable input: the sun's radiation. There is no outlet for waste from the earth. The economic process is an 'entropic flow' in which useful matter is transformed into less useful 'waste' (Altvater, 1993). It is also a spatial and a temporal process. The input to the process comes from somewhere and the waste goes somewhere. The input occurs at a particular time, the waste accumulates at a particular rate. The production of every commodity transforms a piece of the environment somewhere at some time as it passes through the economy.

If we cannot produce something without transforming a piece of the environment, then it makes sense to include that piece of the environment *as part of* the commodity. As Schmidt-Bleek puts it, the commodity carries an ecological rucksack (backpack) consisting of all the material that has to be shifted around in order to produce it (Schmidt-Bleek, 1994). The gold ring on your finger carries a rucksack that weighs three tonnes. The three billion tonnes of coal the world burns every year carry a rucksack of fifteen billion tonnes of material shifted, plus about ten billion tonnes of carbon dioxide waste (von Weizsaacker et al, 1997: 243). Of course there are many less tangible environmental values used up in the process of production which ought to be included in the rucksack: production of *toxic* waste, damage to species habitat, deforestation, damage to the land, rivers, seas, and atmosphere.

Given such a perception of the facts of the economy, how does this effect ethics? We are accustomed to assuming that commodities belong to someone and that the environment belongs to no-one or to everyone. This assumption is not a physical fact but an artifice of the institution of property. Under this artifice, ownership of something confers a set of rights over that thing which amounts to sovereignty over it. But sovereignty demands clear boundaries. We have to be certain where the thing over which sovereignty is exercised begins and ends, otherwise there can be no unambiguous definition of sovereignty and we cannot judge among the rights of different persons over the use of the thing. The environment cannot be subjected to the artifice of property in the same way, for environments have no clear boundaries. Nor do environments belong exclusively to particular persons.

Even so, we can still use the term 'belongs to' *without* evoking property rights. 'Belongs to' in this non-proprietorial sense means being effected by and having a relationship with, being constituted by. 'Be mine tonight', as the song goes, does not invite the partner to become 'my property,' but to enter into a relationship of mutual care. Let us call this the 'constitutive' sense of the word 'belong.' In a very similar way, when we talk about 'our labor,' as Marx and Engels pointed out, that labor constitutes ourselves. Similarly, as we have argued, the environment is constitutive of the self (Low and Gleeson, 1998a: 148). In this sense the environment always belongs to someone, existing in some place at some time. So the flow of commodities through an economic process of transformation takes with it chunks of people's environments. The gold ring contains a proportion of the environment shifted and destroyed to get at the gold. The newspaper contains a proportion of the old growth forest that supplied the woodchips to make the paper. Each liter of petrol consumed contains a portion of the atmosphere used up as a sink. This is the implication of Daly's and Schmidt-Bleek's vision.

Does this vision logically necessitate an ethical change? One may still say that the people, part of whose environment is destroyed to manufacture a gold ring, were willing to exchange that part for the commodities that it becomes possible to buy with the money gained in wages from sacrificing the environment. Saying that, however, conflates the senses of the word 'belong.' It assumes that the environment which 'belongs to' people in the constitutive sense also 'belongs to' them in the proprietorial sense. Of course it does not. What is occurring, and it has been for centuries, is that the environment which belongs to the people in a constitutive but non-proprietorial sense is being expropriated for nothing and incorporated into commodities. Because the environment belongs to no-one (proprietorially) it can be taken at no cost and incorporated into commodities which belong to particular people proprietorially. One class of people and one part of the world have benefited enormously from this process at the expense of the environment of another class and other parts of the world. There is an environmental injustice at the core of the process of economic transformation.

This point is reinforced by T. W. Pogge (1994) who argues for a compensatory 'global resource tax' levied on all consumers of the environment, but of course impinging most heavily on those who consume most—the populations of the affluent countries. Such a tax is justified to fund a 'global resource dividend' whose aim is to guarantee that basic human needs—for food, clothing, and shelter—are met for all people in the world. According to Pogge, such a tax is justified because affluent populations participate in a single system of world economic institutions which generates avoidable poverty, because the affluent derive material benefits from the use of natural resources without compensation for the destruction of the environments of the poor, and because radical inequality is the result of a historical process of environmental exploitation infused with violence and crime—colonialism, slavery, and genocide.

Assuming that the environment belongs to all people in a constitutive sense, to whom does it belong? This is not an easy question to answer. We might say that the atmosphere, for example, belongs to the whole population of the earth. But the climate which the atmosphere creates belongs differently to different people in different parts of the globe. From where we sit the temperate climate of the city of Melbourne belongs to us here. No-one has a right to change 'our' climate! But 'us' *when*? Us now living or us extended over some indefinite time period? Does 'us here' include the rest of the living beings in this area? Which living beings are to be included? Ethical questions arise which we will not attempt to answer here.

To approach these questions Daly advocates a number of steps. The first is to separate out what he regards as three problems of economics, and distinguish clearly between problems of justice and problems of efficiency (Daly, 1996: 159-160):

> We have three economic problems to consider: allocation, distribution, and scale. *Allocation* refers to the apportioning of resources among alternative product uses—food, bicycles, cars, medical care. An allocation is efficient if it corresponds to effective demand, that is, the relative preferences of the citizens as weighted by their relative incomes, both taken as given. An inefficient allocation will use resources to produce a number of things that people will not buy, and will fail to produce other things that people would buy if only they could find them. It would be characterized by shortages of the latter and surpluses of the former. *Distribution* refers to the apportioning of the goods produced (and the resources they embody) among different people (as opposed to different commodities). Distributions are just or injust; allocations are efficient or inefficient. There is an efficient allocation for each distribution of income. Scale refers to the physical size of the economy relative to the ecosystem...

> *Scale* may be sustainable or unsustainable. An efficient allocation does not imply a just distribution. Neither an efficient allocation nor a just distribution, nor both implies a sustainable scale.

This is the response of the welfare economist. The problem of distribution and the problem of scale are both matters where injustice occurs. If the environment is an absolutely scarce resource, a resource that we cannot create any more of, then there is no possibility of applying the convenient fiction of Pareto optimality—a situation of change from the present in which no-one is worse off, but at least one other person is better off. If someone is better off, under Daly's environmental assumptions, someone else is worse off. Scale is a problem of intergenerational justice, distribution is a problem of geographical or intragenerational justice. These problems of justice cannot be resolved by the market. They must be resolved politically. Daly, however, assumes that there can be a political resolution and then the market can be left to get on with the work of efficient allocation. The political system should regulate the total scale of the economy. This regulation should result in the issue of 'permits' to use the environment, for example by using the atmosphere as a sink for waste CO_2. The political system then distributes the permits justly. Then trading occurs in a market for permits to ensure the efficient allocation of environmental use. "The tradable permits idea is truly a paradigm for many sensible policies" (Daly, 1996: 56).

While this approach is appealing compared with that of neo-liberalism (which simply dispenses with politics as far as possible: micro-economic rationality being the validating criterion for all aspects of social life), there are the familiar problems with it. First, political power cannot be separated from economic power. Those who hold the purse strings are predominantly the multinational corporations, the growth of whose power, and their capacity to range all over the globe, assisted the rise of the neo-liberal ideology in the first place. Second, a market facilitates the concentration of power by means which are not subject to market logic. Chance and luck, manipulation of information, violence, theft, and every conceivable misuse of government rules all create concentrations of whatever is traded (such as money or permits). The process of distribution cannot be decided once and for all, or even fifty years at a putative jubilee (see Daly, 1996: 206-7 and The Old Testament: Leviticus Ch. 25).

Distribution by political means must be a continuous process of rebalancing the contingent imbalances which occur in the course of trading.

Hence Pogge's proposal for a tax. Third, while it might be desirable on grounds of efficiency to let resources be allocated by markets with private ownership of production, government ownership has sometimes been used more efficiently than regulation to correct the injustices of distribution (Self, 1993: 253-261).

Daly is surely right, however, in claiming that incentive systems, such as those that typically operate in markets, must have at least as important a place as regulatory (or 'command') systems in an ecologically sustainable and socially just society. This was once the wisdom of the 'mixed economy.' The proposition that there is no alternative between a pure market economy and the regulatory 'Road to Serfdom' of a 'command economy' is part of the rhetoric of neo-liberal politics, not good economics or good public administration.

Arguing that questions of justice should be decided outside market logic does not, of course, tell us anything about what constitutes *just* distribution. Here Daly appeals to common sense founded on the concept of community and the Christian religion. A certain level of distribution inequality is desirable to reflect the need for the incentive to work and commensurate reward for 'irksome' work (Daly, 1996: 210). But there must, in Daly's view be a limit to inequality. If private property is justified on the grounds that it encourages freedom and responsibility and protects individuals against the collective abuse of power, then property must be distributed as widely as possible. The limit to inequality cannot be fixed definitely but the important thing is to recognize the need for a limit. He suggests a factor of ten between the lowest and highest individual incomes. On the crude measure of GDP ($US) per capita the poorest countries hardly changed between 1900 and 1992, while the richest grew by a factor of about four. The disparity between the richest and poorest grew from a factor of about seven in 1900 to a factor of 30 in 1992. For simplicity, the calculation is based on the United States ($4096 per capita GDP in 1900, $21,558 in 1992), and Bangladesh ($581 per capita GDP in 1900 and $720 in 1992), see Table 1.

Daly also points out that the founders of liberalism, David Ricardo and Adam Smith, developed their key concepts ('comparative advantage,' 'invisible hand') against the background assumption that the interests of property owners lay in the prosperity and stability of a national community (1996: 152-3). It was never the intention of either theorist that their ideas should be used in justification of a globalized world of absolute advantage in which, through free trade, capital would flow to the places where wages were lowest and restrictions on industry to protect society and nature least. The unit of community is the nation—the unit in which there are institutions and traditions of collective action, responsibility, and mutual help, and the unit in which government tries to carry out policy for the good of all its citizens equally (Daly, 1996: 165-6).

Daly's ethic does not constitute a coherent logical structure. It is rather a mix of appeals to different sources of ethics. There exist different ethical discourses, each logically consistent in its own terms and giving some access to the truth of our human condition, but conflicting with each other. We cannot see how it is now, or will ever be, possible or desirable to contain ethical discourse within a single logical framework, a foundational system. Rather our view is of ethics as a dialectic. Other theorists have proposed different versions of this dialectic (Davy, 1997; Tully, 2001). The problem, as we have argued, is not the diversity of ethical discourses, but the disappearance of ethical discourse under the cloak of a miserable utilitarianism equipped with an absurdly diminished conception of the self. If all that we are is constituted by some sort of internal homunculus generating preferences, then the best that we can hope for is indeed a mechanism such as the market to negotiate this diminished version of self-interest without resorting to violence. We do not accept such a premise.

Table 1
Richest and Poorest Countries in 1820, 1900, and 1992
in GDP per Capita (1990 US$)

1820		1900		1992	
Richest		Richest		Richest	
UK	1756	UK	4593	USA	21,558
Netherlands	1561	New Zealand	4320	Switzerland	21,036
Australia	1528	Australia	4229	Japan	19,425
Austria	1295	USA	4096	Germany	19,351
Belgium	1291	Belgium	3652	Denmark	18,293
Poorest		Poorest		Poorest	
Indonesia	614	Myanmar	647	Myanmar	748
India	531	India	625	Bangladesh	720
Bangladesh	531	Bangladesh	581	Tanzania	601
Pakistan	531	Egypt	509	Congo	353
China	523	Ghana	462	Ethiopia	300

Source: United Nations Development Programme. 1999. *Human Development Report.* New York, NY: United Nations. Figure 1.6, page 38.

Accepting that debate on ethical principles is not only unavoidable but something to be valued as essential to humanity, we have to find a way of usefully promoting ethical debate. People mostly do not debate ethics for the purpose only of exercising their minds. The ethic has to lead somewhere and have some practical effect. There are certain desiderata of a practical ethics which we discuss more fully elsewhere (Low and Gleeson, 1998: Chap. 8). For example, a practical ethics must not devolve into a simple relativism. If every position is accepted simply because someone asserts it, there can be no argument, but only counterposed assertions. We expect debates to have an outcome leading to action, therefore the debate must find temporary closure so that decisions may be taken. The debate must be open-ended, containing the possibility of learning from the practical results of having taken a decision. The debate on the level of principle gives rise to practical judgments in particular cases. Likewise particular judgments lead to reflection on principles. The judgments must be implemented, otherwise the debate will have no practical effect and there can be no possibility of learning from experience. What these desiderata amount to is a politics of governance. But if environmental justice is to become part of this politics, then the form of governance in the world has to change.

Environmental Justice and Environmental Governance

We have argued that global governance is already a reality (Low and Gleeson, 1998: 175-8). A similar and more empirically grounded argument is put forward by van der Pijl (1998: 160-1). In his analysis, global governance, an outcome of class struggle and transnational planning, is the form of normative integration in which rating agencies and international consultancies channel the transfer of micro-economic rationality across regions and between private and public sectors: "It is our thesis that in this process of synchronizing socialization and institutional behavior under the discipline of capital, consultancies and their equivalents are in effect laying the groundwork for a system of *global governance* ... By this term, we understand the worldwide integration of economic, social, and political organization into a mediated complex of state and quasi-state authority" (van der Pijl, 1998: 163, author's emphasis), in short, *neo-liberal* governance. Under neo-liberal global governance the burden of distribution of environments (good and bad) falls increasingly to micro-economic rationality: poor people are to have poor environments, the environments of the poor are transformed into the commodities of the rich (irrespective of their membership of a nation-state) who are able politically to protect the high quality of their environments (Harvey, 1996; Bullard, 1999).

Micro-economic rationality is opposed by the principle of 'nationhood' and even more by democracy. In contrast with the principle of micro-economic rationality (in which one dollar is one vote in the market place), democracy, based on the idea of national community, is a practical instance of the principle that every person is to have equal resources. Nor is it to say that the principle applies with equal force in every democracy. Its application is determined by the widely varying balance of political and economic powers, dominant beliefs and existing institutions within each nation.

Under neo-liberal governance, the nation state and its government has yielded much of its power to regulate the economy for the benefit of its citizens, regulation which includes both social and environmental protection (see also Falk, 2001). While global oversight of the world economy has been strengthened by organizations such as the World Trade Organisation, the IMF, and regular summit meetings of national and business leaders, transnational authority for protection of the global environment remains a weak congeries of internationally negotiated agreements lacking binding force. The problem is not so much the weakness on the part of the institutions at either global or national levels, but of an unbalanced mix of weaknesses and strengths at both levels. The nation state has plenty of strength to assist the interests of transnational corporations, but not so much strength to assist new businesses exploiting new technologies that may be helpful to environmental conservation. Likewise, global governance is strong in promoting interests vested in the existing global economy and weak in changing the direction of that economy.

In those nations (typically European) where the principle of national solidarity and democracy has most strongly opposed micro-economic rationality, there remains a resistance to the spread of the latter into the social and environmental spheres. Protection of the environment is viewed as a matter for the state to undertake on behalf of the national community. As van der Pijl observes, in the later 1990s there was a resurgence of support in Europe for reassertion of the protective role of the state (van der Pijl, 1998: 164):

> The 'Socialists', representing the fraction of cadres with a background in the state and international organisation ... are seeking to contain the untrammeled forces of private

capital spearheaded by the management consultants, in order to maintain a degree of social cohesion.

By the turn of the century, however, this movement appears to have reached a stalemate, blocked by the market logic imposed by transnational economic governance. It seems unlikely to us that substantial progress can be made towards ecosocialization without a move towards democracy enshrining the principle of equal citizenship at a global level. What is needed is increased authority to pursue social and environmental goals at the national level, and increased authority to harmonize these goals at the global level.

Can this be done without change to global institutions? Dryzek (1999) and others (Lipschutz, 1995; Wapner, 1996) have argued that the study of and struggle for democracy should be focused on civil society rather than the state, and on changing discourses, ideas, rather than changing institutions. Dryzek observes that "Discourses are intertwined with institutions, if formal rules constitute institutional hardware, then discourses constitute institutional software" (Dryzek, 1999: 269). Dryzek recommends attention to the software rather than to the hardware. He argues that to create anything resembling a state at global level would be at best counterproductive: "State-like systems at the global level would be guided by all the economic imperatives that currently constrain states organized at the national level" (Dryzek, 1999: 277).

The process of socialization, we believe, requires struggles 'from below,' in civil society, outside the state, over the discourses of environmentalism and justice. But it also requires action within the state on the institutional rules of governance. At global level there is no state, but there are structures of governance and rules governing the behavior of actors in the global economy. These structures should be the target of struggle from below. Or let us put the matter another way about: it would be absurd to keep the economic rules off the environmental agenda, when it is precisely these rules that are damaging the environment, inhibiting the possibility of ecological sustainability and generating social injustice. While the power of discourse must certainly be engaged, part of that discourse will surely be about the rules of economic governance. One example of this is the campaign waged in 1998 over the Internet against the Multilateral Agreement on Investment. The latter was an attempt on the part of national and international and national bureaucrats, hand in glove with transnational corporations, to change the rules of trade. It was successfully resisted, but the struggle over the rules continues.

State-like institutions grow because they are needed. The objection that state-like institutions always favor economic over environmental and social development can be met by creating and empowering institutions with specific purpose, such as that of protecting the environment. Such institutions would be state-like in that they would represent the common interest in the environment of humankind, perhaps with the addition of advocates of future generations and non-humans, but they would counterbalance existing economic institutions.

The failure to have state-like institutions at global levels tells us much about our failure to express community feeling at that level. Why should we not conceive of a global community: a 'community of communities' as cosmopolitanism proposes? The world has changed irreversibly since Neville Chamberlain could say of Czechoslovakia before the Second World War: "It is a faraway country of which we know little." Multilateral intervention in state affairs on ethical grounds is now a well-established fact: in Somalia, Rwanda, Kuwait, Cambodia, Kosovo, Timor and now Afghanistan. The action has been alloyed with national interests, it has often been crude, violent, and less than successful, but cynicism about these actions seems unwarranted. The fact that political leaders of democracies can take such action, spend large amounts of public money, and get public applause for it suggests that there is a feeling of 'global community' abroad today. The problem is that we do not have the institutional means to give it appropriate expression, and for this we need more global state-like institutions, institutions with the authority of representative democracy.

Finally, rules enacted by authoritative state-like institutions have a particular role in coordinating civil society in a just manner. The 'rule of law' posits transparent rule sets applying equally to all. Economic actors have an interest in ensuring that they apply to all so that fair competition occurs. Such rules provide the market with its political context. If, as Daly argues, questions of environmental and ecological justice are to be desired politically, then we must have the authoritative institutions wherein debates can occur and decisions can be made. It should be made clear today that, such is the scope of environmental problems, the nation state (though still necessary) is not sufficient for their resolution.

These arguments should not be construed as a demand for comprehensive world government, even a government equipped with the highly developed checks and balances that Falk, Mendlovitz, and Kim built in to their preferred model for world order (Falk, 1975). Hempel concludes his discussion of the prospects for global environmental governance with these words (1996: 176-77):

> Utopian as it may seem, a constitutionally based world federation that can link communities and regions, without decimating or strengthening nation states, may be the only way to ensure that the policy and institutional responses needed for effective global environmental governance do not undermine the world's growing but fragile impulse for democracy.

Hempel may well turn out to be right, but our view of how the world will arrive at such a federal system is a little different. A federation may be the eventual, but highly contingent, outcome of a process of democratization of global institutions of global governance. This democratization will occur because of the need for increased authority of existing institutions, which in turn arises because of a growing appreciation of the environmental threat to humanity from continued quantitative economic growth according to the existing pattern. To propose a fully developed concept of comprehensive global government, however democratic, is to suggest a process of institutional design that is unlikely to occur short of world revolution. Socialization is a more incremental process. To think about global governance in terms of socialization removes its utopian character and by definition focuses attention on the political process. At the same time it leads us away from analyzing the stupefying complexity of a policy-making process for the global government whose politics can neither be predicted nor controlled (Hempel, 1996: 124). What then might be the first steps towards institutional change which would assist ecosocialization?

Our proposal is twofold: a representative World Environment Council (with representatives directly elected) and a World Court of the Environment (see Low and Gleeson, 1998). The purpose of these institutions is to instantiate the principle of rule of law on the environment, to declare environmental law, and to arrive at impartial judgments based on that law. To select these two institutions as a first step is not an arbitrary decision. Together they would create a unified set of mandatory rules for exploitation of the environment within which all economic actors can feel secure in planning their future business. The rules should be openly debated and transparent. Once enacted they require interpretation and enforcement by legal process. The two institutions are therefore inseparable. If there is to be environmental law of the kind necessary to set limits on economic growth, then it must be law for all. Accordingly, the views of all should be heard in its making and agreement reached by all on its form and substance—'quod omnes tangit ab omnibus comprobetur' or QOT (see Tully, 1995: 123). The principle heralds an extension of democracy, perhaps towards deliberative forms, but we will not pursue the matter here (see Eckersley, 2000).

Now although QOT is a good maxim for a constitutional process, producing global law governing the economic exploitation of the environment, it is not one that can be immediately put into effect in a process of socialization. The agreement of 'all' should be something to work towards in setting up the proposed institutions, rather than a prior condition for their creation. The agreement of 'all' in Europe was not feasible or necessary to set in motion a process which eventuated in the European Union. The point of departure was a decision to create a 'community' in specific policy arenas: coal and steel. Here we return to a different part of the argument developed by van der Pijl. His analysis tracks the modern history of international relations in terms of the relationship between what he calls the 'Lockean heartland' and the 'Hobbesian contender states.'

The system of society-state relations which developed in Britain after the 'Glorious Revolution' of 1688 established the principles of a market economy regulated by law, the sovereignty of an elected assembly, and the separation of powers (a separate and independent executive, legislature, and judiciary). The system further came to embody the separation of politics from economics, the 'level playing field' in competition, 'consumer sovereignty,' and the freedom of the individual under law (van der Pijl, 1998: 71). This system may be termed 'Lockean' after the author the Two Treatises of Government, the English philosopher, John Locke. The roots of the British system which Locke codified are to be found in medieval governance, but, as van der Pijl points out, the system happened to 'combine the preconditions to become the cradle of capital'. The Lockean system (adopted by Montesquieu) spread to the U.S.A. and eventually to the whole of Europe, so that we may speak of a 'heartland' of liberal democratic capitalism with a trading system which facilitated the growth of international capital, but gradually weakened the autonomy of the nation states within it. Of course by the end of the nineteenth century, leadership of the heartland had passed from Britain to the U.S.A.

In opposition to this growing international system, van der Pijl identifies a series of challenges from 'contender states' which found themselves marginalized and sought to seize or regain power in the trading system. In each case the opposing system involved a powerful, integrated state authority, termed 'Hobbesian,' after the author of *The Leviathan*. First came Napoleonic France, then the Fascist powers of Nazi Germany, Japan, and the communist Soviet Union and China. Are we today witnessing a new challenge from parts of the Islamic world? In every case to date the Hobbesian contenders have been defeated or eclipsed and eventually absorbed in the Lockean international, and now global, capitalist production and trading system.

The claim is not that the Lockean system is morally superior to other systems, but rather that it happens to have fostered the 'implacable play of free competition' (Gramsci, 1977: 46), to have neutralized the harmful aspects of state power, and to have dealt with class conflict effectively "by deflecting popular aspirations into a...moral internationalism in which export and overseas investment ambitions of capital imperceptibly merged with a missionary concept of democracy, human rights, and other 'universalist' aspects of the Lockean doctrine" (van der Pijl, 1998: 69). It remains to be seen how effective the Lockean system will prove in dealing with the challenge of ecological decay. However, given its continuing dominance, it seems reasonable to expect any move to deal with the problem to be centered on the heartland and to be consistent with its principles of governance.

Our proposal for the reform of global governance, although it seeks to enhance and extend democracy beyond the liberal minimalism, is nevertheless founded on Lockean principles and stems from authentic liberalism. One would not, however expect the proposal to be immediately attractive to the Hobbesian contenders, the major one today being China. What is more likely is for a group of the heartland Lockean states to bring the proposal to life through a multilateral treaty. We envisage here a different kind of EC, an Environment Community created by a treaty involving as a start, say, the European Union, the NAFTA states, and Japan. There would be no reason to exclude any state which found the 'Lockean' system agreeable. India, whose polity has already partly embraced Lockean principles, might well be a founding member. These states would set up the Council and Court to govern the conditions of their exploitation of the environment within their own borders.

Once the Environmental Community was created under treaty and equipped with an Environment Council and Court, the environmental law ensuing would apply with mandatory force only to the member states of the Environmental Community. The ultimate sanction would be exclusion from the Community and its law. The QOT maxim would be applied in the formation of the environmental law of the community. However, the law of the community would certainly impinge upon the economic relations between the participant states and the rest of the world. An interesting question then, is whether the Environmental Community would eventually grow to become a World Environmental Community. Of course, we can hardly guess whether this would be likely to occur, but one scenario could run as follows.

The participant states might eventually be tempted to erect barriers to trade with non-members who might not comply with the environmental law of the member states. For those nations which initially chose to remain outside, the question would then arise whether it would now be in their interest to join, much as Britain, which initially refused to join the European Community, was eventually persuaded by the force of its own interest to do so. China, Indonesia, and Russia, with large populations, would appreciate that they could in fact dominate the World Council. But, because the Council would consist of directly elected representatives, it would be citizens and not governments of these countries that would dominate. The government of China, for example, would have to ask if it could trust its citizens' representatives to vote in their nations' interest as seen by the leadership. But then, with such a Treaty in existence, China's interests would be different from what they are under a global neo-liberal economic regime dominated by the U.S.A.

Such a scenario raises a host of political questions. Plainly there would be a strong tendency for the participant states to become an exclusive club. Part of the founding constitution would therefore have to announce at the start the aim of global membership. An inclusive constitution is absolutely required and a key principle would have to be that no state that agreed to abide by the Treaty conditions shall be denied membership. The question of free trade would arise and be debated. There would be opposition to free trade on environmental grounds but also powerful advocacy from those who supported free trade on grounds of economic efficiency and fairness to developing nations. Such a debate would be healthy. At present there is little—free trade is simply accepted in elite circles as the rule.

Finally, the European Union grew from a decision to create a particular regime for a particular purpose. What purpose is sufficiently pressing to begin the process of creating an Environmental Community? There is one such purpose which appears to be immediately in need of a new kind of regime: the regulation of greenhouse gas emissions. International change at the global level is likely to proceed from the agreed failure of existing institutional arrangements. Young (1994) regards the climate regime as something of a test of the efficacy of the negotiated order of environmental governance. If it fails, he says, we may need to move from 'governance' to 'government,' that is from a negotiated and voluntary regime to an authoritative, compulsory regime. If government in some form is necessary to reduce global warming and cope with its effects, it seems likely that other environmental issues may also in time be brought within its scope: biodiversity questions may well be seen as linked to climate issues. Rather in the way the European Union began as a result of the need for efficacy in a specific functional area (the European coal and steel Community), so global government for the environment might start as a much strengthened climate regime. The first step to reinventing global governance should therefore be the formation of a Climate Union of those states that agree to harmonize the transformation of their economies to attain effective targets for the reduction of emissions of greenhouse gases to put a brake on global warming.

At present, the U.S.A. stands as the great obstacle to the formation of a Climate Union and indeed to any solution to the crisis of climate change. But this is perhaps because the crisis is denied in the U.S.A. History has shown twice in the last century that America joins Europe when the security of the Lockean heartland is plainly threatened. Perhaps, as NATO becomes irrelevant in the absence of a military threat, we may still hope for a new kind of Atlantic alliance to take shape against a new kind of global threat.

Conclusion

In this Chapter we scanned the landscape of environmental justice and political change and in the process tried to demonstrate a connection between ethics and politics. We first argued that the discourse of ecologically sustainable development (ESD) represents the emergence of a new turn in the socialization of capital. Under the rubric of 'sustainable development' can be found a number of perceived requirements for saving the natural and social substratum or 'life support system' of the capitalist economy. Sustainable development advocates commonly combine them—as the economic, ecological, and social pillars of sustainability—but without satisfactorily explaining the relationship. The future impact of this discourse remains very much an open question to be decided by political struggles at different levels, but there is some reason for hope that ESD will come to mollify or replace the ecologically and socially destructive phase of socialization of 'neo-liberalism.'

We then examined the connection between sustainable development and environmental justice in the interests of clarifying the relationship between the social and environmental aspects of economic development. We argued that environmental justice should not be seen as merely pertaining to the end result of industrial processes, a matter of the distribution of good and bad environments to be settled after the event, so to speak, by political decision. Rather the question of environmental justice and injustice, we argued, lies at the heart of commodity production. This relocation of the question resulted from thinking about the nature of property and belonging and how things outside the person can constitute 'personhood' or individuality, without becoming the person's property in the liberal sense of the word. If we think in these terms, then we must also recognize that environments have been taken, and are still being taken, from some people and places and transformed into commodities at no cost to the purchasers.

We did not go on to spell out the principles of justice, which might be developed to regulate such a seemingly unjust economic system. Such principles, though they follow from familiar principles of justice based on deserts, rights, and needs, must be worked out and institutionalized in practice. Instead, we considered how the process of socialization might proceed to develop institutions capable of rectifying the environmental injustice at the core of the economy. We reiterated our proposal for a World Environment Council to enact authoritative environmental law and a World Court of Environmental Justice to give effect to this law. It was suggested that such institutions might eventuate as a result of the formation of an Environmental Community, which in turn develops out of a Climate Union with significant powers and mechanisms for implementation and monitoring the responses of its members.

We stand at the threshold of new century and at such a point we can no longer postpone the necessary response to the threat to humanity. Optimism is in order. We have to win. Let us go to work.

References

Adams, J. 1997. "Globalisation, Trade and Environment." In OECD. *Globalisation and Environment, Preliminary Perspectives.* OECD Proceedings. Paris: OECD. pp. 179-197.

Altvater, Elmar. 1993. *The Future of the Market, An Essay on the Regulation of Money and Nature after the Collapse of 'Actually Existing Socialism.'* London: Verso.

Athanasiou, Tom. 1998. *Slow Reckoning: The Ecology of a Divided Planet.* London: Verso.

Bellah, Robert Neelly, Richard Madsen, William M. Sullivan, A. Swidler, and Steven M. Tipton. 1985. *Habits of the Heart: Individualism and Commitment in American Life.* New York: Harper and Row.

Bhaskar, R. 1993. *Dialectic, The Pulse of Freedom*, London: Verso.

Booth, A. L. 1999. "Does the Spirit Move You? Environmental Spirituality." *Environmental Values.* Volume 8, Number 1: 89-105.

Bullard, Robert. 1999. "Environmental Justice Challenges at Home and Abroad." In Nicholas Low (ed). *Global Ethics and the Environment.* London and New York: Routledge. Pp. 33-46.

Christoff, Peter and Nicholas Low. 2000 "Recent Australian Urban Policy and the Environment: Green or Mean?" In Nicholas P. Low, Brendan J. Gleeson, Ingemar Elander, and Rolf Lidskog (eds). *Consuming Cities: The Urban Environment in the Global Economy After Rio.* London: Routledge. pp. 241-264.

Cockett R. 1995 *Thinking the Unthinkable, Think-Tanks and the Economic Counter-Revolution, 1931-1983.* London: Fontana

Daly, Herman. 1996. *Beyond Growth: The Economics of Sustainable Development.* Boston: Beacon Press.

Davy, Benjamin. 1997. *Essential Injustice: When Legal Institutions Cannot Resolve Environmental and Land Use Disputes.* Wien, New York: Springer.

Dryzek, John S. 1999. "Global Ecological Democracy." In Nicholas P. Low (ed). *Global Ethics and Environment.* London and New York: Routledge. pp. 264-82.

Durkheim, Emile. 1976. [1912] *The Elementary Forms of the Religious Life.* London: Allen and Unwin.

Eckersley, Robyn. 2000. "Deliberative Democracy, Ecological Representation and Risk: Towards a Democracy of the Affected." In Michael Saward (ed). *Democratic Innovation: Deliberation, Representation and Association.* London and New York: Routledge. pp. 117-132.

Falk, Richard. 2001. 'Humane Governance and the Environment: Overcoming Neo-Liberalism' in Brendan J. Gleeson and Nicholas P. Low (eds). 2001. *Governing for the Environment.* Basingstoke, UK and New York: Palgrave. pp. 221-236.

_____. 1996. "Environmental Protection in an Era of Globalisation." *Yearbook of International Law.* Volume 6: 1-25.

_____. 1975. *A Study of Future Worlds.* New York: Free Press

Gelbspan, Ross. 1997. *The Heat is On: The High Stakes Battle Over the Earth's Threatened Climate.* New York: Addison-Wesley Publishing.

Georgescu-Roegen, Nicholas. 1971. *The Entropy Law and the Economic Process.* Cambridge, MA: Harvard University Press.

Gleeson, Brendan J. and Nicholas P. Low (eds). 2001. *Governing for the Environment.* Basingstoke, UK and New York: Palgrave.

Gramsci, Antonio. 1977. *Selections from Political Writings 1919-1920.* Translated and Edited by Q. Hoare and G. N. Smith. New York: International Publishers.

Gray, John. 1998. *False Dawn: The Delusions of Global Capitalism.* London: Granta.

Harvey, David. 1996. *Justice, Nature and the Geography of Difference.* Oxford: Basil Blackwell.

Hayek, F. A 1944. *The Road to Serfdom.* Sydney: Dimocks Book Arcade.

Hempel, L.C. 1996 *Environmental Governance, The Global Challenge.* Washington, DC: Island Press

Krugman, Paul. 1999. *The Accidental Theorist, and Other Dispatches from the Dismal Science.* London and New York: Penguin Books.

Lake, Robert W. 2000. "Contradictions at the Local Scale: Local Implementation of Agenda 21 in the USA. In Nicholas P.Low, Brendan J. Gleeson, Ingemar Elander, and Rolf Lidskog (eds). *Consuming Cities: The Urban Environment in the Global Economy After Rio.* London and New York: Routledge. pp. 70-90.

Levine, M. P. 1994. "Pantheism, Ethics, and Ecology." *Environmental Values.* Volume 3, Number 2: 121-138.

Lipschutz, Ronnie, D. 1995. *Global Civil Society and Global Environmental Governance: The Politics of Nature from Place to Planet.* Albany, NY: State of University Press.

Low, Nicholas (ed). 1999. *Global Ethics and the Environment.* London and New York: Routledge.

Low, Nicholas and Brendan Gleeson. 1998a. *Justice, Society and Nature: An Exploration of Political Ecology.* London and New York: Routledge.

Low, Nicholas and Brendan Gleeson. 1998b. "Situating Justice in the Environment: The Case of BHP at the OK Tedi Copper Mine." *Antipode.* Volume 30, Number 3: 201-226.

Low, Nicholas P., Brendan J. Gleeson, Ingemar Elander, and Rolf Lidskog (eds). (2000). *Consuming Cities: The Urban Environment in the Global Economy After Rio.* London and New York: Routledge.

Luke, Timothy W. 2000. "A Rough Road Out of Rio: The Right-wing Reaction in the United States against Global Environmentalism." In Nicholas P. Low, Brendan J. Gleeson, Ingemar Elander, and Rolf Lidskog (eds). *Consuming Cities: The Urban Environment in the Global Economy After Rio.* London and New York: Routledge. pp. 54-69.

Martin, Hans-Peter and Harald Schumann. 1997. *The Global Trap: Globalization and the Assault on Democracy and Prosperity.* London and New York: Zed Books.

OECD (Organization for Economic Development and Cooperation). 1997. *Globalisation and Environment: Preliminary Perspectives.* OECD Proceedings. Paris: OECD.

Orbach, T. and C. Leidtke. 1998. *Eco-management Accounting in Germany.* Wuppertal papers. Wuppertal: Wuppertal Institut für Klima, Umwelt, Energie.

van der Pijl, Kees. 1998. *Transnational Classes and International Relations.* London and New York: Routledge.

Pogge, Thomas W. 1994. "An Egalitarian Law of Peoples." *Philosophy and Public Affairs.* Volume 23, Number 3: 195-224.

Polanyi, Karl. 1957 [1944]. *The Great Transformation: The Political and Economic Origins of Our Time.* Boston, MA: Beacon Press.

Prades, Jose A. 1999. "Global Environmental Change and Contemporary Society: Classical Sociological Analysis Revisited." *International Sociology.* Volume 14, Number 1: 7-31.

_____. 1993. *Durkheim.* Paris: Paris Universitaires de France.

Roth, G. 1967. *Paying for Roads: The Economics of Traffic Congestion.* Harmondsworth, UK: Penguin Books.

Scheicher, S. P. 1997. "Borders in a Borderless World." In OECD. *Globalisation and Environment: Preliminary Perspectives.* OECD Proceedings. Paris: OECD. pp. 173-178.

Schmidt-Bleek, F. 1994. *Carnoules Declaration of the Factor Ten Club.* Wuppertal Papers. Wuppertal Institut für Klima, Umwelt, Energie: Wuppertal.

Self, Peter. 1993. *Government by the Market? The Politics of Public Choice.* London: Macmillan.

Shiva, Vandana. 1999. "Ecological Balance in an Era of Globalisation." In Nicholas Low (ed). *Global Ethics and the Environment.* London: Routledge. pp. 47-69.

Smith, Adam. 1759. *The Theory of Moral Sentiments.* London: Millar, Kincaid, and Bell.

Spangenberg, J. H. 2001. "Towards Sustainability." in Brendan J. Gleeson and Nicholas P. Low (eds). 2001. *Governing for the Environment.* Basingstoke, UK and New York: Palgrave. pp. 29-43.

Spangenberg, J. H., Scharnagl, A., with F. Hinterberger. 1998. *The SuE Model – A Decision-Support Tool.* Wuppertal papers. Wuppertal: Wuppertal Institut für Klima, Umwelt, Energie.

Tully, James. 2001. "An Ecological Ethics for the Present: Three Approaches to the Central Question." in Brendan J. Gleeson and Nicholas P. Low (eds). *Governing for the Environment.* Basingstoke, UK and New York: Palgrave. pp. 147-164

_____. 1995. *Strange Multiplicity, Constitutionalism in an Age of Diversity.* Cambridge, UK:Cambridge University Press.

UNDP (United Nations Development Program). 1999. *Human Development Report.* New York: United Nations.

Wapner, Paul Kevin. 1996. *Environmental Activism and World Civic Politics.* Albany, NY: University of New York Press.

Von Weisäcker, Ernst, Amory B. Lovins, and Hunter L. Lovins. 1997. *Factor Four: Doubling Wealth, Halving Resource Use.* Sydney: Allen and Unwin.

Young, O. R. 1994. *International Governance, Protecting the Environment in a Stateless Society.* New York and London: Cornell University Press.

10

globalization.com vs. ecologicaljustice.org: Contesting the End of History

Leigh Glover

Introduction

Globalization either enhances or diminishes the prospects for ecological justice. Expanding international trade is extending the range and scale of industrialized economic development, and its consequences, across the globe and into the future. Promoted by conventional economic theory, the concepts of free trade and increased international economic activity enjoy the support of most national governments and their centrist political parties, international economic agencies, and transnational corporations. Globalization has a direct relationship with ecological sustainability, as the form, type, and scale of resource use and waste production is allied to industrial economic activity. Although lauded as an engine of economic growth, globalization's supporters have neglected its capacity to generate social and environmental costs. Because of a social connectivity through the medium of the environment, the lifestyles of some peoples produce environmental consequences borne by others and by Nature itself. Far from generating random and isolated effects, trade, investment, and industrial activity act in accord with ecological processes to produce patterns of ecological injustice.

This chapter explores the relationship between the process of globalization and the concept of ecological justice (as defined by Low and Gleeson, 1998), with particular concern for disadvantaged peoples, future generations, and for Nature. We consider the overall question of whether these two phenomena can be reconciled and ecological justice increased or whether the obvious antagonisms between economic growth and environmental values will remain and prevailing injustices exacerbated. Three related issues appear central to this debate: 1) the fate of the world's indigenous peoples; 2) management of the environmental and cultural commons; and 3) global economic development's effect on eco-logical values. Additionally, we briefly consider the claims that the new information and communication technologies have opened new possi-bilities to realize ecological justice.

Globalization and a Contracted World

So what exactly is 'globalization?' In one sense, globalization may be considered as the 'natural' functioning of modernity, with its propensity for economic growth mediated and facilitated through nation-states, in-dustrial capitalism, modern science and technology, and liberal-demo-cratic governance. Extending and deepening global economic interac-tions and networks are without precedent in scale, velocity, reach, and social influence: Modern 'progress' has a tendency to progress. Global-ization represents, therefore, the geographic diffusion of modernity through primarily economic relationships.

Globalization is variously considered as a process entirely coexistent with the long sweep of history; as accompanying the process of modern-ization and capitalism, with a recent acceleration; or coeval with the post-industrial, postmodern, or contemporary phase of capitalism (Wa-ters, 1995). At one end of a continuum is Wallerstein's (1979) world-system (as prefigured by Polanyi, 1957) and the progression towards a unitary global economy (after Karl Marx) and at the other, Lash and Urry's (1987) concept of an economic devolution into 'disorganized capi-tal.'

Economically, statistical markers of globalization abound. While pro-portionally the extent of world trading may not yet rival that of pre-1914, the value of world trade is without precedent, as is world eco-nomic production. Global output of goods grew in value from US$5 trillion in 1950 to $29 trillion in 1997, and as Brown notes, the growth of US$5 trillion between 1990-97 matched the growth from the "beginning of civilization to 1950" (1998: 3). World exports were 7% of world out-put in 1950, rising to around 17% today (Held et al, 1999: 168). Mea-sures of the intensity of trade links (i.e., the number of nations trading with each other) show a continual increase through the 20th century, reaching 66% of the possible maximum in 1990 (Held et al, 1999: 167). For developed nations, trade as a proportion of GDP has also increased through the last century (Held et al, 1999: 169).

Globalization is a contentious concept that its promoters identify as radically transforming the global future into an era of great prosperity, in which they foresee a near-Utopian prospect (e.g., Bryan and Farrell, 1996; Freidman, 2000; and Thurow, 1999). A skeptical few consider it to be a fraud, misnomer, or mythical (e.g., Krugman, 1996; Hirst and Thompson, 1999), whilst a more substantial group recognize globalization as a real phenomenon (although contest its 'global' appellation) which is producing a world with many undesirable features (e.g., Greider, 1997; Mander and Goldsmith, 1996; and Schrecker, 1997). This latter grouping typically derive their position from nationalist, populist, or environmentalist perspectives ('communtarians' to use Rodrik's (1997) phrase). Environmentalists have been prominent in their objections, protesting individual trade and industrial activities, free trade and trade liberalization in general and now, globalization as a normative social and economic goal.

As a deterministic concept, globalization may have few modern rivals. Not only are increasing world trade activities bringing forward the original goal of the Enlightenment, it is claimed, but also this process is being driven by momentum beyond human control. Worldwide extension of capitalism, in this vision, is identical with that of democratic reform within nation states (e.g., Dahl, 1998). One of the most famous claims made for contemporary global politics, and from which part of the title for this Chapter is drawn, comes from Fukuyama (1989:2):

> What we may be witnessing is not just the end of the Cold War, or the passing of a particular period of postwar history, but the end of history as such: that is, the end of mankind's ideological evolution and the universalization of Western liberal democracy as the final form of human achievement.

Globalization is rendered here as the process that delivers a political, economic, and ethical certainty.

Yet the claims that globalization produces globalized effects are questioned. Some analysts consider that globalization is the outcome of a dominant process, citing the inherent character of industrial capitalism or the "cultural logic of modernity" (Yearly, 1996: 141). For others, globalization is a product of the elements that comprise modernity. Technology has been a key factor: Technological innovation and access to more-widely dispersed sources of raw materials, labor, and manufacturing capacity have seen commodity chains lengthen considerably under globalization. And while economic factors predominate, there are ". . . multiple, interacting spurs to the globalization of environmental awareness and environmentalism" (Yearly, 1996: 143).

Technological development is often cited as a major determinant of this process, in which it is bestowed with both political neutrality and a normative role as an agent of social progress. With the revolution in communications technology and services supporting the expanding international trade activity, especially in the finance and banking sectors, there has been a revival of the concept analyzed by Winner in which technology is viewed as being both autonomous and 'out of control' (Winner, 1977).

Overall, the future of the nation state has absorbed the majority of attention from the scholars of political economy and international relations. While globalization is no longer the outcome of empire building, its institutional basis still involves nation states interacting with systems (unilateral, regional, and international) of governance. Additionally, those assertions that nation state development is automatically inclined towards democracy have been questioned. Cerney (1999), for example, considers the opportunities for democratic governance in decline, with globalization leading not to global pluralism, but to ever-widening inequality and the fragmentation of governance.

Politically, some witness in globalization the attenuation of nation state powers, in which choices at this scale are confined and shaped by international forces. Others, such as Hirst and Thomson reason (1999: 277):

> Paradoxically then, the degree to which the international economy has internationalized (not globalized) reinstates the need for the nation-state, not in its traditional guise as the sole sovereign power, but as a crucial relay between the international levels of governance and the articulate public of the developed world.

Even globalism's proponents and admirers often stress that the process is, in fact, not actually global, as Gilpin (2000: 294) notes: "Moreover, integration of the world economy has been highly uneven, restricted to particular economic sectors, and not nearly extensive as some believe." During this, the second great modern phase of international economic activity, trade, investment, and financial flows are primarily the business of the U.S., Western Europe, and Japan (Gilpin, 2000). Certainly, it makes little sense to talk glibly of the benefits of globalization when the income of 1.2 billion people is less than US$1 a day and over one billion lack access to safe drinking water (UNDP, 2000: 4).

Frequently presented an as ideology by its proponents, their depiction of globalization is a process by which the diffusion of Western culture and capitalism is inevitable, carried forward by a deterministic logic beyond any intervening powers. McMurtry equates this global market ideology with fundamentalism (1997: 194):

> No amount of human suffering or natural destruction exacted by the doctrine's implementation can alter its prescriptions or prove it false. This is because its truths are eternal and not subject to falsifying evidence.

Indeed, what might strike a newcomer to this field of scholarship is the confident appearance of doctrines and attitudes that one might have assumed anachronistic by this time. For example, Gilpin opines (2000: 293):

> Although a few prominent economists believe that unregulated international finance poses a serious threat to the world economy, almost all economists and other proponents of free markets believe that globalization promises a world of increasing prosperity and international cooperation; they argue that no obstacles should be allowed to prevent the free flow of goods, services, and capital.

Such sentiments of mainstream economics would conform seamlessly with the rhetoric of the free trade liberals of the nineteenth century and subsequent debates over imperialism and colonialism. Attitudes towards indigenous peoples, commons resources, and ecological values held by present-day free trade exponents also seem reminiscent of those from that earlier period, and it is to these issues that we now turn.

'New as Better': Erosion of Traditional Lifestyles and Indigenous Cultures

Globalization's recent history is dominated by the spread of western culture. Divining between diffusing western culture and global capitalism has become a hairsplitting exercise—the distinctions between them are subtle and particular. Globalization is spreading economic relations to unprecedented scales, with commodity chains ever lengthening, resource exploitation spreading, and production becoming more dynamic in processes, ownership, and location. Western popular culture has been recording the impacts of its globalization with a frequency that reflects its rate of dissemination around the globe. Considerably less popular interest has been shown by modernity in cataloging cultural losses, especially when located in developing nations.

Transmission of Western culture is being facilitated by the new communication and mass media technologies (including the Internet, electronic information transfer, digital communication technology, satellite and cable communications systems, and highly portable devices), which

"... have created the arteries through which modern entertainment conglomerates are homogenizing global culture." (Barnet and Cavanagh, 1996: 71). Champions of globalization tend to downplay the 'Western' aspect of globalization and stress the multiplicity of new cultural forms arising from cultural 'cross fertilization': "In a dynamic system, differences persist, but they enrich each other. Verges do not extinguish variety; they create plenitude." (Postel, 1998: 194).

It may be that globalization's 'winners' witness multiplicity of the familiar, but not the extinction of the 'other.' For each advance in global culture, there must be a diminution of its local forms. Cultural homogenization continues apace as the decline in the world's languages indicates. Crystal reckons that 96% of the world's languages are spoken by 4% of its population, and although estimates of the next 100 years' language deaths vary greatly, he endorses predictions of at least a 50% loss being likely (2000: 15-19). In light of this prospect, it is difficult to perceive much plenitude and enrichment arising from globalization.

For many in the developing world, globalization is but the latest manifestation of economic and cultural colonialism. Globalization brings a set of imposed social relationships, including the creation of industrial class structures associated with gender, ethnicity, income, religion, education, and other factors, it is argued (e.g., Mander and Goldsmith, 1996; Sachs, 1993). Capitalism connects distant resources, cultures, and locations with its dominant sources of capital production in the developed world. Concomitant with this connection is the infiltration of the systems of industrialization, such as in manufacturing, agriculture, energy production, transport, medicine, and education. Accordingly, a number of writers, especially from the South, consider the effects on developing nations' environments and cultures as exemplifying a new form of exploitation by the developed nations, known as 'ecological colonialism' (e.g., Shiva, 1988).

Schumpeter (1975 [1942]) coined the phrase 'creative destruction' and this notion has re-entered the discourse on economic activity in recent years, making its author, as Krugman (2000) suggests, a "... sort of new economy icon." Economic competition is not merely that of price differential, argued Schumpeter, but more fundamentally generated by the entry of new commodities, technologies, resources, and forms of organization. Capitalism's prosperity depends on creating new products, services, and markets and the destruction of that which preceded it. In this sense, markets cannot be distinguished from the cultures in which they are embedded; consequently, indigenous culture is invariably destroyed once it fully embraces capitalism.

Presented thus, the elimination of aboriginal cultures is the outcome of conflict with a superior system of economics, whereby economists tend to envisage history as the march of economic systems and competing market forces. From this perspective, globalization simply quickens the pace of the march and the speed of the inevitable conquests by market-based capitalism. Fukuyama associates this process not with destruction, but with the inevitability of the victory of cultural superiority: "The triumph of the West, of the Western *ideal*, is evident first of all in the total exhaustion of viable systematic alternatives to Western liberalism." (1989: 2). Hence, democracy as a laudable social goal can only realized in tandem with industrial capitalism in the context of a world economy. Cultural losses, in such reckoning, must be overwhelmingly offset by the imposition of Western culture—although pinning down that 'Western ideal' is no mean task.

Fukuyama was considering the rivalries of nation-state ideologies in the above quotation, but most free market proponents welcome the market's indifference to scale and culture, with its ability to infiltrate individual lives, local communities, and nation states. For many individuals, communities, organizations, and even nations, whether to become involved in world markets is not a decision of their making. Workers in a typical manufacturing plant, for example, no more decide whether their products should be exported than they participate in decisions of whether their plant itself should be re-located in another nation. Indigenous peoples rarely have a say in what happens to their lands, waters, and resources when subject to imposed economic forces, as the environmental justice literature attests. As Clifford Geertz once noted, the choice over whether to adopt modernity over pre-modernity, is always stark and unitary.

Even if capitalism and democracy are inexorably linked, participation in world markets is hardly a guarantee of being able to participate in decisions about the preservation of local culture, retain access to commons resources, or influence the production of pollution from another jurisdiction. Integration of indigenous peoples into liberal democratic relationships, therefore, is one that undermines traditional cultural forms, especially where these are most closely tied to resources being drawn into the market system. In other words, the path towards liberal democracy through an imposed economic system leads away from investing rights in indigenous peoples, unless those rights accord with the interests of capital.

Cox (1995) sees a parallel between the Polanyi's (1957) description of capitalism in the last two centuries—which experienced a transition from a self-regulating market to that of neo-liberalism through the imposition of social and political controls—with contemporary circumstances. Cox writes (1995: 39):

> So now the market appears to be bursting free from the bonds of national societies, to subject global society to its laws. The results on the global level are like those Polanyi saw in the nineteenth-century Britain: greater polarization of rich and poor, disintegration of pre-existing social bonds, and alienation.

Expiration of autonomous, independent, and traditional culture is therefore the hallmark of modernity. For Fukuyama, capitalism is creating the conditions for its eventual global sweep of liberal-democratic governance, while Polanyi considered the uncontrolled growth of capitalism as eroding its environmental and social foundations. However, in a cultural sense, both positions may hold true, for traditional culture is replaced or infused by western popular culture, and the world seemingly offers diminished support for traditional associations with ecological systems.

By suggesting that liberal capitalism is the universal social goal, and alluding to the absence of significant rivals, the small matter of how such superiority might be philosophically or practically demonstrated becomes overlooked in the broader discourse. Accepting that economic and political systems cannot be divorced from their social settings, how can it be possible to demonstrate economic superiority, given those economic criteria for assessment could be agreed?

At this time in Western culture much intellectual opinion and popular culture questions the ability of 'modernity' to produce universal 'progress.' Progress has become a term more likely to be applied with ironical, rather than literal, connotations. Casting a glance over the preceding century of two world wars, the Cold War, the Great and many minor economic depressions, the legacy of colonialism, and environmental destruction, it takes a special myopia to claim that western culture has reached a moral zenith to which all should aspire. While there is little doubt that western culture is superior at being dominant, this is something less than claiming it to be somehow superior per se over indigenous cultures.

Ironically, much within the liberal tradition would deny even the concept of cultural 'superiority'—yet this very notion is being promulgated as the basis for a revised world economy that increasingly adopts western culture. One foundation for doubting capitalism as a primary organizing principle for all social relations is articulated by Heilbroner, and is widely accepted in liberal circles, namely the ethical void in market activity (Heilbroner, 1985: 140):

> It is part of the nature of capitalism that the circuit of capital has no intrinsic moral dimension, no vision of art or idea aside from the commodity form in which it is embodied. In this setting, ideas thrive, but morality languishes . . .

Driving that circulation of capital are several presumptions about the market place, such as that social progress occurs through consumption, that competition is superior to cooperation, and that social choices can be rendered in economic terms. Nevertheless, while capitalism may suffer the absence of a moral compass, it is deemed morally acceptable by globalization's defenders as an economic system uniquely capable of delivering a morally desirable political system.

Although globalization is seemingly justified on the premise of its superiority, the decline in ecological conditions that can result from its imposition undermines this position. Even the claim of modern economic superiority over the pre-modern can be falsified. Governments create institutions that favor capitalist relations even where existing social institutions may be environmentally and socially benevolent, more efficient, and economically of lower cost. On the grounds of managing commons resources, traditional cultures have much to offer sustainable management (WCED, 1987). Disappearance of such knowledge can result in the degradation of land and water management practices, sometimes to the extent that subsequent scientific management cannot restore (The Ecologist, 1993; Shiva, 1988, 1994). Furthermore, to argue that the new cultural forms resulting from interaction with global culture are of the same integrity and meaning as those they replace is contestable. Entities and symbols from traditional culture that have a market value may be identified and protected in global culture through commodification, but this in itself need not empower the traditional possessors.

There are grounds, however, for questioning this economic 'inevitability' that seeks to create a dominant cultural form. Several important aspects of the spread of Western culture are often omitted from the glowing accounts of the march of progress, such as that economic relations are rarely a simple expression of economic contest, but an outcome of factors that include coercion, corruption, military threat, inducement, political strategy, and diplomatic influence. Considerable international efforts though organizations such as the International Monetary Fund, World Bank, World Trade Organization, Association of South East Asian Nations, and the North American Free Trade Agreement, further promote the global economy and intensifying international economic activity. Indigenous cultural losses, therefore, cannot be merely attributed to economic inferiority, as the market advocates suggest.

Globalization's regard of indigenous people pays scant regard to the ethical dimensions of their eradication or the erosion of their cultures and knowledge by insisting on its version of progress. Ethical issues aside, globalization cannot demonstrate its superiority on its own terms. Indigenous peoples and traditional ecological knowledge possess both intrinsic worth and instrumental value as preservers of ecological conditions and attributes, for which modernity's substitution of scientific management has been shown to be inadequate and incomplete. Advocates of globalization take refuge from the implications of cultural and ecological destruction with rationalizations based around the philosophy of 'the end of history.' Assumptions of industrialized society's superiority are ethnocentric and mechanical, and are based on a determinism that is both ahistorical and teleological.

If indigenous peoples are recognized as having rights similar to those living in wealthy nations, then ecological justice offers them a future with a different trajectory to that grim fate generated by globalization. Ecological justice contains the insight that self-determination and the protection of ecological values can be aligned within the same ethical frame, providing a means by which local and global commons management can be considered. Recognizing a basic set of values that western society purports to be the hallmarks of civilization as also residing in indigenous peoples is to acknowledge that their 'history' is not at an end, but they should have the same opportunities to flourish as the wealthy nations assume for themselves.

Making 'Ours' Theirs: Commodification and the Commons

Capitalism's ability to create markets where none previously existed is one of its most remarkable features and this capacity has reached unprecedented realms. Environmentalists have been particularly concerned over the commodification and trading of a range of natural resources and ecosystem services, particularly the 'commons.' One set of commons is that of open access, and these common property goods include the atmosphere and oceans, material and energy cycles, and biological entities and processes. That other set of commons includes those areas, services, and goods shared and managed by local communities (and include land, water, flora, fauna, and a plentitude of other materials and benefits). This latter group are not based on either state or private property systems, but are organized around local, small-scale social systems of management (The Ecologist, 1993). Commons resources may also comprise cultural entities, but in the context of traditional or indigenous culture, the material, spiritual, and cultural interactions with the natural world are effectively indivisible.

Globalization has produced a complex set of influences on these resources: it both appropriates commons, but can also serve to foster organizational arrangements for environmental protection and management. Irrefutably, globalization has extended the reach of capitalism into the realm of that which was previously available for communal use and made the access and use of commons dependant on purchase or hire (Chatterjee and Finger, 1994). Community dispossession may take the form of material, cultural, spiritual, aesthetic, and educational deprivations. Governments have legitimized the conversion of the public commons into private property either willingly, as political favor or to promote economic activity, or implicitly, by failing to protect commons. Examples of the 'marketization' of commons include tradable licenses to pollute the sky and waters, ownership of genetic materials and life forms, and the appropriation of commons lands and waters for commercial use (such as commercial mining, forestry, farming, fishing on public lands and waters).

Western systems of property law rarely acknowledge the place of commons, but are well attuned to dealing with ownership of privatized public goods (The Ecologist, 1993). Where there is no pre-existing acceptance of commons' ownership, there are few parties empowered in a legal sense to contest the appropriation of commons at the macro scale. So for open-access commons, their appropriation often passes unnoticed. Cooperation by nation states and their international authorities to seize and partition commons resources generates few opportunities for legitimate contestation by non-nation state entities, such as NGOs. In effect, the open-access status of these resources becomes immediately sublimated as nation-state property over which nations cooperatively determine the fate of the resource within global management regimes.

Commons that are not 'open access' have a communal or collective ownership. Communities manage these resources so as to ensure the sustainable stream of benefits for multiple users. Claims of the 'tragedy of the commons' (Hardin, 1968, 1977) that depicted commons as inevitably vulnerable to abuse are largely recognized as a misleading allegory. Where environmental destruction of commons does occur, the cause is more likely associated with conditions that diminish communal controls, not the manifestation of a selfish instinct. A common antecedent of the failure of local communal management is the injection of capitalist economics, which promotes the systematic production of short-term surplus and disregard of longer-term supply.

Not that communal or traditional commons management is without environmental costs or even the possibility of the elimination of ecological values. It can be argued that commons management is not inherently sustainable, despite long narratives of continual natural resources use. On balance, a reasonable generalization is that traditional commons management (part of traditional ecological knowledge) always has as its primary directive the continuation of those goods and services derived from the commons. Preserving the world's extant indigenous cultures and biodiversity, in all likelihood, is now identical with protecting indigenous peoples, their lifestyles, and traditional ecological knowledge. Communal management does the best it can with what it knows—but where environmental conditions produce effects beyond the limits of available knowledge, then communal management is no better than scientific or economic management.

Communal commons resources are being eroded at an accelerating rate as globalization extends the reach of industrial capitalism, although conventional economic accounts of globalization have remarked little on this phenomenon. Although usually small, these local losses of commons are often fiercely contested—local welfare and survival, material, and spiritual culture are dependent on the retention of commons goods under local management. Vanishing commons resources translate into the loss of someone's traditional way of life. Appropriation typically involves indigenous peoples' resources ceded to central government or directly to corporate ownership or control. World attention is occasionally given to these contests, such as oil drilling in Nigeria, China's Three Gorges water resource projects, and tropical timber harvesting. However, for the most part, the diminution of local common property goods comprises a multitude of local events that pass largely unnoticed by those not immediately affected.

Under the logic of globalization, common resources have only two basic future conditions, either as private goods or entities under state control. One irony of globalization is that global environmental crises, the outcome of industrialization, have found nation states considering the aforementioned choices as a means of addressing these problems. As private property, commons resources can acquire all the protection afforded any asset of equivalent value. Privatized commons can then be managed so as to include the goal of ecological and cultural sustainability. Alternatively, structures of governance can be established for the management over these resources. As Goldman postulates, the environmental vulnerability of the globalized commons has ". . . created new demand for regulatory institutions and sciences, staffed by global technocrats and scientists. The creation of this global-commons discourse justifies the conditions for their problem-solving tools: global experts unconstrained by provincial traditions, metaphors, politics and local ecosystems." (1998: 4-5). Against this background of emerging global management regimes are those NGOs struggling to create a place for civic society institutions in order to assert the causes of ecological justice.

Both these conditions essentially require the powers of governance in capitalist states to exert unprecedented controls over the globalized world economy and those of individual nation states. This challenge usually produces a paradoxical solution. For nation states to apply environmental modernization goals over corporations and the market economies, they create various control mechanisms. However, it has been shown to be very difficult for liberal-democratic states to hold ecological sustainability as a goal and not be diverted into designing market control systems that maximize market-based goals, such as economic efficiency.

Modern states' role in securing resources for economic development conflicts with their responsibilities for community welfare and environmental protection. Governmental efforts in exercising protection over communities and the environment are usually reactions to injustices already perpetrated (e.g., Bullard, 1994; Camacho, 1998; and Faber, 1998a). Nowhere is this conflicted task of promoting commons appropriation and providing justice for the affected parties more apparent than in the management of ecosystems to preserve valued ecosystem services. Protecting both traditional rights of access to commons resources and restricting the reach of new markets is necessary to promote sustainability, yet contrary to the character and purpose of globalization. Making sustainability and globalization part of the same dynamic, therefore, is riven by contradiction.

Globalization seemingly offers the choice of privatization or governmental regulation for commons' management, even though neither offers substantial recognition of ecological values or the rights to self-determination by local communities or global civic society. Market-based approaches to common's management seek to sever communities from commons, despite the evidence of mutual harm. Resolving environmental problems and addressing such issues as biodiversity, however, finds an indisputable place for traditional knowledge and local autonomy. Furthermore, the values of autonomy and equity that ecological justice promotes have a place in global regimes to manage commons resources, as well as for local resources. Ecological justice seeks to assert the primacy of political dialogue over resources management and ecological protection at all scales, a role that the forces of globalization cede to the anonymity of global capitalism.

Materials regarded as inputs in economic reckoning are the basis for ecosystem processes and life itself. Loss of these resources is necessarily injurious, and many times, permanently so. Ecological justice requires that consideration of these losses be assessed against the impacts on ecological and social interests, both contemporaneously and for the future. Social justice is part of ecological justice, so that human and natural interests are not assumed oppositional, but share common goals (Low and Gleeson, 1998). Environmental justice commentators have identified the costs of modernization through industrialization in measures and descriptions of the health and psychological damage accompanying the demise of the traditional, familial, tribal, and indigenous culture (e.g., Bullard, 1994; Sachs, 1993; and Shiva, 1994).

Ecological justice also requires consideration of issues of community autonomy when commons resources are lost. As an increasing number of communities and social organizations become enmeshed in world economic markets, their fate lies increasingly in the hands of persons and forces at some distance from themselves and indeed may reside in the instructions to an automated system. Expanding economic relations connect distant entities and locate them within a decreasing number of markets, so that previously autonomous communities and individuals necessarily become subject to external corporate priorities and decisions.

Economic Creativity and Ecological Destruction: A New Paradigm or Recycled Rhetoric?

Contemporary debate over the ecological implications of globalization is reminiscent of that over the 'limits to growth' in the late 1960s and 1970s, and indeed it features many of the protagonists of that discourse repeating their earlier nostrums. Then, as now, effectively all developed nation states (and many developing nations), global financial and development institutions, and major corporations favor economic growth and trade liberalization with equal enthusiasm, assuming one to be axiomatic of the other. What has shifted in the discourse is a lessening of attention to resource abundance and a deepening of concern over the ecological implications of industrial (and post-industrial) development, especially following the revelations of global environmental crises.

Economic growth ultimately has a material basis in ecological resources and services (Daly, 1996) and certainly the modern era has seen global resource consumption match production increases, with corresponding demands on ecology. From 1950 to 1997, Brown summarized key aspects of resource consumption as follows: ". . . the use of lumber tripled, that of paper increased sixfold, the fish catch increased nearly fivefold, grain consumption nearly tripled, fossil fuel burning nearly quadrupled" (1998: 3), and so on. Industrial lifestyles have transformed the world, diverting much of the globe's primary production and consuming vast quantities of resources. For example, in 1990, the average American consumed or moved 50 kilograms of material per day (Warnick, 1996: 112).

Globalization leads the world's consumers with the promise that all can 'live like Americans,' despite the fact that there are insufficient global resources for this to occur: "If all countries followed the industrial example, five or six planets would be needed to serve as "sources" for the inputs and "sinks" for the wastes of economic growth." (Sachs, 1996: 241). Industrial capitalism may continue its effectiveness in being "very adept at substituting relatively plentiful substances for scare ones" (Yearly, 1996: 48), but this in itself doesn't address the ecological effects of the extraction, processing, consuming, transporting, and disposing of the materials essential to industrial life.

Environmental conditions have suffered correspondingly, with global ecological crises in climate change, biodiversity, and stratospheric ozone depletion, and adding to the regional and local impacts on aquatic, marine, wetland, forest and woodland, and alpine ecosystems, including those areas used for agriculture and other productive activities. NGOs and international organizations, such as the United Nations Development Programme, have presented empirical descriptions of environmental quality at the global and sub-global levels that reveal the deleterious effects of industrial practices (e.g., the Worldwatch Institute's annual 'State of the World' series and the UN World Development Index). Industrial activity has ensured that no substantial part of the globe is free of human influence, the exceptions being a few remote areas.

Helleiner summarizes the issue for environmentalists: "… globalization intensifies many of the negative trends they associate with the industrial age" so that as a result, "The phenomenon is seen to be encouraging more economic growth, mass consumption, and large-scale economic activity, plus the global spread of industrial production process." (2000: 61). Industrialization has failed to become conciliated with the protecting environmental values, so that globalization must extend the unsustainable quality of modernity in various ways: "While economic indicators such as investment, production, and trade are consistently positive, the key environmental indicators are increasingly negative." (Brown, 1998: 4). In other words, markets can't replace lost environmental values, nor can technology substitute for ecological services, except at the trivial level.

Economic growth and expanding globalization under free trade are not necessarily or invariably destructive argue its supporters, and that such growth may be compatible with the recovery of degraded ecological conditions. Conventional economics approaches to the environmental problems of growth are exemplified by international institutions dedicated to fostering international economic growth, such as the World Bank (1992) and the OCED (1994). Environmental problems arise from economic problems, the OECD argues, so that market distortions in themselves are partly responsible for pollution problems. Structural restraints can be overcome through free trade, so that those policy interventions giving rise to environmental problems are eliminated. Freer trade encourages the transfer of environmental technologies and services, and enables greater access to more environmentally benign production inputs (OECD, 1994).

And, of course, free trade creates wealth that can be directed towards rectifying those problems created by economic activity: "In general, it is easier to raise levels of environmental protection in a growing economy." (OECD, 1994: 15). Where there are cultural and environmental threats resulting from corporate and state influence exceeding that of communities or citizen groups, globalization itself lays claim to providing a solution: "We need to demonstrate to the herd that being green, being global and being greedy can go hand in hand. If you to want to save the

Amazon, go to business school and learn how to do a deal." (Friedman, 2000: 283). Globalization takes as its starting point for the resolution of environmental issues and other social problems the primacy of the market as the basis of social relations. Freidman's reasoning may not amount to philosophy, but it does embody the spirit of the dominant ideology within the globalization *boosterism*. Two broad outcomes of economic growth within high-income nations are therefore advanced as 'solutions' to its associated ecological costs: 1) surplus income for investing in restoration; and 2) structural economic changes that shape production towards less harmful activity.

Taking a global comparison of nation states, it is possible to argue as Bhagwati does, that: "Growth can then be asserted to be tightly linked neither to the improvement of the environment nor with its degradation . . ." so that it is ". . . incorrect to assume that the growth per capita of income necessarily, or even overwhelmingly damages the environment." (1993: 163). This conclusion conveniently overlooks the manifestation of global environmental problems and takes no interest in the international patterns of income growth and environmental investments. While Bhagwati's claim may be taken as nothing more than a brazen apologia for industry's self-appointed (and usually state-sanctioned) right to pollute, conventional economics lays claim to a more solid foundation for the necessity of economic growth.

Empirically, much of the conventional economic position rests on the proposition that pollution increases with economic growth until income crosses a threshold after which additional growth results in increasing environmental restoration (i.e., the environmental Kuznets curve (EKC) hypothesis). Early empirical studies demonstrated instances of the EKC effect in high-income nations for select environmental variables, mostly of air and water pollution variables correlated against per capita GDP (e.g., Grossman and Krueger, 1995; Selden and Song, 1994).

Extrapolating the results of such studies into generalizations of the environmental benefits of economic growth has prompted research identifying the shortcomings of the EKC thesis:

- Only a few environmental variables have been studied for relatively few locations and these indicate little of overall environmental conditions, as does average national wealth of overall social welfare;

- Typical environmental variables selected are those of local problems with low costs of remediation where success is relatively facile, while those variables that increase continuously with income have been little investigated (see Rothman, 1998);

- 'Embodied' resources and pollution associated with goods and resources imported and exported are not included (Suri and Chapman, 1998); trade is not usually part of these studies, nor the phenomenon of the movement of heavy industry away from industrialized nations;

- Broader issues of resource consumption, ecological sustainability, carrying capacity, and ecosystem resilience are not considered (Arrow et al, 1995); and

- Different studies of the same pollutant show differing responses to income and nations of similar incomes have different pollutant levels and responses.

Furthermore, its critics note, few explanations were advanced in the empirical EKC studies describing the causal relationship between economic growth and environmental restoration. Mechanisms that might account for any relationship between pollution and income cannot generally be revealed by the variables that index a small number of pollutants and national income (de Bruyn et al, 1998). Wernick's (1996) findings that the consumptive response to economic growth varies greatly over time and between commodities and economic sectors undermine any assumptions that economic growth in different locales and sectors produces a common or uniform response. Structural economic change, efficiency improvements, 'dematerialization' and reduced consumption of rare resources by substitution, and technical and managerial improvements are necessary economic factors that can all play a role in reducing the environmental impacts of economic growth, although their implementation depends greatly on government policy and incentives (World Bank, 1992).

As Stern et al (1996), Rothman (1998), Suri and Chapman (1998) and others suggest, neglect in the EKC hypothesis of the export of polluting industries to developing nations is a major oversight, if not a fatal flaw. If developed nations continue to consume manufactured goods at high levels through imports from developing countries, while simultaneously transforming their economies away from secondary production and into tertiary activities (involving dematerialization and transmaterialization), then the developed nations' environmental improvements are achieved at the ecological cost of the less developed. By implication, developing nations will remain with high-pollution economies because they are the world's lowest-cost sites for manufacturing, and their continued growth could not result in improved environmental conditions. Changes recorded by the EKC studies could therefore reflect transformation in developed nations' "composition of production without accompanying changes in the composition of consumption" (Rothman and de Bruyn, 1998: 141).

Economic growth in developing nations, facilitated by globalization and free trade initiatives, has generally failed to cause improving environmental conditions. Rock (1996) described empirically how developing nations with greater trade orientation tend to have higher levels of pollution per GDP, so that increasing openness to trade has not reduced pollution. Such a finding is consistent with Suri and Chapman (1998) and Stern et al (1996), who found that poorer nations have been attracting dirtier industries, while richer nations remain essentially unaltered. Northern economic growth is not de-linked from imports of non-renewable resources from developing countries (Muradian and Martinez-Alier, 2001) and the extraction and processing of these natural resources entails much ecological destruction. These and other factors led Stern et al (1996: 1159) conclude that it did ". . . not appear to us that the EKC approach has much to offer in the way of informing the choices arising for policy makers," whilst Ayres (1995: 97) thought the general proposition that growth is good for the environment to be "false and pernicious nonsense."

Defenders of economic growth have largely defined their argument with environmentalists as being one confined to the effects of economic activity, so that pollution, resource and ecosystem destruction, and other problems represent 'market failure.' Orthodox economic reasoning offers two solutions to this problem: the insights of 'environmental economics' and economically rational standards of protection. For example, Wathen claims that environmentalists and citizen groups ". . . worry that a deregulated, free trade system will undercut existing environmental protection laws" and that the incentives for ". . . increased specialization will cause developing countries to base their economies on export commodities, like timber, or on certain agricultural crops, like bananas or coffee, which can be environmentally damaging." (1993: 10). Consequently, attaching market values to environmental phenomena though the techniques of environmental economics is held as a promising repair to market failure, making the primary economic challenge that of affixing appropriate price signals to environmental goods and services.

Burtless et al typify the economic rationality that concerns environmentalists, when finding a place for (properly restrained) environmental standards (1998: 94):

> But as long as standards reflect the outcome of a legitimate political process in each nation, the outcome should improve aggregate welfare, both at home and abroad. The countries with tougher pollution standards will get what they want: less pollution. The countries with lenient standards will get what it wants: more output from pollution-intensive industries.

Suffice to note that ethically such logic is troubling; "aggregate welfare" is best served by further harming poor nations for the benefits of richer ones.

Hence, the market 'works' if that by using various pricing techniques, markets reflect the 'value' of the environment, including its spiritual, educational, aesthetic, historical, ecological services, and other attributes. A nagging problem for market supporters is that economic theory has not yet shown how markets can readily incorporate intrinsic environmental values. Ultimately, when environmental values are affixed with prices within a market system, all that remains is their comparison with the competing values of economic development—and whenever economic values exceed environmental values, economic orthodoxy demands that the higher values be favored (see, e.g., Byrne et al, 1994). Environmentalists draw little comfort from such techniques, for the fate of the earth becomes invested in a market system and political debate becomes merely arbitration over price setting.

Some of globalization's advocates seek not only a primacy of market interests in social and environmental life, but exhort a pure form of unfettered market activity, namely *laissez faire* economics, which in the hands of some adherents seemingly becomes tangled with the virtues of liberal democracy. Globalization helps those who can already help themselves: "In a dynamic, decentralized system of individual choice and responsibility, people do not have to trust any authority but their own." (Postel, 1998: 168). Characteristic of globalization espousal is the denial of alternatives to globalization or to liberal capitalism as a universal social goal, despite the variety of competing alternatives within ecologism. Promoters of globalization often identify potential opportunities for achieving sustainability goals, and again the recourse to determinism lies close at hand. Lewis states that: ". . . capitalism, despite its social flaws, presents the only economic system resilient enough to see the development of a more benign presence on the earth." (1992: 9).

A future world comprising autonomous individuals charged with the responsibility of protecting their own well being would certainly differ from existing 'mixed' economies, welfare states, and social democracies. How the global economic market—free of the 'authorities' of public education, consumer protection, health and safety provisions, environmental protection, and other measures designed to protect the environment, communities, and individuals from corporate and state malpractice and negligence—would empower the poor, protect the environment, and secure the future, is left open. Such a prospect may not even appeal to the corporate sector. Equally importantly from the economic perspective, is the corporate need for state authorities to order and control overall economic activity. Bello (2000), for example, argues that most multilateral and international trade agreements favor developed nations and provide the cheapest means of protecting the international market system from which developed nations draw disproportionate benefit.

Postulating that the market system can be free of governance seems fanciful, no less so for considering that the legitimacy of the global free market can be maintained in the absence of the pursuit of democratic goals. Fukuyama's (1989, 1992) aforementioned proposition is therefore an indispensable foundation for global capitalism, for without the promise of democratic governance, those advocating globalization are only left with Postel's thin economic rationalizing that markets alone produce socially-optimal outcomes. Making sense of this contest necessitates distinguishing between the theoretical solutions offered by globalization's advocates (e.g., the 'business school' option) and approach that has dominated the real practice of developed nation states—namely, environmental management by democratic governments and their agencies. Responses to environmental problems and environmental injustice have seen most of the world's governments engaged in control activities based around legislation, regulation, and planning to varying extents.

Ecological justice has not been priority of the private sector. Corporations tend to interpret their civic responsibilities narrowly in this regard, rarely initiating environmental protection, resisting community demands and governmental controls, and consistently failing to meet required environmental protection performance standards. Even when required to act: "The corporate response has focused on two areas: point of production regulation and hazardous waste management. In both, the market model predominates." (Buell and DeLuca, 1996: 31). Employee, community, and environmental welfare have not featured highly in market models of corporations, as numerous examples from the literature on environmental justice attest.

Communities and firms have initiated successful actions, but government policy, regulation, and legislation dominate the 'big picture.' Indeed, the 'improvements' in environmental quality to date reflect the outcomes of this activity, and which have become part of the routine responsibilities of 'ecological modernization' by Western governments (Hajer, 1995). And here we touch on an obvious, but frequently overlooked, factor, namely that economic surplus usually only results in ecological repair via the agency of governments committed to that task (together with the necessary other factors, such as community engagement). Within this era of rapidly extending economic activity and increased commercialization of features of the natural and social realms, the application of capital to the task of environmental remediation is planned, directed, and mediated mostly by the state. Initiatives by grassroots activists and communities for environmental justice have often sought resolutions within the bounds of civic society, but frequently their efforts have involved interaction with government authorities.

Ecological modernization acknowledges the reality of the environmental crisis and the part that existing forces of production play in its creation, but holds that through the modernization of production as informed by ecological concerns and restraints, that the crisis can be resolved. Therefore, institutional changes could inform capitalist economies to achieve a shift to an ecologically sustainable state through ecological modernization. Such changes include market revisions to reflect ecological requirements, technological changes to prevent pollution and waste generation, and social and corporate adoption of environmentalist values. Dryzek (1997), Weale (1992), and others have identified the advantages of this approach, such as the economic savings resulting from early intervention and the gains in efficiency through less damaging industrial activity, which few environmentalists would dispute. Restoration of environmental values by such means have been successful, but usually within relatively narrow bounds of the solutions being relatively inexpensive, amenable to regulatory control, of small scale and short-term, usually urban, and linked to issues of human health or industrial production. Environmental remediation and protection of this sort leaves the modern state's alliance with corporate activity largely undisturbed.

That tension between current ecological modernization and the market solutions being proffered under the rubric of free trade is expressed in the current public policy discourse in environmental management. As a generalization, developed nations have not thrown out ecological modernization in response to free-market lobbying, but have increasingly incorporated more explicit market measures into existing state policies and apparatus as environmental management tools. Although environmental NGOs and community groups have consistently remained skeptical of such approaches, a considerable literature now exists advocating the economic benefits of environmentalism, of which *Factor 4* (von Weisacker et al, 1997), *Natural Capitalism* (Hawken et al, 1999), and *Hard Green* (Huber, 2000), are better-known examples. Admirable as such optimism may be, there are grounds for questioning the rectitude of the market's ecological sympathies, especially once the lowest-cost gains in efficiency have been won form any specific initiative. More fundamentally, market-based approaches cannot resolve the problem of aligning industrial activity within ecological limits; we don't know how to translate sustainability limits into prices (Common, 1995), and even if this were possible, there is no guarantee that social behavior would follow market instruction.

Assessment of individual instances of environmental injustice reveals that communities and environments at risk from industrial activity have little recourse from corporations and very limited success in having government authorities successfully resolve existing problems (exemplified in the collections of Bullard, 1994; Camacho, 1998; Faber, 1998a; Hofrichter, 1993; and Shiva, 1994). Accordingly, even in developed nations, the likelihood of ecological modernization reliably producing ecological justice is, at best, dubious. Local successes are important, necessary, and worthy of celebration, but cannot yet be counted as constituting a cultural movement or typifying an automatic social mechanism that responds to ecological problems in the U.S. (Faber, 1998b) or in the developed world generally. Typically neglected by state and corporation is the production of risk, pollution, ecological harm, and resource exhaustion—issues which have become central to the environmental justice movement.

Commitment to economic growth lies at the heart of globalization, a condition that cannot be made compliant with the values of ecological justice. As Daly (1996) suggests, such a commitment entails a denial of ecological limits. Justifying the continual expansion of the world's industrial economy using the 'grow, then repair' logic is inherently unsustainable because of the following:

- Global economic growth and increasing resource consumption show no sign becoming 'decoupled;'

- Present growth undermines the resource foundation and ecological services necessary for future growth; and

- There are no substitutes for the species, communities, and ecosystems destroyed or altered by industrial growth.

This results in the circumstance where no technical 'fix,' as Arrow et al (1995) state, can enable existing patterns of resource use to continue. Escalating resource consumption and waste generation as a consequence of globalizing industrialization therefore deprives current and future species and ecosystems of the space, materials, conditions, and energy necessary for their survival. Furthermore, as Sachs (1993), Shiva (1994), and others suggest, the current formulations of global industrial expansion have an inescapable bias against the welfare of the developing world. Aligning industrial activity with ecological values remains crucial for the planet's ecological future; what globalization has yet to realize is a strategy that does not involve forfeiting future ecological values and the interests of poorer nations for current exploitation of natural resources and ecological services—a seemingly impossible task.

Symbolic Disputes and the Rise of 'Virtual' Justice

Finally, let us briefly examine the notion that one dimension of globalization, at least, offers considerable hope for those engaged in the struggle against its deleterious effects. Within the rapidly expanding reach of the new information and communication technologies (ICT), some find encouraging prospects for promoting ecological justice (O'Meara, 2000). Cyberspace offers an unprecedented realm for exchanging information, leading to claims that a new epoch of reform and civic empowerment has begun. Certainly, environmentalists have extended their organizations, outreach, and interconnection through these technologies. Despite such benefits, there are several limitations on the capability of cyberspace to promote ecological democracy and ecological justice.

At present, a 'digital divide' exists between those with access to digital communications technology and those without, clearly demarcating a territory of inequity. Africa, South and Latin America, developing Asia and the Pacific are clearly disadvantaged. And within the developed world, there exist great differences in digital access. Conspicuous by their absence in this new 'electronic global village' is the number of real villages excluded. It seems likely, therefore, that a new layer has been added to the filters that determine which issues, locations, communities, species, and ecosystems become the subject of environmental activism.

Access and equity concerns also evoke the specter of traditional 'Hobbesian' concerns when these new ICT become a normal feature of political discourse, a time rapidly approaching for the developed world. Goldman wrote of the 'information superhighway' that (1996: 137-138): "It will be lavishly sponsored by corporate, governmental, and academic institutions, and supplied with an elite squad of independent experts to establish proper standards, definitions, methods, measures, and questions." ICTs are therefore politically empowering, but not equally so. As Ogden pointed out: ". . . in the emerging cyberdemocracy, where information is a source of social power, those who are typically the downtrodden (many minorities as well as the poor) are not even aware that they are on the verge of being disenfranchised." (1998: 79). Greater volumes of protest should not, therefore, be automatically assumed to be the product of more numerous voices and a positive sign of enhanced democratic activity.

Optimism for the benefits of ICTs assumes that empowerment occurs through knowledge, a claim that may be more relative than absolute. Such beliefs hold that cyberspace as a medium, in and of itself, offsets the power relationships within 'real' social discourse. For this to be the case, the outputs of cyberspace activity have to be realized. 'Virtual' justice is merely that until electronic messages are formed into political acts. Clearly, these technologies enable new coalitions and opportunities to build social movements of opposition with unprecedented access to technical information and research (which is nearly always a essential element in environmental disputation). Such changes may shift the distribution of power in individual disputes, but invariably the political influence of these technologies will be assessed not just by the facility to connect those with common political purposes, but also to increase the number and influence of those holding such beliefs. Pragmatically, the final test will be whether these social changes are registered in mainstream political activity.

Further, the limits of the liberationary capacity may arise from the type and form of communication occurring in cyberspace and the sort of knowledge conveyed. Along with much of contemporary communication and popular culture, the use and manipulation of symbols dominate cyberspace. Asserting the cause of justice in such a setting depends on its expression in symbolic form in order to counter those in opposition. Although space does not permit here, we might ponder the identity and allegiances of the emerging 'global citizens' of cyberspace who are to assume the responsibilities of defending ecological justice. If cyberspace were to confer greater justice in this world, then this must be on the basis that justice's symbolic representation has power equivalent to that of rival arguments. Cyberspace discourses may draw on the motivated and aware members of civic society able to enter this world of electronic discourse, but corporations and states share the ease of this entry, and are likely to have greater resources to direct towards specific campaigns.

Symbols likely to find widest appeal are those of the cultures that dominate the Internet, namely the industrialized, developed, English-speaking nations. Promoters of the Internet as a liberationary force need to consider the implications of the necessity to convert the substance of diverse indigenous cultures into the symbols of Western popular culture in order to seek justice for these groups. Careful differentiation is needed between knowledge useful for engaging in political strategies of resistance, protest, and influence necessary to protect commons resources and traditional societies, with traditional knowledge itself. Internet access doesn't cater for traditional and indigenous knowledge vested and ingrained in land and culture, in oral traditions, in familial relationships: cyberspace isn't place for these kinds of values. So although cyberspace has an emancipatory role, in practice this is bounded by several constraints. It may be that cyberspace constitutes a commons resource and one that has also to be defended against appropriation by the political interests supporting globalization.

Conclusion

Environmentalists are rightly troubled by globalization: it degrades ecological entities and processes; promotes ecological injustice; and impoverishes future prospects for the flourishing of Nature and civic society. If liberal democracy is the end of history, then globalization is the end of justice and the eulogy of Nature. Yet this need not be so. Ecological justice asks us to think expansively about justice—drawing us away from contests over the distribution of disbenefits—and towards a questioning of globalization's manufacture of ecological injustice and the pursuit of the interests of indigenous peoples, future generations, commons resources, and natural entities and processes. An alternative future that features ecological justice, therefore, will actively resist globalization. Examining the applications of traditional ecological knowledge, the management of commons resources at the local scale, and the resistance of grassroots environmental movements we see opportunities for resisting the effects of globalization. New information technologies can assist this effort. Justice, however, ultimately cannot be found within the virtual world of cyberspace, but will result from contesting the real grip of global markets. An ecologically just world may be found in a justice that responds to local, immediate, and specific needs, but can also counter globalization with an awareness of global ecology and the rights of 'others' in the most expansive sense. For if anything is to be made global by human invention, what could have a stronger claim than justice?

References

Arrow, Kenneth, et al. 1995. "Economic Growth, Carrying Capacity, and the Environment." *Science.* Volume 268: 520-521.

Ayres, Robert U. 1995. "Economic Growth: Politically Necessary but *Not* Environmentally Friendly." *Ecological Economics.* Volume 15: 97-99.

Barnet, Richard and John Cavanagh. 1996. "Homoginization of Global Culture." In Jerry Mander and Edward Goldsmith (eds). *The Case Against the Global Economy and For a Turn Toward the Local.* San Francisco: Sierra Club Books. pp. 71-77.

Bello, Walden. 2000. "The Iron Cage: The World Trade Organization, the Bretton Woods Institutions, and the South." *Capitalism, Nature, Socialism.* Volume 11, Number 1: 3-32.

Bhagwati, Jagdish. 1993. "Trade and the Environment: The False Conflict." In Durwood Zaelke, Paul Orbuch, and Robert F. Housman (eds). *Trade and the Environment: Law, Economics, and Policy.* Washington, D.C. and Covelo, CA: Island Press. Pp. 159-190.

Brown, Lester. 1998. "The Future of Growth." In Lester Brown et al. *State of the World 1998.* London and New York: W. W. Norton. pp. 3-20.

Bryan, Lowell and Diana Farrell. 1996. *Market Unbound: Unleashing Global Capitalism.* New York: John Wiley.

Buell, John and Tom DeLuca. 1996. *Sustainable Democracy: Individuality and the Politics of the Environment.* Thousand Oaks, CA: Sage.

Bullard, Robert D. (ed). 1994. *Unequal Protection: Environmental Justice and Communities of Color.* San Francisco: Sierra Club Books.

Burtless, Gary, Robert Z. Lawrence, Robert E. Litan, and Robert J. Shapiro. 1998. *Globaphobia: Confronting Fears about Open Trade.* Washington: Brookings Institution.

Byrne, John, Constantine Hadjilambrinos, and Subodh Wagle. 1994. "Distributing the Costs of Global Climate Change." *IEEE Technology and Society.* Spring: 17-32.

Camacho, David E. (ed). 1998. *Environmental Injustices, Political Struggles: Race, Class, and the Environment*. Durham, NC: Duke University Press.

Cerney, Philip G. 1999. "Globalization and the Erosion of Democracy." *European Journal of Political Research*. Volume 36: 1-26.

Chatterjee, Pratap and Mattias Finger. 1994. *The Earth Brokers: Power Politics and World Development*. London: Routledge.

Common, Michael. 1995. *Sustainability and Policy: Limits to Economics*. Cambridge, New York, Melbourne: Cambridge University Press.

Cox, Robert W. 1995. "Critical Political Economy." In Björn Hettne (ed). *International Political Economy: Understanding Global Disorder*. London and New Jersey: Zed Books. pp. 31-45.

Crystal, David. 2000. *Language Death*. Cambridge, UK: Cambridge University Press.

Dahl, Robert A. 1998. *On Democracy*. New Haven: Yale University Press.

Daly, Herman E. 1996. *The Economics of Sustainable Development*. Boston: Beacon Press.

Dryzek, John S. 1997. *The Politics of the Earth: Environmental Discourses*. New York: Oxford University Press.

Faber, Daniel (ed). 1998a. *The Struggle for Ecological Democracy: Environmental Justice Movements in the United States*. New York: Guildford Press.

_____. 1998b. "The Political Ecology of American Capitalism: New Challenges for the Environmental Justice Movement." In Daniel Faber (ed). *The Struggle for Ecological Democracy: Environmental Justice Movements in the United States*. New York: Guildford Press. pp. 27-59.

Friedman, Thomas, L. 2000. *The Lexus and the Olive Tree: Understanding Globalization*. New York: Anchor Books.

Fukuyama, Francis. 1992. *The End of History and the Last Man*. Free Press: New York, NY.

_____. 1989. *Have We Reached the End of History?* Santa Monica: Rand.

Gilpin, Robert. 2000. *The Challenge of Global Capitalism: The World Economy in the 21st Century*. Princeton, New Jersey: Princeton University Press.

Goldman, Benjamin A. 1996. "What is the Future of Environmental Justice?" *Antipode*. Volume 28, Number 2: 122-141.

Goldman, Michael (ed). 1998. "Introduction: The Political Resurgence of the Commons." *Privatizing Nature: Political Struggles for the Global Commons*. New Brunswick, NJ: Rutgers University Press. pp. 1-19.

Greider, William. 1997. *One World, Ready or Not: The Manic Logic of Global Capitalism*. New York, NY: Simon and Schuster.

Grossman, Gene M. and Alan B. Krueger. 1995. 'Economic Growth and the Environment." *The Quarterly Journal of Economics*. May: 353-377.

Hardin, Garret. 1977. *Managing the Commons*. San Francisco: W. H. Freeman.

_____. 1968. "The Tragedy of the Commons." *Science*. Volume 162: 1243-1248.

Hajer, Maarten A. 1995. *The Politics of Environmental Discourse: Ecological Modernization and the Policy Process*. Oxford, UK: Oxford University Press.

Hawken, Paul, Amory Lovins, and L. Hunter Lovins. 1999. *Natural Capitalism: Creating the Next Industrial Revolution*. Boston: Little, Brown, and Company.

Heilbroner, Robert. 1985. *The Nature and Logic of Capitalism*. New York and London: W.W. Norton.

Helleiner, Eric. 2000. "New Voices in the Globalization Debate: Green Perspectives on the World Economy." In Richard Stubbs and Geoffrey R. D. Underhill (eds). *Political Economy and the Changing Global Order*. Second Edition. Oxford: Oxford University Press. pp. 60-69.

Held, David, Anthony McGrew, David Goldblatt, and Jonathon Perraton. 1999. *Global Transformations: Politics, Economics and Culture*. Stanford, CA: Stanford University Press.

Hirst, Paul and Graeme Thompson. 1999. *Globalization in Question: The International Economy and the Possibilities of Governance*. Second Edition. Cambridge, UK: Polity Press.

Hofrichter, Richard (ed). 1993. *Toxic Struggles: The Theory and Practice of Environmental Justice*. Philadelphia, PA: New Society Publishers.

Huber, Peter. 2000. *Hard Green: Saving the Environment from the Environmentalists: A Conservative Manifesto*. New York: Basic Books.

Krugman, Paul. 2000. "Create and Destroy." *New York Times*. 8 October.

_____. 1996. *Pop Internationalism*. Cambridge, MA; London, England: MIT Press.

Lash, Scott and John Urry. 1987. *The End of Organized Capitalism*. Cambridge: Polity Press.

Lewis, Martin W. 1992. *Green Delusions: An Environmentalist Critique of Radical Environmentalism*. Durham, NC: Duke University Press.

Low, Nicholas and Brendon Gleeson. 1998. *Justice, Society and Nature: An Exploration of Political Ecology*. London and New York: Routledge.

Mander, Jerry and Edward Goldsmith (eds). 1996. *The Case Against the Global Economy and For a Turn Toward the Local*. San Francisco: Sierra Club Books.

McMurtry, John. 1997. "The Global Market Ideology: Anatomy of a Value System." In Ted Schrecker (ed). *Surviving Globalism: The Social and Environmental Challenges*. New York, NY: St. Martin's Press. pp. 177-198.

Muradian, Roldan and Joan Martinez-Alier. 2001. "Trade and the Environment: From a 'Southern' Perspective.'" *Ecological Economics*. Volume 36, Issue 2: 281-297.

Ogden, Michael R. 1998. "Technologies of Abstraction: Cyberdemocracy and the Changing Communications Landscape." In Cynthia J. Alexander and Leslie A. Pal (eds). *Digital Democracy: Policy and Politics in the Wired World*. Toronto, Oxford, New York: Oxford University Press. pp. 63-86.

O'Meara, Molly. 2000. "Harnessing Information Technologies for the Environment." In Lester R. Brown et al. *State of the World 2000*. New York and London: W.W. Norton. pp. 121-141.

Organisation for Economic Co-Operation and Development (OECD). 1994. *The Environmental Effects of Trade*. Paris: OECD.

Polanyi, Karl. 1957. *The Great Transformation: The Political and Economic Origins of Our Time*. Boston: Beacon Press.

Postel, Virginia. 1998. *The Future and its Enemies: The Growing Conflict over Creativity, Enterprise, and Progress*. New York, NY: The Free Press.

Rock, Michael T. 1996. "Pollution Intensity of GDP and Trade Policy: Can the World Bank be Wrong?" *World Development*. Volume 24, Number 3: 471-479.

Rodrik, Dani. 1997. *Has Globalization Gone Too Far?* Washington, D.C.: Institute for International Economics.

Rothman, Dale S. 1998. "Environmental Kuznets Curve—Real Progress or Passing the Buck? A Case for Consumption-Based Approaches." *Ecological Economics*. Volume 25, Issue 2: 177-194.

Rothman, Dale S. and Sander M. de Bruyn. 1998. "Probing into the Environmental Kuznets Curve Hypothesis." *Ecological Economics*. Volume 25, Issue 2: 143-145.

Sachs, Wolfgang. 1996. "Neo-Development: Global Ecological Management." In Jerry Mander and Edward Goldsmith (eds). *The Case Against the Global Economy and For a Turn Toward the Local*. San Francisco: Sierra Club Books. pp. 239-252.

_____. (ed). 1993. *Global Ecology: A New Arena of Global Conflict*. London: Zed Books.

Schrecker, Ted (ed). 1997. *Surviving Globalism: The Social and Environmental Challenges*. New York, NY: St. Martin's Press.

Schumpeter, Joseph A. 1975. [1942] *Capitalism, Socialism and Democracy*. New York: Harper and Row.

Selden, Thomas M. and Daqing Song. 1994. "Environmental Quality and Development: Is there a Kuznets Curve for Air Pollution Emissions?" *Journal of Environmental Economics and Management*. Volume 27, Number 2: 147-162.

Shiva, Vandana. 1988. *Staying Alive: Women, Ecology and Development*. London: Zed Books.

_____. (ed). 1994. *Close to Home: Women Reconnect Ecology, Health, and Development Worldwide*. Philadelphia, PA: New Society Publishers.

Stern, David I., Michael S. Common, and Edward B. Barber. 1996. "Economic Growth and Environmental Degradation: The Environmental Kuznets Curve and Sustainable Development." *World Development*. Volume 24, Number 7: 1151-1160.

Suri, Vivek and Duane Chapman. 1998. "Economic Growth, Trade and Energy: Implications for the Environmental Kuznets Curve." Ecological Economics. Volume 25, Issue 2: 195-208.

The Ecologist. 1993. *Whose Common Future?: Reclaiming the Commons*. Philadelphia, PA: New Society Publishers.

Thurow, Lester C. 1999. *Building Wealth: The New Rules for Individuals, Companies, and Nations in a Knowledge-Based Economy*. New York, NY: HarperInformation.

UNDP (United Nations Development Programme). 2000. *Human Development Report 2000*. New York, NY and Oxford: Oxford University Press.

von Weisacker, Ernst, Amory B. Lovins, and L. Hunter Lovins. 1997. *Factor Four: Doubling Wealth – Halving Resource Use*. London: Earthscan.

Wallerstein, Immanuel. 1979. *The Capitalist World-Economy*. Cambridge: Cambridge University Press.

Waters, Malcolm. 1995. *Globalization*. London and New York: Routledge.

Wathen, Tom. 1993. "A Guide to Trade and the Environment." In Durwood Zaelke, Paul Orbuch, and Robert F. Housman (eds). *Trade and the Environment: Law, Economics, and Policy*. Washington, D.C. and Covelo, CA: Island Press. pp. 3-21.

Weale, Albert. 1992. *The New Politics of Pollution*. Manchester: Manchester University Press.

Wernick, Iddo K. 1996. "Consuming Materials: The American Way." *Technological Forecasting and Social Change*. Volume 53: 111-122.

Winner, Langdon. 1977. *Autonomous Technology: Technics-Out-of-Control as a Theme in Political Thought*. Cambridge, MA: The MIT Press.

World Bank. 1992. *World Development Report 1992: Development and the Environment*. New York: Oxford University Press.

World Commission on Environment and Development (WCED). 1987. *Our Common Future*. New York: Oxford University Press.

Yearly, Steven. 1996. *Sociology, Environmentalism, Globalization: Reinventing the Globe*. London: Sage.

11

The Production of Unequal Nature

John Byrne, Leigh Glover, and Cecilia Martinez

Introduction

Nature is reacting to the activities of modern society in unique and largely unexpected ways. The spread of acidified rain to every continent, a worldwide decline of forested lands, and the ubiquitous presence of persistent organic pollutants due to industrial experiments in biochemistry suggest that the contemporary nature-society relation includes phenomena unlike any that were previously known in human, or geological, history. These reactions are surprising since human impacts on nature have traditionally been ascribed a minor role in determining the course of ecological change. While humanity has long discarded its wastes in nature, the "predominant view in the natural sciences was that life on Earth is primarily passive, responding to nonliving forces like volcanic eruptions, severe storms, droughts, and even drifting continents" (Schneider, 1990: 6).

This conception of passivity is under increasing challenge, but until recently, physical and biological debates about global change presumed its validity (Price, 1989). Accordingly, modernity can be characterized as the era guided by an ecological theory of nature's inexhaustibility at the broad scale, and certainly for those processes necessary to sustain overall human expectations. Such an understanding has fostered the belief that human reason is a superior instrument for the design of nature compared to the 'passive' forces of physical and biological change. In essence, modernity asserts that society can 'know' nature and apply that knowledge to shape a better future. Human progress, in this view, is identical with and dependent on the mastery of nature. Hence, in a landmark work of modernist environmental consciousness, the problem was framed thus (Ward and Dubos, 1972: 1):

> Man inhabits two worlds. One is the natural world of plants and animals, of soils and air and waters which precede him by billions of years and of which he is a part. The other is the world of social institutions and artifacts he builds for himself, using his tools and engines, his science and his dreams to fashion an environment obedient to human purpose and direction.

Breaking with this orthodoxy, a growing number of scientists have begun to doubt the adequacy of the modernist thesis. A prominent example is the reconceptualization of climate change now underway in which science bodies assert that the cumulative effects of human activity are overwhelming natural processes that until very recently were responsible for variation in climate (see, e.g., IPCC 1990, 1996a, and 2000). But even in this instance, discussion of the social and political organization of nature is strangely absent. Thus, the case of global warming is commonly debated in terms of nature-society interactions expressed almost exclusively in units of carbon (or other chemicals), with the aim of establishing a natural limit on gaseous releases that humanity should not exceed.

The nexus of society and nature cannot be captured by studying the chemical content of industrial emissions alone. Indeed, the social content—the political economy—of this nexus is likely to be key to unraveling the sources of, and responses to, global change. Perhaps the most difficult challenge is to consider whether nature is undergoing a process of social capture which eventually may make it in effect a social subsystem subject to political attitudes and ideologies, and a functioning part of the world political economy. It is readily admitted that modernist ideals of progress endanger indigenous cultures throughout the world. Mounting evidence suggests that the same argument now needs to be applied to ecosystems. Although the present society-nature regime is only about 300 years old (dating to the spread of a coal-based energy regime, steam technology, wage labor and capitalist political economy), it has reached a level of sophistication which may render its operations a threat to several million years of climate and biological, as well as social, evolution.

A clear implication of rejecting modernist premises of natural passivity and society-nature autonomy is that physical and biological phenomena must be reconceived as outcomes, to some degree of political-economic, as well as ecological, processes. One needed theoretical addition, in this vein, would be an explanation of nature as a medium of social advantage and disadvantage. In other words, while observations of environmental injustice are hardly new (consider, for example, Engel's accounts of the Irish working class in Manchester (Engels, 1993 [1845]), the slave trade of European nations, or conditions in colonial primary production), the concept of *unequal nature* as a contemporary invention of political economy needs systematic explanation. In effect, this would mean the pursuit of an explanation of modernization as a pattern of con-comitant, 'co-produced' (O'Connor, 1994a) social and ecological change with a distinctive distribution of effects on and in the natural and social worlds. Together, these changes and effects can be understood as creat-ing the levels of justice and injustice that are found in modernized ecol-ogy and society. Pursuing this theoretical strategy promises an explana-tion of the evolution of unequal nature that is ecologically, as well as sociologically, informed. Below we offer our initial efforts in this direc-tion.

Social Structure and Nature

Three hundred years of industrialization have rendered social and eco-logical relations[1] largely commodity-based. Human existence transpires within a reality of production and consumption of commodities which together release into the air and water, and deposit on plants and the soil, pollutants more numerous than we know and, certainly, more complex in their effects than we understand. This reality is structured and moti-vated by the logics of technology and capital; environmental conse-quences are, at best, a residual concern. We depend for our lives and our experience of life upon a collective capacity to produce goods and ser-vices and upon individual capacities to obtain and consume goods and services, as though nature was incidental to the human drama. As Mumford (1970) argued, society has become a 'megamachine' with its members existing as so many machine parts. In the techno-logical milieu, natural experience has all but evaporated except as a reproduction or 'sign' (Barthes, 1972) that romanticizes the natural world as variously a pastoral retreat, a pristine, pre-human order of life, or a wild, primordial state (see, e.g., Merchant, 1980; and Borgmann, 1993).

In a world where adverse environmental and social consequences of industrial production and consumption are considered as unavoidable events along the way to modernity, dirty skies and the dirty lungs of society's members elicit little concern other than the need to fashion or strengthen regimes of management and treatment. Conceived in this con-text, much of social theory concerns itself with the travails and clean up ('remediation') of the mess of modern life. Few efforts are made to develop social analyses which can both characterize the commodification process and challenge its hegemony over social and ecological relations. Even several of the more comprehensive social frameworks conceive only the possibility of social activities which degrade the environment. Structural transformation of the environment is presumed to be beyond the reach of social influence. Theories of political economy by and large regard the 'laws of nature' as operating literally beyond the 'laws of social motion' (as Karl Marx termed them).

This is not to say that the analytic boundary between society and nature assumed in most social theory precludes significant impacts as a result of their interaction. But efforts to conceive the difference between nature-society relations and putatively social ones (especially, political and economic relations) typically embody an assumption of a duality of structures. For example, it is possible to develop a structural analysis of social activities producing pollution: social behaviors can be conceived as structurally organized to continuously disrupt or degrade environmental quality; and changes in social structure can be shown as necessary to remedy the pattern of polluting behavior. Mainstream analysis, though, leaves intact the distinction between society and nature as separate phenomenal structures.

Natural inquiry in its most general form likewise observes an analytic boundary between the two spheres. The influence of human beings on natural operations, and vice versa, is recognized in the paradigms of biology, chemistry, and physics. But again, the architectures of social and natural order are understood as maintained by relations and rules that are distinct to each sphere. In this respect, much of natural inquiry, like its social counterpart, operates on a premise of dual realities—one social and one natural.

Guided by the dual-realities premise, social theory presumes that virtually anything can be socially practiced and repeated with the principal environmental consequence being a natural disturbance or degradation of environmental quality. To speak about environmental 'spillover effects,' 'externalities,' and 'social costs,' it is essential to the very logic of the language in which these ideas are conceived that one can reliably believe in the natural reservoir as, in effect, bottomless; and that the problems of environmental disruption or degradation, eventually, can be internalized within the social structure. Accordingly, the natural world is bestowed with a resolute capacity for reproduction by individual species, life forms, and ecosystem processes. Their self-perpetuation then is counted upon in the social sphere to provide the range of resources that humanity can acquire and transform to meet its needs. Nature, we assume, takes care of itself in the manner that it takes care of human needs. This does not preclude social catastrophe—the starvation of large populations, the spread of epidemics, annihilation of societies, or even the human species—but, ultimately, such disasters are confined to the social sphere. The permanence of nature is not obviated or negated by human calamity.

The natural point of view is similarly predicated on nature's analytic permanence. Only with this characteristic can nature provide the grounds, literally, for validation/falsification of the supposed rules and laws of natural order, the epistemological centerpiece of this mode of inquiry. We cannot think about natural order within the reigning paradigms of science without, at the very least, assuming a distinct order for nature. It is the ability of science to uncover 'laws' that places it atop the hierarchy of human knowledge. Indeed, for most practitioners of natural inquiry, a hierarchy of orders is implied between the natural and the social, with the former setting, broadly, the conditions and constraints for actions in the latter, a so-called ecology of order.

However, a range of environmental issues, such as the depletion of stratospheric ozone, climate change, and other phenomena traceable to the changing chemical composition of the earth's atmosphere, point to the difficulties, to say the least, of maintaining the assumption of a dual reality—one natural and one social—at the structural level. For our purposes, the most important scenario for the breakdown of the dual reality thesis is that a 'commodification' process[2] has functionally spread to the architecture of nature itself. In this possibility, the potential for social activity to affect its own context is thought to be great enough to redesign nature. This potential is in part an outgrowth or legacy of social behaviors under the structural guidance of industrial capital; and in part a result of the achievements of certain scientific and technological insights. Under this scenario, the forces of technology and capital are not limited to acts of natural disturbance or degradation. Rather, the very structure of nature is subjected to the design principles of these social forces. In the design of nature through science, technology and political economy, the fuller meaning of environmental and ecological injustice is also to be found.

A contrast exists between decisions guided by capital and technology to endanger the health of workers and whole communities by pollution practices at various industrial sites (which enhance profit, market position, etc.) and the collected practices of technological societies which *in toto* valorize a particular atmospheric chemistry (specifically, one richer in CO_2). The difference is fundamental. In the former case, a social structure—technological society—guides behaviors which adversely impact nature at the behavioral level: air, water, and human tissue are poisoned to some degree. But the natural order, which produces air, water, and living matter, is not itself altered; the effect of the pollution is too small to restructure nature; and the force of technicization and capitalization are too specific in their goals to alter natural order. In the latter, social structure threatens to cause a different natural order to evolve. This interpretation conceives commodification as having breached the nature-society duality and is now encroaching on the structural organization of nature itself. This prospect lies beyond the theoretically possible for social and physical analysis as presently organized. Apparently, however, it is not outside the reality of contemporary nature-society relations.

A similar contrast is identifiable with respect to issues of justice, environment, and society. In one instance, the environment is used as a weapon against those devalued by capital and the state—the shipment of toxic wastes generated in the U.S. to Africa is a poignant example of environmental injustice. But in another instance, ecological and social forms are threatened with elimination in the interest of a 'capitalized nature' (Escobar, 1996; and O'Connor, 1994b). The sacrifice of indigenous communities and ecologies for so-called ecological modernization comes to mind here. Explaining injustice in the latter sense and effectively challenging an era of capitalized nature will necessarily require theories that drop the pretense of nature-society duality. A reconceived theory of commodification offers one pathway to explain environmental justice/injustice without the dualism presumed by many current arguments.

Three Phases of Commodification

Three phases of the commodification process and its evolution to the capitalization of nature can be identified. As we conceive them, these phases represent a process of increased 'co-dependency' in nature-society relations (O'Connor, 1994a). The reach and range of commodification embedded in these relations successively expands and manifests an accretive quality in its evolution. But there are also transformative elements that alter the structures of nature-society relations themselves. We do not intend in this analysis to suggest that one era 'rationally' supercedes the previous. Nor do we believe that one era dramatically ends a prior one. Instead, we argue that a common core of relations and transformations can be detected across the three periods of order and change. These occur *together* and constitute the whole of modernist nature-society relations and explain the realities of justice/injustice in those relations.

Normal Pollution

In his comprehensive examination of global urban industrial growth, Lewis Mumford argued that modern society had simultaneously lost all semblance of balance with the natural order while reducing the focus of human life to the mere production of things (Mumford, 1934, 1961). With the Industrial Revolution, an alliance of science, capitalism, and carbon power reorganized social order on the pervasive principle of *quantification* (Mumford, 1961: 570):

> Quantitative production has become, for our mass-minded contemporaries, the only imperative goal: they value quantification without qualification. In physical energy, in industrial productivity, in invention, in knowledge, in population the same vacuous expansions and explosions prevail.

The new social order produced goods at an unparalleled rate and magnitude, but also pollution of a type and scale hitherto unknown (Mumford, 1934: 168-169):

> In this [industrial] world the realities were money, prices, capital, shares: the environment itself, like most of human existence, was treated as an abstraction. Air and sunlight, because of their deplorable lack of value in exchange, had no reality at all . . . the reek of coal was the very incense of the new industrialism. A clear sky in an industrial district was the sign of a strike or a lock-out or an industrial depression.

The nature and content of what Mumford called the 'atmospheric sewage' of modern industry changed in the 20th century, but the chain of energy combustion-to-environmental degradation was not altered. The alliance of science and technology, the power complex, and the industrial economy ushered in a social order in which pollution was a functional element of human progress. In effect, pollution was "normalized."

Lasting into this century, the phase of *normal pollution* is distinguished by its rationalization of nature as alternately a resource mine and a bottomless sewer into which the afterthought of industrial production can be deposited. The industrial degradation of nature, of course, does not exempt human life from the damage. Indeed, industrial tolerance for pollution has presupposed that human suffering is a necessary part of the equation.

As the air was fouled with technological and economic advance, 20th century cities were afflicted with the worst pollution. Circulating through an industrially manufactured cloud of chemical waste, urban air worldwide exacted the price of modern existence—life threatened by the involuntary, heretofore life-giving, act of breathing. Chronic bronchial, lung, circulatory and heart problems were and are the special mark of industrial civilization.

When the industrial elites worried at all about pollution or social health, it was to assure that popular efforts to address these problems were kept strictly local and posed no threat to profit-making. In this objective they were assisted by the 'new thinking' of economics which abstracted environmental abuse from the workings of the production regime, assigning it the residual status of an 'externality' (Marshall, 1946 [1890]; and Pigou, 1924). In this treatment, those who profited from pollution or threatened human health were exempted from responsibility for cleaning up; society as a whole was to bear the burdens of progress. Policy and law followed the 'analytic' view of the economists, giving institutional permission for the waters, land, air, and the human body to be used as dumps.

Environmental costs of production and wealth creation were considered, when considered at all, in the aggregate and not the particular. Accordingly, pollution became a 'social cost,' implying that the burden was collective, as were the benefits. Nothing could be more misleading; the costs and benefits of pollution were sharply and equivocally divided within society and between societies from the onset of industrialization to the present day. Arguably, the tendencies of early capitalism described by Mumford (and others), have become the habits of mature capitalism under the strategies of globalization.

Economics provided a *post hoc* rationale for the acceptance of unequal nature in parallel with unequal society. The distribution of the spoils of industry to the rich and the spoiled landscapes to the poor was justified by the circular assertion of productivity: those who accumulated the most wealth were able to do so because their services to society were highly valued; the poor deserved poverty because they had little to offer of value. That nature conspired in this rewards-for-productivity scheme seemed logical to economists: the wealthy could afford the princely rent of clean air, as though nature was organized to provide its 'services' to the highest bidder.

By leaving industry unfettered in its operations, overall economic gains would be optimized, economists averred, and through the realization of national economic growth, all would eventually benefit. Raw materials and resources for the industrialized world came increasingly to be drawn from the European colonies in the New World and poorer independent states during the era, while capitalism's productivity rationale was extended to these trading partners. Trading inevitably boosted the economic performance of some parties, although there was obviously great differentiation in those benefits within and between participant nations. Polluting capitalism was both an historical era and a development stage. As a result, many of the hallmarks of the era remain in the contemporary world and are spreading to societies on the eve of their being 'modernized.' Using trade to globalize the model, Western nations have been able to reduce their risks and discomfort from polluting capitalism through the displacement of many industrial practices to the developing world.

Essentially this has created a dualism within the industrial regime. Spurred on by the search for lowest cost, and most profitable, production, industrialization has predictably meant locating the most harmful activities in the poorest communities and nations. Lawrence Summers' infamous proposition (while employed by the World Bank) about poor nations being under-polluted (Foster, 1993), exemplifies exactly the economic rationale for shifting pollution away from the rich. Such social engineering through economic rationality formed the antecedent to globalization and its quest to organize a world wherein development choices are primarily dictated by global profitability.

The legitimation of pollution and disease, while defining facets of the first era of commodification, must be understood within the broader historical context. The target of capitalist development in the 19th and 20th centuries was the transformation of all social activities into commodities to be valorized in markets and exchanged for cash. Labor, leisure, sexuality, emotion and, above all, the human experience of time were stripped of their intimacy and personality, and reconstituted as anonymous units of market value. The reduction of nature to a supplier of resources and a repository of wastes was an instrumental component of the commodification process; but exploitation (of humanity and nature) was the driving force of the period.

The resulting class division of industrial society *and* nature set in motion forces of inequality that privileged certain lives and landscapes and denied or marginalized others. While many analyses of the period dwell on the social dimensions of injustice, a smaller number discuss the environmental implications, and only a few realize the intimate relation between the two, Mumford representing this last group. His depiction of worker-river injustice brilliantly captures his insight in this regard.

> Nothing seems more characteristic of [Manchester] . . . than the river Irwell, which runs through the place . . . The hapless river—a pretty enough stream a few miles up, with trees overhanging its bank and fringes of green sedge set thick along its edges— loses caste as it gets among the mills and print works. There are myriads of dirty things given it to wash, and whole wagonloads of poisons from dye houses and bleachyards thrown into it to carry away; steam boilers discharge into it their seething contents, and drains and sewers their fetid impurities; till at length it rolls on— here between tall dingy walls, there under precipices of red sandstone—considerably less a river than a flood of liquid manure (Mumford, 1934: 459-460).

From upstream communities of wealth, a healthy Irwell descended into industrial districts where low-cost production through low-wage labor re-defined the river, and the communities and factories housed alongside it, as 'working class.' The nexus of social and environmental injustice could not have been clearer. Capital's hegemony and labor's alienation were expressed not only in social relations, but ecological ones as well. A half-century after Mumford's landmark analysis, Crosby (1988) has documented the international scale of the class division of lives and landscapes (and species) that occurred with the imperial thrust of capitalism. The "demographic takeover" of the Americas and Oceania by Europeans recorded capitalism's social *and* environmental aims. Steward cultures that had sustained life for millennia were attacked and, in some cases, enslaved, in capital's pursuit of advantage. Equally important, biological warfare waged by European invaders, sometimes inadvertently and at other times by design, released pests and pathogens that Europeanized ecologies in the same degree that military and economic contests Europeanized human populations.

Technological Authoritarianism

The first era of commodification left Western society transformed, non-Western society under economic siege, and many ecosystems polluted and infested with the species and landscape preferences of capitalist elites. But a second era emerged during the 20th century that advocates claimed would right the social and ecological wrongs of polluting capitalism. Scientific knowledge and technological organization would increasingly make it possible to divorce human activity from its past and travel along a new course. In the new era, society's needs could be designed in cooperation with nature and with a socially more equitable order. Old constraints on progress that had led to the failures of the first era of commodification were to vanish.

Why should anyone expect that the injustices of social and environmental commodification, which had permeated the first era of modernization, could be corrected by *deepening* the commitment to modernity? For modernization's believers, the answer was (and is) clear: the source of progress lay in the advance of scientific and technical knowledge. Modernity's first era had preempted civilizational success by yielding too much authority to the institutions of polluting capitalism and settling for a regime that simply exploited labor and nature with the tools of modern thinking (e.g., Bell, 1967; and Drucker, 1993). It was promised that the displacement of capital with science and technology as the guiding forces of society would realize a new era of cornucopian, yet egalitarian, modernity. Humanity's impact on nature would be considerably softened as societies replaced the first era's legacy of pollution with an intelligent ideology of nature conservation and management. At least for those confident that science and technology could be progressive rulers of modernity, the new era was anticipated to quiet social fears of inequality, end class antagonisms, and bring to a swift conclusion the unfortunate chapter of polluting capitalism.

Certainly, the Global North[3] has experienced some of the triumphal effects promised for the new era. A string of intellectual revolutions has brought about an extended period of scientific and technological breakthroughs that have meant much longer lives and the eradication of major diseases for elite communities (and, in some cases, for non-elites as well). Suddenly, the length of human life—if you are wealthy—seems less dependent on fate than the advance of scientific knowledge. With the appearance of exceptionally productive crops and crop management strategies, and the invention of hybrid varieties that could grow food almost anywhere, minding nature has lost its compellingness. Human sustenance is no longer a matter of soil and water, but of chemistry and biology (and the wealth to afford their implementation). The spread of digital, wireless networks has enabled much greater and faster volumes of interaction, while computers have made calculation ubiquitous. Together these innovations have supplanted materiality with the limitlessness of post-material virtuality. A 'space of flows' has dissolved the traditional 'space of places' (Castells, 1984, 1996) and time is no longer rooted in experience but in the far more 'precise' atomic measure of its meaning. A radical transformation of the relation between idea and reality has resulted from these 'revolutions' as well as the fundamental progress made recently in the understanding of energy-matter and the genome. For many in the sciences and engineering, human intelligence has been elevated by the advance of knowledge to a determinant, rather than simply an inquirer, of phenomena. Indeed, the frequency and depth of change realized in the new era has led many in the Global North to believe that scientific and technological revolution is now the *privilege* of being modern.

But the dream-state of 'knowledge society' can mask only for a time the existence of another phenomenon that accompanies achievement of breakthrough science and technology—the catastrophic environmental risks that are ineluctably embedded in the world built on our genius.

For example, a state-of-the-art oil derrick erected in the 1960s off the coast of Santa Barbara, California was able to drill for its product to depths of 3,500 feet while balancing pressures of nearly 600 pounds per square inch—a feat that would have been unthinkable until extraordinary achievements in materials science (and other branches of knowledge) that had occurred by the mid-20th century. But in January 1969, when tolerances of the piping material were exceeded, the drilling column burst and an eruption of 1.3 million gallons of oil sent a 'black tide' ashore, sliming more than 800 square miles of coastline. The toll on wildlife was substantial: 6,000 to 15,000 birds died as a result of the blowout, as well as 74 elephant seals and five whales (Easton, 1972: 257-261). Seepage from seabed fissures caused by the blowout continues 30 years after the event. While politically important for the U.S., the Santa Barbara 'spill' no longer qualifies as a major event in the cavalcade of modern oil spill spectaculars (Oil Spill Intelligence Report, 2001). This is because the Santa Barbara catastrophe stimulated improvements in oil extraction technology that increased safety—and risk. Now, platforms balance much higher pressures and drill in far more 'challenging' areas (e.g., the North Sea). And when mistakes occur, the consequences are much greater.

A second environmental warning on March 23, 1989 suggests how greatly the scale of damage has escalated. On that date, the Exxon Valdez oil tanker hit a reef in the Alaskan Prince William Sound and spilled nearly 10 million gallons of crude. The oil spread to five National Wildlife Refuges and three National Parks, covering an area of 900 square miles. Again, hundreds of miles of shoreline were washed with a black tide. The estimate of bird kills was 100,000, including 150 bald eagles. Approximately 1,000 sea otters were also lost. Debris from the clean up of the oil spill was in excess of 50,000 tons. Importantly, the Exxon Valdez represented one of the most sophisticated ships in the world fleet at the time of the accident. Steered by a massive computer system and complex software, the enormous ship could not sail without scientific data. That 'pilot error' played a role in the accident misses the larger point: a vessel of that size would not have attempted to navigate off the section of the Alaskan coast where it crashed unless modern science had created the possibility.

Oil spills are only one category of environmental catastrophe experienced as part of the normal operations of the 'knowledge society.' For example, there is the ubiquitous destruction of forests and lakes as part of modernity's outdoor experiments in chemistry. Unlike the earlier era's penchant for dumping its wastes in streams, rivers, and lakes, and clear-cutting forests, the manufacture of 'acid rain' is a thoroughly modern technique for fouling these ecosystems.

The important elements of acid deposition—sulfur dioxide and, to a lesser degree, nitrogen oxides—are deposited in the atmosphere where they are transformed chemically and then fall to earth as acidic rain, snow, fog or dry particles. Damage to aquatic resources, estuaries and coastal waters, timber and recreational resources, buildings, monuments and statues, and public health are the result.

In many respects, this form of pollution repeats the practice of polluting capitalism in which environmental degradation is treated as a normal activity. The acid belt in China's heartland (Smil, 1993) is a testament to the triumph of industrial development and the ubiquity of modern technology in transforming what was the world's largest agricultural civilization into yet another concrete jungle. Socialist principles ushered forward this change with no less vigor than the capitalist ones that engineered European and North American industrialism. In this respect, even the contest of socialist and capitalist states over the aims, direction, and structure of society—which had dominated the first era—does not override the tendency to produce acid rain. Science and technology reach beyond the era of polluting capitalism to commodify nature and society in a distinctly new way.

In the U.S. and Europe, acid rain is produced not simply to bolster short-term business profits. Rather, it is the result of a practical strategy informed by scientific studies of wind mechanics, soil composition and chemistry. When concerns about polluting capitalism began to take the form of national regulation of industrial activity (e.g., with the passage of so called 'clean air' and 'clean water' laws in the United States setting volumetric standards for the amount of pollution that could be released), science and technology were called upon to solve the problem. Industrial locations would now be assessed scientifically for environmental impact, and 'scrubbing' equipment, tall smokestacks, and other technologies would be added to factory 'tailpipes,' and chemicals would be injected in industrial processes in order to disperse and dilute pollution from traditionally 'dirty' industries.

But in the reform of polluting capitalism, acid rain *became* an outcome. While dispersing sulfur pollution, for example, tall smokestacks also allow transport of the pollutant higher into airsheds which, in turn, facilitates its mixing with water vapor for transport to wider geographical areas. Similarly, chemical treatment of industrial processes introduces new emittants that can interact with water vapor and promote acidification. In this way, chemical change of rain, fog, and snow can actually be traced to efforts to use science for the purpose of reducing old-fashioned pollution. The result is a new pollution regime with a scale of damage that is distinctive to our technological civilization. Large swaths of the Canada-U.S. border, the U.S. Midwest and East, Germany's Ruhr Valley, and eastern Russia are infected with this new disease created from the exercise of human intelligence. Only modernist political economies could manufacture continental and transcontinental acid pollution as a product of environmental management. While not a failure of a spectacular technological kind (like oil spills), acid rain in the Global North nevertheless derives from technological progress and is itself a stimulus for remediation by still more sophisticated technological means. In this respect, our social and natural futures are revealed in the case of acid rain as increasingly contingent upon the result of scientific and technological trial and error.

A prominent symbol of modern environmental pollution—Love Canal, a residential development in New York State close to Niagara Falls—offers a further lesson on our scientific and technological dependence. Between the early 1940s and early 1950s, some 21,800 tons of liquid and solid chemical waste were buried in an abandoned canal project, together with municipal waste from the city of Niagara Falls. Owned and operated by Hooker Chemical, the site was sold to the local board of education, which built a school there in 1954. Despite knowledge that the site was contaminated, between 1966 and 1972 the area also became the location for residential development.

After a few years of occupation, residents began to complain of odors and other problems. Subsequent chemical analysis revealed that highly toxic chemicals from the waste had contaminated groundwater sources and migrated to the surface of the area's soils. However, there was considerable resistance by officials to take action and accept responsibility for the problem. Instrumental in bringing the issue to local and national prominence was the activity of a local group of concerned residents (Gibbs, 1982). Their efforts to have the extent of the health impacts researched were frustrated by officials, but investigations eventually revealed exceptional rates of miscarriage, birth defects, and epilepsy in the community living atop the chemical (and municipal) refuse dump. Finally, a federal emergency was declared and owners of over 1,000 houses were ordered to abandon them. The canal was capped and subsequently some $250 million was spent on relocation and remediation efforts.

The saga of Love Canal commanded special attention precisely because it was so ordinary that it could be repeated everywhere—and it was. By the 1980s, it was learned that modern development transpires within a reality of ever-present invention and use of chemicals, and their disposal, in ways which threaten lives and ecologies as a normal part of its operations. The least powerful in society had been and would continue to be the 'lab mice' for the societal experiment in modern development (Lee, 1987). Repair of this situation could not include a cessation in the use of these substances—such action would be tantamount to trying to repeal progress, since toxic chemicals are in everything and found almost everywhere in modern life. Instead, social confidence in expert management of chemicals was favored as national legislation enlisted scientists and engineers to assume permanent responsibility for 'societal risk assessment and mitigation.' In fact, Love Canal reveals just how dependent modern society had become on science and technology, not only for products, but also for the investigatory powers necessary to discover and affect its impacts. The irony of technological risk and the 'normal accident' could not have been more transparent, thanks to Love Canal: to diagnose the problem of risk and accidents, activists turned to science and technology; to reduce risks and restore society and the environment in the wake of accidents, government and industry turned to science and technology; yet, the greater use of science and technology will bring new risks and accidents… that only science and technology can understand and act upon.

Initially, the risks and damage evident in the Santa Barbara and Valdez catastrophes, the acid rain debacle, and the Love Canal disaster (and its imitated conditions throughout modern societies) might have been seen as episodes of excessive confidence in the progressive capacities of the new era. But as the essential features of these environmentally and socially calamitous events have proliferated, it has become increasingly difficult to treat them as isolated cases. For those who doubted the globality of the phenomenon, the evidence of pervasive risk was undeniable after yet another display of advanced knowledge gone awry.

The manufacture of methyl isocyanate is a distinctly modern enterprise. Its use to manage pests as part of a high-yield cropping regime has assisted the globalization of scientific agriculture. Production of this chemical compound depends upon a sophisticated industrial scheme that required the invention of advanced technology and breakthroughs in agrochemistry. Only an organization with the most modern research and development infrastructure could have commercialized pest management of the kind offered with methyl isocyanate; and only a large, multinational company could afford its manufacturing requirements and organize its production regardless of geographic location.

A plant built by Union Carbide experienced a leak on December 3, 1984 in a large storage tank. The interaction of methyl isocyanate with the night air produced a toxic gas that drifted over shantytowns in Bhopal, India. By morning, there were more than 3,500 deaths and in the coming months, over 150,000 injuries caused by the 'leak' would be recorded, many permanently disabling. The awful sacrifice of human life at Bhopal to profit an 'advanced' industry is inexcusable. Yet, modernity necessarily excuses it. Such an 'accident' can now occur on any continent on any day because the technology linked with the Bhopal factory is so widespread. However, it would not have been possible in India before the 1970s and could not have happened without scientific and engineering progress earlier in the 20th century. And the prevention of a 'Bhopal-like' disaster also rests with scientific and engineering progress.

One further insult, in 1986, left only true believers to champion the new era as necessarily progressive. The origins of this catastrophe lay in the use of one of the iconic achievements of the era—the discovery of the atomic structure of matter. From the outset, even some in the scientific and engineering communities worried about the implications of our new knowledge and of the institutional machinery evolving to assure its permanent expansion. With the knowledge of nuclear fission, the human race was seen to have acquired the permanent capacity to destroy the basis of life on earth (Schell, 1982). This capacity renders obsolete 'nature' as we have traditionally known it. No society can escape the threat of nuclear annihilation, but must depend upon the mutual decisions of the community of nations to forego use of certain applications of atomic knowledge. A parallel condition of dependency upon social decisions/ actions exists for the natural order as well, all of which became evident in 1986.

In early April of that year, *The Economist* (1986), citing the latest probability studies and in-depth engineering analyses, declared to its worldwide readership that a nuclear power plant is "as safe as a chocolate factory." A few days later, the lid blew off the No. 4 Reactor at the Chernobyl nuclear power complex. A cloud of radioactive debris swept across Europe and eventually circled the Northern Hemisphere. An estimated 300 million people in 15 nations experienced elevated radiation levels as a result of the explosion. Locally, 130,000 then-Soviet citizens were evacuated within a 30-mile radius of the site. An area within a 10-mile radius of the reactors became a 'dead zone' where nothing grows; nor can anything be allowed to grow because the radioactive soil could transfer its toxicity up the food chain (e.g., via bird transit to and from the site). The World Health Organization monitored at-risk populations for a decade and found that: 600,000 persons had suffered significantly increased levels of radiation exposure in the months after the 'accident;' 238 Ukrainian residents and emergency workers had contracted acute radiation syndrome (which is often fatal) and 31 individuals had lost their lives because of the explosion; and childhood thyroid cancers were eight-fold higher in the region after the Chernobyl blast (Medvedev, 1991; WHO, 1995; and Yamashita and Shibata, 1996).

Of course, the startling dilemma is that a nuclear power plant that suffers *no accidents* and is successfully retired after 40 years of operation has absorbed enough radioactivity in all of its equipment and building structure to require the entire site's designation as a highly toxic waste dump. The plant, with the spent fuel accumulated during the plant's operation, poses a far worse biological and human risk than the Chernobyl disaster unless contact with all living things is prevented for 10,000 to 100,000 years. Obviously, nuclear risk is like nothing that previously existed in human history (Byrne and Hoffman, 1996). Curiously, only our most sophisticated science—the physics of energy-matter, could produce the knowledge that informed the engineering that designed the Chernobyl reactor (and 212 similar and different reactors operating around the world).

Santa Barbara, Prince William Sound, transnational acid rain, Love Canal, Bhopal, and Chernobyl exemplify an environmental geography of accidents that are tragic but normal. They represent what is necessary to maintain the whir of modernity. Catastrophes such as these may be exceptional in the scale of their potential ecological and societal consequences, but in all other regards they represent what is routinely risked while in the embrace of science- and technology-driven progress. Only the vigilance of experts can be expected to protect society from technological risk and the omnipresent catastrophic accident. When management by expertise fails, the illusion of an autonomous social order is revealed. Unfortunately, in the face of such revelations we have all too often redoubled our efforts to create even more compelling illusions with pronouncements of new fail-proof management and technology innovations.

Thus, in the second era we arrive at a curious point where only advanced knowledge is regarded as capable of protecting the natural and social order from destruction. Yet, the source of destructive threats is traceable to the exercise of the very same expertise. The continued spread of modern technology will necessarily increase the frequency of accidents, and the stockpile of long-lived, toxic wastes, bringing into sharp focus the hegemony of commodity values over life-affirming ones. Notwithstanding the escalation of catastrophic risk and destructive potential, the momentum of modernity hinges upon continuation of a Faustian gamble that our firm conviction in scientific objectivity is more right than believing the contrary but supposedly 'temporary' evidence of the arrogance of that conviction. Of course, society could go without oil retrieved from beneath the sea; it could reduce electricity consumption; it could close all nuclear facilities and adopt a sustainable development path; it could preclude use of toxic chemicals.

But such choices would mean repudiating the very quantification ideology which undergirds modern ideals of progress. Leaders of our 'knowledge society' know instinctively of the dangers of such Luddite thinking. The only acceptable alternative in such a society for meeting its needs is to resort to risky advances. In this respect, modern society increasingly struggles with itself: it is a captive of the environmental problems that it is uniquely capable in all of social history of creating; and likewise a captive of the technological solutions which, once employed, invariably breed new, more difficult social and environmental problems.

Beck (1992, 1995, and 1997) has impressively described the contradiction. He contends that one of the major functions of the state in modernity is to respond to the hazards and dangers generated and perceived by society, by insuring the ongoing production of the risk information and assessment expertise necessary to promise the public that solutions for its benefit will be discovered.

Technological requirements are paramount in the modern order. Human existence has been broken into endless acts of commodity production and consumption which in turn depend for their accomplishment upon networks of technology. In an explicit sense, society is governed by technological institutions that create and manage the conditions of human experience. Nature is reduced in this phase to a technical problem. An authoritarianism of technique prevails in the social and, increasingly, natural spheres. To realize progress in this era, decisions about technology-society-nature relations are removed from spheres of democratic activity and considered instead in the domains of science and economics.

In the new era, nature and its evolution is no longer phenomenally independent of the evolution of human knowledge. Nature is now imbued with knowledge—and the escalating risks that only advancing knowledge can create. Thus, to Lyotard's observation that knowledge is a "force of production" (Lyotard, 1984), there must now be added the recognition that it is likewise a 'force of nature.' In essence, nature has a "social structure" that is expanding with the advance of the knowledge society (Byrne et al, 1991). Justice or its violation, in the new era, is a property of nature, as well as society. In particular, nature and society now evolve together based on an institutionalized condition of unequal risk that reflects the unequal interests of advanced knowledge both in its creation (e.g., in the problems that are selected as meriting attention of the leading knowledge 'producers' such as universities and government and corporate laboratories) and its use (e.g., the services it does, and does not, provide). But when management and design errors unexpectedly surface, faultlines in the premise of life outside nature are starkly revealed.

The construct of environmental injustice operating in the globalized technological milieu socially and geographically maps the logic of the era. The least powerful are endangered because structuring risk differently would impede progress. The social order continues to rely on class, gender, race, and culture to decide its victims, but environmental injustice spreads in the second era to encompass not only material conditions, but knowledge structures which manage modern life. Endangering communities and ecologies generally is normalized as the fate of modern life—a necessity regardless of its implications for justice. An ideal of 'efficient' risk is sought in which the problems of communities and ecologies are allowed to stimulate scientific and technological interest in a 'just' solution—only so long as it is cost-effective and objectively based. Ellul pointedly summarized the matter: "Efficiency is a fact; justice is a slogan" in the modern era (1964).

Living in the Anthropocene

Crutzen and Stoermer (2000) have proposed a new geological era—the Anthropocene—in recognition of the fact that human activity has transformed the path of Earth's history. Human activity has altered surface conditions of the planet at the landscape scale, has disturbed biophysical processes and conditions at the global scale, constitutes a major evolutionary factor determining planetary biodiversity, and is creating new life forms through genetic modification. Crutzen and Stoermer suggest that the new era began in the latter part of the 18th century when geology first manifested a macro-scale imprint of our presence.

We would like to borrow their suggestion for a different purpose. Seen from the perspective of commodification (as developed here), until very recently the human imprint was confined to the geography of nature-society relations. Specific areas and discrete social and ecological systems were exploited and/or risked by modernity. However, a third phase of commodification may now be conceived in which all of nature has become available to human ends. A crucial attribute of this phase is that the 'total reach' of human impact is now recognizable, at least among members of expert sections of knowledge society. Empowered by this recognition, projects in knowledge society anticipate an ability to *embody* nature as a whole in human knowledge. From genetic modification to global ecological management, the Global North aspires to realize nature as a system organized and managed by human intelligence.

Nature will no longer be merely exploited for its particular attributes or its evolution risked in the name of progress. Rather, the possibility is being investigated of its transformation entirely from a phenomenal order to a value vector that meets the needs and interests of technological civilization. As a result, the future cannot resemble the past—nature, social relations with nature, knowledge of nature, and the purpose of social action must assume new meanings.

In this idea of an Anthropocene, human use and understanding of the natural world may no longer be based on natural ecosystems that are distinct from social ones. Nature routinely bears the imprint of human influence and the phenomenon of nature 'beyond influence,' in essence, cannot finally exist. Not only is nature denied autonomous standing and development, but its future becomes dependent upon social direction. Such an anthropomorphized nature presents humanity with 'decisions' to select which species and ecosystem attributes are to survive human influence—it is, some argue, our choice to leave aspects of nature 'as is' or to valorize them in some other way.

In this respect, nature broadly contains two modern forms of value: one that is reflected in its direct use as a commodity—its production/consumption value; and one that represents its capital value, both as a source of reproduction of ecological services and as a source of knowledge. In the Anthropocene, these values compete (Escobar, 1996) and social institutions decide the proportion of 'as is' and modified nature.

As in the previous era of commodification, scientific knowledge and technical organization provide the foundations for diagnosis of and response to environmental problems. However, living in the Anthropocene will differ from the past in significant respects.

There is the obvious matter of scale: in this era, environmental management extends to the limits of the natural order—from the genetic to the global. Furthermore, the design of social systems can be expected to evolve to 'efficiently' exploit natural resources and systems for the normal functioning of the global industrial system, while also seeking to transform the deleterious ecological effects of this activity into forms that can be managed. Hence, the advent of 'natural capitalism' (Hawken et al, 1999) and 'ecological moderization' (Hajer, 1995) can be predicted in which the repair and restitution of a harmed ecology is incorporated into the productive cycle of the global economic system.

As well, commodification will frequently become the key to managing the interaction of natural systems: the most effective means of satisfying planetary management goals is likely to be the assignment of value to all relevant elements, including those of risk, ecological harm, community well-being, ecological services, and so on. In many instances, commodification is now assumed when devising management regimes for such diverse resources as water, seeds, fish, rangelands, and forests. Once ceded to scientific and technological control, the existence of an ecological and social commons vanishes. In anthropomorphized nature, 'as is' nature and modified nature will be co-managed by coordinated social protocols.

From the perspective of this era, ecological justice is a challenge that can be addressed by manipulation of nature and society. It is a value added to the many values managed by the global political economy, global service, and global technology networks. In this system, if a value can be attached to ecological justice, then it can be made part of the machinations of the management process.

No current issue better presages life in the Anthropocene and its implications for ecological justice than anthropocentric climate change. As is now widely known, the combustion of fossil fuels in industrial energy systems has increased the atmospheric concentrations of key gases, including carbon dioxide, methane, and nitrous oxide, resulting in a warming of 0.6°C of the planet over the last century (IPCC, 2001). Indisputably structural in character, the anthropogenically-enhanced greenhouse effect will produce higher global surface temperatures, changes in the patterns of precipitation, and other climatic factors, together with rising sea levels for at least the next few centuries.

Consequently, natural ecosystems will be affected with both the abundance and distribution of indigenous and introduced species altered (IPCC, 1996b), and the prospect of accelerated biodiversity loss assured. Terrestrial aquatic ecosystems will change; as will stream flow and flooding characteristics (IPCC, 1996b). Human systems of resource harvesting in agriculture, forestry, and fishing will experience changes in yield and location of production activities: other industries and activities, such as transport, will be altered (IPCC, 1996b). Human health will respond to climatic changes and be indirectly affected by changes in the distribution and abundance of pathogens (IPCC, 1996b).

Both the production and applications of knowledge about climate change differentiate the contemporary era from its predecessors. Only science at its most global could detect an atmospheric warning about the planet's climate, identify the anthropogenic causes, and speculate on and estimate the range of potential physical, biological, social and economic impacts. Understanding the processes and timing of global climate and its potential impacts is an enterprise of vast intellectual complexity, entailing a broad range of scientific disciplines, computer modeling that is as sophisticated as any yet attempted by humanity, and a virtual army of researchers that rivals in sophistication the one already assembled for military 'research.'

In response to this global environmental issue, an international agreement—the United Nations Framework Convention on Climate Change (FCCC)—was created. Its overall goal is to limit the concentrations of greenhouse gases in the atmosphere so as to prevent a dangerous level of climate change, defined specially as an unpredictable pattern of temperature variation. Under the FCCC, an international protocol (known as the 'Kyoto Protocol') has been negotiated to set a global target for greenhouse gas emissions reduction and to apportion this reduction among participating nations.

Having global ambitions is a characteristic shared by a growing number of international agreements, and in this respect the FCCC is unremarkable. However, in seeking to mange the global energy system that underlies modernization, the FCCC is arguably unique in the scope of its aspirations and likely effects. Two features of the FCCC stand out as signals of life in the Anthropocene; one is the role of science in attempting to understand the global climate system and human effects on it; and a second is the emergence of a global management system for greenhouse gas abatement centered on market-based tools.

Human-caused climate change now appears certain; at stake is the magnitude of change and the rate at which it occurs, which are functions of the historic and future characteristics of greenhouse gas releases. A key output from the scientific process has been the production of a series of global emission scenarios with the resulting levels of atmospheric concentration of greenhouse gases estimated (e.g., IPCC, 1990, 1996a, and 2000). Future generations and the natural environment have already been compromised by greenhouse gas releases to date, making the management of future releases a major determinant of future ecology and human prospects. Such is the character of the social structure that the manufacturing and release of greenhouse gases across the global political economy, and the understanding and management these emissions, is an issue of science-based control with few, if any, precedents. In essence, a virtual reconstruction of the technology-nature-society relation is being contemplated as a 'policy question'—How to convert the atmosphere from a commons, as it existed for all of geological time, to a commodity available for capitalization in the time frames modeled by science and valorized by society?

The outlines of the new regime are evident in recent international negiotations centered on creating markets for managing the sky. Favored strategies include emissions trading, carbon sink investments, and the transfer of emission abatement technology from wealthy nations (where emissions are high) to poor nations (where emissions are low)—all justified under the rubric of economic efficiency. A system of commercial rights of access to atmospheric 'services' is under design (Costanza et al, 1997) with advanced science enlisted to monitor performance.

In the late 1980s, Harvard economist Thomas Schelling reasoned that it might be better for the U.S. to respond to the future impacts of forecasted global warming when they occur, rather than to invest in contemporary measures to reduce greenhouse gas emissions (Schelling, 1989). A decade later, the Chair of the U.S. President's Council of Economic Advisors (CEA) described research that estimated meeting the greenhouse gas reduction targets set by the Kyoto Protocolwould increase each U.S. household's annual energy bill by US$70-110 in 2008-2010 (Yellen, 1998). In spring 2001, a newly elected U.S. President concluded that a precautionary stance similar to that in the 1998 CEA report was too costly and a 'no regrets' strategy—as Schelling's approach is often termed—would be premature. Instead, the U.S. government withdrew from international negotiations, preferring to wait for further scientific proof that global action is needed. All three pronouncements evoked criticism from those alarmed at the apparent readiness of the world's largest national source of greenhouse gas emissions to base social action on the value of 'atmospheric services.' However, modern management justifies evaluations and considerations such as these in order to produce acceptable decisions.

Ecological justice is poorly served by the existing response to climate change. The impacts of modernist progress on climate are likely to disproportionately harm poorer nations and communities and the ecosystems not favored by the wealthy. The failure of the world's wealthiest nations to reduce their greenhouse gas emissions to date is, in this respect, an act of "environmental colonialism" (Agarwal and Narain, 1993). Existing environmental agreements wrangle over 5% reduction targets under the Kyoto Protocol, when 60% reductions are estimated to be needed to stabilize atmospheric concentrations of greenhouse gases (IPCC, 1992 and 1996c). Even here, the intent of the wealthy is to transfer technology—and the burden of change—to the poor in order to meet targets unrelated to ecological sustainability (Byrne et al, 1998; and Byrne and Glover, 2000). Future generations and future ecological conditions will bear the burdens of climate change resulting from present practices, due to the lag effect in the climate system, so that the consequences of current modernization are saddled on those not responsible for their creation.

While the biophysical processes of the atmosphere for millions of years had no design feature producing such unequal consequences, life in the Anthropocene changes this circumstance. Having altered the chemistry of the atmosphere *and* globalized a social system of unequal conditions and unequal risks, the modern order now promises to turn climate into a problem of political economy. The atmosphere needs scientific management, at a minimum, to determine if human-induced changes to its chemistry can alter global temperature. This minimal activity has already engendered a potential triage situation as discussion of significant action is postponed until scientific understanding of such factors as clouds, water vapor, and pollutant aerosols improves. In the meantime, islands are threatened by the early warning signal of sea level rise and continental populations, which are less harmed in the early stages, survey their rational options.

However, the forces of environmental colonialism and triage are simply a prelude of the management project immanent in the Anthropocene. The semeiotic conquest (Escobar, 1996) of the sky in the context of efforts to rescue the planet from the consequences of modernization will mean that problems of ecological injustice associated with climate change will *inhabit* the atmosphere in the way that these problems now inhabit urban neighborhoods. Of course, the totality of the atmosphere makes its capture and use in the production of unequal political economy and unequal nature a distinctively new order of commodification; and as far as we can see, the completion of the process of transforming the phenomenal order into a vector of commodity values.

Thus, in the Anthropocene we will be confronted with a form of world political economy in which global warming and other totalizing commodifications are risked in the pursuit of progress. Whereas the initial stages of commodification tested the statics of nature (namely the absorption capacities of land, water, and air), the Anthropocene challenges the dynamics of nature, in particular, the seasons, the tides, the breathing of the planet, and the reproductive cycles of living things. While the emblems of advancing industrialism remain waste, pollution, and risk, there has been a fundamental breach of the nature-society relation in the Anthropocene. Modern life transpires not simply outside the constraints of nature, but relegates nature to commodity status, to be purchased and sold in the world along with other products and services.

The contemporary world political economy presumes that sustainability is a scientific, technological, and economic matter. Although this presumption is typically manifested in economic terms and thus continues to be most concretely presented in discussions of trade-offs between environmental protection and material progress, its deeper implication is the demise of any idea of the inviolability of nature. There is *nothing* in the modern logic beyond the reach of knowledge and its manipulation: not the climate, not the atmosphere, and not the diversity of species. Nature is stripped altogether of an autonomous status.

The issues of ecological justice that accompany third-era commodification are, literally, inescapable. Ecological justice can only find a place in the Anthropocene by assuming a commodity value itself and becoming part of the emerging management regime. In this way it would join the atmosphere, which is already well underway in its transition from a commons to a commodity, as a mere value, competing with other expressions of value for the right to shape the nature-society relation. The endless contest for the efficient result determines the final meaning of ecological justice.

The transformation of social and ecological existence into a value vector is far from complete. The Athropocene, in our view, is an evolving, not a completed era. Yet, recent experience with the global climate offers a sobering view of the meaning of a world that finally values only commodities.

Conclusion

The scientific revolution and the rise of capitalism initiated the reconceptualization of the relation between society and nature. A new worldview emerged which emphasized rationality, order, and power as the underlying principles of human and natural development. This worldview demystified the physical and biological worlds so that nature could be "construed as ordered systems of mechanical parts subject to predictability through deductive reasoning" (Merchant, 1980: 214). Scientific knowledge about the environment has been achieved through the conceptual "death of nature" and the use of analytic methods predicated on the deconstruction of nature into its constituent parts (Merchant, 1980). In this view, nature is made up of "modular components or discreet parts . . . the parts of matter, like the parts of machines being dead, passive, and inert" (Merchant, 1980: 229).

The emergence of the modern view has led directly to the legitimation of the commodification process and the repudiation of earlier organic visions of the unity of social and natural reality. In contrast to the normative structures of organicism which regarded the exploitation of nature as a violation of life, the modern order treats nature and its exploitation as objective reality; there can be no normative content in nature when "matter is made up of atoms, colors occur by the reflection of light waves of differing lengths, bodies obey the law of inertia, and the sun is the center of the solar system" (Merchant, 1980: 193). With the embrace of modernity, civilization seeks to act without normative constraint. Limits on society's actions are almost exclusively instrumental: economy, efficiency, and scientific validity identify the boundaries of action. It is in this context that contemporary nature-society relations have evolved.

In an initial era of commodification, ecological conditions aligned with wealth; pollution and resource depletion became the habitat of poor families, poor communities, poor regions, and poor nations. Aided by science and technology, industrialization became global in reach, generating risks commensurate with its scale, and a pattern of injustice that was class, race, gender, and culture-focused.

Spawning a second era of commodification, progress necessitated commitments to advancing knowledge and its application, along with the distinctive threats that only modernity could augur. Societies are obliged to place their faith in experts, technocratic systems, and management institutions in the expectation that these offer social and environmental protection. At the same time, catastrophe-scale 'mistakes' are inevitable. Here, justice becomes a technical problem with analysis as the source of 'solution sets.' Those least equipped to 'model' their problems become the 'lab mice' as human intelligence works out management schemes to respond to objectively discovered cases of injustice.

In a third phase of commodification, we embark on a project in which ecological justice is allocated through our manipulation of the structure of nature and society. Interactions between human and natural systems in the era of the Anthropocene will require global management so as to temper the effects of modernization on nature and society. One rationale for the management regime will almost certainly be to shape and control nature to meets the aims of a rhetoric of ecological justice. In this phase, ecological justice becomes a commodity whose value must compete with others for modern attention.

Recognition of the Anthropocene might be regarded as fatalistic. We would agree that, conceptually, the transformation of phenomenal nature to commodified nature signifies a crossing of commodification's final frontier. Moreover, it is evident that powerful institutions of the global regime have an interest in, and potent capabilities for, the pursuit of an Anthropocene. And it is clear that human existence outside earth's atmosphere is technologically plausible.

However, these facts hardly justify the destruction of the basis of life on earth, as all species have ever experienced it. In this respect, rather than being fatalistic, our diagnosis of the Anthropocene offers ideas on how to oppose and prevent its completion. The discourse of ecological justice to which it contributes is necessarily rooted in resistance. Indeed, the viability of the discourse would appear to depend on a successful challenge to the onset of the Anthropocentric "death of nature."

Notes

1.   Social relations refer here to collective relations among human beings; while ecological relations refer to the interaction of humanity with all other forms of life and with the natural order as a whole. Regarding the terms environmental and ecological justice, we follow the approach used by Low and Gleeson (1998) and others. Environmental justice refers specifically to human transformations of nature that institutionalize social disadvantage. Ecological justice is applied more broadly so as to embrace the presence of existing social disadvantage, the interests of future generations, and the intrinsic interests of nature in the present and future. Ecological justice cognizes a commonality of interests between nature and society, thereby reflecting a radical reconceptualization of the human regard of ecology.
2.   The term 'commodification' is used here to refer to a social process by which phenomena (social and natural) are transformed from their intrinsic and autonomous existence into a social, political, and/or economic value. This transformation from phenomenon to value delivers a thing, person, etc., to society as a fungible object available for use and exchange.
3.   The phrase "Global North" is used here to refer to urban communities and societies throughout the world that rely on science and technology development since the Enlightenment, along with industrial wealth, to organize economic, political, and intellectual life.

References

Agarwal, Anil and Sunita Narain. 1993. *Global Warming in an Unequal World: A Case of Environmental Racism.* New Delhi: Centre for Science and Environment.

Beck, Ulrich. 1997. "Global Risk Politics." In Michael Jacobs, (ed). *Greening the Millennium? The New Politics of the Environment.* Oxford, UK, Malden, MA: Blackwell. Pp. 18-33.

_____. 1995. *Ecological Politics in an Age of Risk.* Cambridge: Polity.

_____. 1992. *Risk Society: Towards a New Modernity.* London: Sage.

Barthes, Roland. 1972. *Mythologies.* Translated by Annette Lavers. New York: Hill and Wand.

Bell, Daniel. 1967. "Notes on the Post-Industrial Society (I and II)." *Public Interest.* 6 and 7 (Winter and Spring): 24-35 and 102-118.

Bogard, William. 1989. *The Bhopal Tragedy: Language, Logic, and Politics in the Production of a Hazard.* Boulder, San Francisco, and London: Westview Press.

Borgmann, Albert. 1993. *Crossing the Postmodern Divide.* Chicago: University of Chicago Press.

Byrne, John and Leigh Glover. 2000. *Climate Shopping: Putting the Atmosphere Up for Sale.* TELA Issue 5. Melbourne, Australia: Australian Conservation Foundation.

Byrne, John and Steven M. Hoffman. 1996. "The Ideology of Progress and the Globalization of Nuclear Power." In Byrne, John and Steven M. Hoffman, (eds). 1996. *Governing the Atom: The Politics of Risk.* New Brunswick, NJ: Transaction Publishers. pp. 11-46.

_____. 1988. "Nuclear Power and Technological Authoritarianism." *Bulletin of Science, Technology and Society.* Volume 7: 658-671.

Byrne, John, Steven M. Hoffman, and Cecilia R. Martinez. 1991. "The Social Structure of Nature." *Proceedings of the Sixth Annual Meeting of the National Association of Science, Technology and Society.* pp. 67-76.

Byrne, John et al. 1998. "Equity- and Sustainability-Based Policy Response to Global Climate Change. *Energy Policy.* Volume 26; 4: 335-343.

Castells, Manuel. 1996. *The Rise of the Network Society.* Cambridge (UK): Blackwell.

_____. 1984. "Space and Society: Managing the New Historical Relationships." In Michael P. Smith (ed). *Cities in Transformation: Class, Capital, and the State.* Beverly Hills, CA: Sage Publications. pp. 235-259.

Costanza, Robert et al. 1997. "The Value of the World's Ecosystem Services and Natural Capital." *Nature.* Volume 387, (May 15): 253-260.

Crosby, Alfred W. 1988. *Ecological Imperialism: The Biological Expansion of Europe, 900-1900.* New York, NY: Canto. (Originally, Cambridge: Cambridge University Press, 1986).

Crutzen, Paul J. and Eugene F. Stoermer. 2000. "The "Anthropocene."" *Global Change Newsletter.* Number 41 (May): 17-18.

Drucker, Peter F. 1993. *Post-Capitalist Society.* New York: HarperColins.

Economist, The. 1986. "The Charm of Nuclear Power." March 29.

Easton, Robert. 1972. *Black Tide: The Santa Barbara Oil Spill and its Consequences.* New York: Delacorte Press.

Ellul, Jacques. 1964. *The Technological Society.* Translated by John Wilkinson. New York: Knopf.

Engels, Friedrich. 1993. *The Condition of the Working Class in England in 1844.* (First published in German, in Germany, 1845.) Oxford and New York: Oxford University Press.

Escobar, Arturo. 1996. "Constructing Nature: Elements for a Postindustrial Political Ecology." In Richard Peet and Michael Watts (eds). *Liberation Ecologies: Environment, Development, Social Movements.* London and New York: Routledge. pp. 46-68.

Foster, John Bellamy. 1993. "'Let Them All Eat Pollution': Capitalism and the World Environment." *Monthly Review.* January: 10-20.

Gibbs, Lois Marie. 1982. *Love Canal: My Story.* Albany: State University of New York Press.

Hajer, Marteen J. 1995. *The Politics of Environmental Discourse: Ecological Modernization and the Policy Process.* Oxford: Oxford University Press.

Hawken, Paul, Amory Lovins, and L. Hunter Lovins. 1999. *Natural Capitalism: Creating the Next Industrial Revolution.* Boston: Little Brown and Co.

IPCC (Intergovernmental Panel on Climate Change). (2001). *Climate Change 2001: The Scientific Basis.* J. T. Houghton, Y. Ding, D. J. Gripps, M. Noguer, P. J. van der Linden, and D. Xiaosu (Eds.) New York, NY: Cambridge University Press.

_____. 1996a. *Climate Change 1995: The Science of Climate Change.* John T. Houghton et al. (eds). Cambridge, UK: Cambridge University Press.

_____. 1996b. *Impacts, Adaptations and Mitigation of Climate Change: Scientific-Technical Analyses.* Robert, T. Watson et al. (eds). Cambridge, UK: Cambridge University Press.

_____. 1996c. *Climate Change 1995: Economic and Social Dimensions of Climate Change.* J. P. Bruce et al. (eds). New York: Cambridge University Press.

_____. 1992. *Climate Change 1992: The Supplementary Report to the IPCC Scientific Assessment.* John T. Houghton et al. (eds). New York: Cambridge University Press.

_____. 1990. *Climate Change: The IPCC Scientific Assessment.* John T. Houghton et al. (Ed.). Cambridge (UK) and New York: Cambridge University Press.

Jasanoff, Shelia, (ed). 1994. *Learning from Disaster: Risk Management After Bhopal.* Philadelphia: University of Philadelphia Press.

Kurzman, Dan. 1987. *A Killing Wind: Inside Union Carbide and the Bhopal Catastrophe.* New York: McGraw-Gill.

Lee, Charles. 1987. *Toxic Wastes and Race in the United States: A National Study of the Racial and Socioeconomic Characteristics of Communities with Hazardous Waste Sites.* New York, NY: United Church of Christ Commission on Racial Justice.

Low, Nicholas and Bredan Gleeson. 1998. *Justice, Society and Nature: An Exploration of Political Ecology.* London and New York: Routledge.

Lyotard, Jean-Francois. 1984. The *Postmodern Condition: A Report on Knowledge.* Translated by G. Bennington. Minneapolis: University of Minnesota Press.

Marshall, Alfred. 1946. *Principles of Economics: An Introductory Volume.* (Originally published 1890). London: Macmillan. Eighth edition.

Mazur, Allan. 1998. *A Hazardous Inquiry: The Rashomon Effect at Love Canal.* Cambridge, MA and London, England: Harvard University Press.

Medvedev, Grigori. 1991. *The Truth about Chernobyl.* New York: Basic Books.

Merchant, Carolyn. 1980. *The Death of Nature: Women, Ecology and the Scientific Revolution.* New York, NY: Harper and Row.

Mumford, Lewis. 1970. *The Myth of the Machine: The Pentagon of Power.* New York: Harcourt Brace Jovanovich.

_____. 1961. *The City in History: Its Origins, Its Transformations, and Its Prospects.* New York: Harcourt Brace Jovanovich.

_____. 1934. *Technics and Civilization.* New York: Harcourt Brace.

O'Connor, Martin. 1994a. "Codependency and Interdependency." In Martin O'Connor (ed). *Is Capitalism Sustainable? Political Economy and the Politics of Ecology.* New York: The Guilford Press. pp. 53-75.

_____. 1994b. "On the Misadventures of Capitalist Nature." In Martin O'Connor (ed). *Is Capitalism Sustainable? Political Economy and the Politics of Ecology.* New York: The Guilford Press. pp. 125-151.

Oil Spill Intelligence Report. "Oil Spills Involving More Than 10 Million Gallons." Available online at: http://www.cutter.com/osir/biglist.htm

Pigou, A. C. (1924). *The Economics of Welfare*. Second edition. London: Macmillan.

Price, Martin F. 1989. "Global Change: Defining the Ill-defined." *Environment*. (October): 18-43.

Schell, Jonathon. 1982. *The Fate of the Earth*. New York: Knopf.

Schneider, Stephen H. 1990. "Debating Gaia." *Environment*. (May): 5-32.

Shrivastava, Paul. 1982. *Bhopal: Anatomy of a Crisis*. London: Paul Chapman Publishing.

Smil, Vaclav. 1993. *China's Environmental Crisis: An Inquiry into the Limits of National Development*. Armonk, NY: ME Sharpe.

Ward, Barbara and Rene Dubos. 1972. *Only One Earth: The Care and Maintenance of a Small Planet*. New York: WW Norton.

WHO (World Health Organization). 1995. *Health Consequences of the Chernobyl Accident. Results of the IPHECA Pilot Projects and Related National Programs*. Geneva: WHO.

Yamashita, Shunichi and Yoshisada Shibata, (eds). 1996. *Chernobyl: A Decade*. Proceedings of the Fifth Chernobyl Sasakawa Medical Cooperation Symposium, Kiev, Ukraine, 15-15 October 1996. Amsterdam: Elsevier.

Yellen, Janet. 1998. Chair, Council of Economic Advisors. Testimony. The Kyoto Protocol —The Undermining of American Prosperity? *United States House of Representatives Small Business Committee*, June 4. Available at: http://www.house.gov/smbiz/ hearings/105th/1998/ 980604/ yellen.htm

Contributors

Anil Agarwal

Anil Agarwal is Director of the Centre for Science and Environment in New Delhi, India and is internationally renowned as an environmental journalist, advocate, community organizer, and the author of books, articles, and reports on a wide array of environment and development issues. He has authored, co-authored, and edited some 19 books on these subjects. Amongst his more recent outputs have been India's Citizen's *State of India's Environment* (a series he conceived), co-authoring *Global Warming in an Unequal World,* and co-editing *Green Politics: Global Environmental Negotiations.* Agarwal is the recipient of 11 Indian and global awards, including the Global Environment Leadership Award (2000), the Indian Padma Bhushan (2000), Environmentalist of the Year (1994), and India's National Citizen Award (1991). He has held some 18 honorary positions in India, as well as 8 international positions on organizations and activities dealing with environmental and social issues.

John Byrne

John Byrne is Director and Professor at the Center for Energy and Environmental Policy at the University of Delaware. He is also co-founder and Co-executive Director of the Joint Institute for a Sustainable Energy and Environmental Future, an innovative research and advocacy organization headquartered in Seoul, Korea with the mission of promoting peaceful and sustainable policy options in Northeast Asia. He is general editor of the Energy and Environmental Policy book series, published by Transaction Publishers. He has published over 100 articles and 11 books, including *Energy and Environment: The Policy Challenge*, which addresses the global warming debate and appropriate policy responses.

Daniel Faber

Daniel Faber is an Associate Professor of Sociology at Northeastern University in Boston. Between 1984-1990, he was Research Director of the Environmental Project On Central America, which he co-founded. He is currently Director of the Philanthropy and Environmental Justice Research Project, and was co-founding editor of the journal *Capitalism, Nature, Socialism*. His research interests include political economy and crisis theory, environmental sociology, development and underdevelopment, social theory, social movements, ecological justice, and Central America. He is the author of numerous works on these subjects, especially environmental politics in Central America and the United States, including the volume *Environment Under Fire: Imperialism and the Ecological Crisis in Central America,* and he edited *The Struggle for Ecological Democracy: Environmental Justice Movements in the United States.*

Brendan Gleeson

Brendan Gleeson is Deputy Director of the Urban Frontiers Program at the University of Western Sydney in Australia. His research interests include the political economy of planning, urban social policy, environmental theory and policy, democracy, and ecological justice. In recent years he has authored *Geographies of Disability* and co-authored with Nicholas Low the award-winning *Justice, Society and Nature: An Exploration of Political Ecology*, as well as *Australian Urban Planning: New Challenges, New Agendas*, and was also co-editor of *Governing for the Environment: Global Problems, Ethics, and Democracy* and *Consuming Cities*, along with numerous other published works in these fields.

Leigh Glover

Leigh Glover is a Research Associate at the Center for Energy and Environmental Policy, University of Delaware. He has published in the fields of energy and environmental policy, climate change, and sustainable development, and worked in several Australian state and federal government environment and resource agencies undertaking administration, research, and policy development.

Steven M. Hoffman

Steven Hoffman is a Professor of political science at the University of St. Thomas in St. Paul, Minnesota, where he directs the University's

Environmental Studies program. He is also an Adjunct Research Professor at the Center for Energy and Environmental Policy at the University of Delaware. His research interests include energy policy, renewable energy, governance and policy formulation, democracy and ecology, and environmental justice. He is co-editor of *Energy and Sustainable World Development* (a special issue of *Energy Sources*) and has published numerous articles on energy and environmental policy. He is also active in environmental policy and community action in Minnesota through his role in several statewide advocacy and policy organizations dealing with energy and ecology.

Nicholas Low

Nicholas Low is a Senior Lecturer in the Faculty of Architecture, Building and Planning at the University of Melbourne, Australia. He teaches planning theory, urban studies and environmental ethics in the Faculty of Architecture, Building, and Planning. He has published many international journal articles and books including *Planning, Politics and the State*. In 1997 he organized the University of Melbourne Conference on Environmental Justice and his 1998 book (co-authored with Brendan Gleeson), *Justice, Society and Nature,* won the Harold and Margaret Sprout Award of the International Studies Association of the USA for the year's best book on ecological politics. In the recent years he edited Global *Ethics and the Environment*, and with Adrian Gleeson co-authored *Australian Urban Planning,* and they co-edited *Governing for the Environment*, and Low was an editor of *Consuming Cities.*

Cecilia Martinez

Cecilia Martinez is Assistant Professor of Ethnic Studies at Metropolitan State University, St. Paul, Minnesota. She is also an Adjunct Research Professor at the Center for Energy and Environmental Policy at the University of Delaware. Her principal research interests include American Indians, energy and environmental policy, energy and nuclear policy, and the political, economy of social inequality, especially as it pertains to the issues of environmental justice. She has worked with the U.S. Department of Housing and Urban Development, was a member of the Sustainable Communities Initiative sponsored by the Minnesota Environmental Quality Board, and has a long association with the American Indian Policy Center.

Sunita Narain

Sunita Narain is the Deputy Director of the Centre for Science and Environment, New Delhi, India, Director of the Society for Environmental Communications, and the Publisher of the fortnightly environmental magazine "Down to Earth." She has worked on a variety on environmental and development issues, but is best known for her work on water resources, forests, and climate change, with an emphasis on democracy and sustainable development. She has contributed to several of India's *State of the Environment* Reports and co-edited the fifth Report in 1999. Narain has written numerous articles, papers, and books, including co-authoring *Towards Green Villages*, *Global Warming in an Unequal World*, and *Towards a Green World*, and co-edited *Green Politics* and *Dying Wisdom*. She also holds a number of honorary positions with Indian and international organizations and has lectured widely on environmental and development topics.

John Poupart

John Poupart is President of the American Indian Policy Center, a non-profit organization that serves the Midwest Indian communities through research, policy development, and education. Poupart is an advocate of community-based participatory research and community projects. He has supervised many AIPC studies including *Reflections on Traditional American Indian Ways*, *Traditional American Indian Leadership*, and *Threats to Tribal Sovereignty* and led many forums and research investigations on subjects including American Indian elders, sovereignty, treaty rights, American Indian home ownership, and tribal governments.

Wolfgang Sachs

Wolfgang Sachs is Senior Research Fellow at the Wuppertal Institute for Climate, Environment and Energy in Wuppertal, Germany. He has a long involvement in activist circles in Germany and Italy, and in academic institutions in the U.S. and Europe. He has published extensively in the fields of environment, development, society, justice, and culture. Two works he edited are famous in development literature: *The Development Dictionary: A Guide to Knowledge as Power* and *Global Ecology: A New Arena of Political Conflict*. A recent work co-authored by Sachs, *Greening the North: A Postindustrial Blueprint for Ecology and Equity*, adds much empirical evidence to the arguments surrounding global environmental justice and has drawn much critical praise. Sachs is widely considered as one of the leading intellectuals in these fields.

Anju Sharma

Anju Sharma is with the Centre for Science and Environment in New Delhi where she is involved in a variety of issues, notably those involving the international environment, global governance, women and environment, development, climate change, pollution, and human health. She has written many articles and papers, and is the co-author of *Slow Murder: The Deadly Story of Vehicular Pollution in India* and co-editor of the CSE volume *Green Politics: Global Environmental Negotiations*.

Subodh Wagle

Subodh Wagle is President of Prayas, a non-governmental research and advocacy organization in Pune, Maharashtra, India. He is internationally prominent for his involvement in the Namada Dam and Dabhol power station issues. Official reviews and the popular press have recognized Wagle's role in exposing the economic and environmental implications of the Dabhol proposal. He is widely published in the fields of energy, sustainable development, environmental justice, multinational corporations, international aid and development finance, and authored *The Enron Story* on the dispute involving corruption in the Enron Corporation-Maharashtra Government negotiations over Dahbol.

Index